MECHANICS' INSTITUTE
❦ MECHANICS' ❦
MERCANTILE LIBRARY

WHITE-COLLAR SWEATSHOP

WHITE-COLLAR SWEATSHOP

The Deterioration of Work and Its Rewards in Corporate America

Jill Andresky Fraser

W. W. NORTON & COMPANY
New York · London

For information about permission to reproduce selections from
this book, write to Permissions, W. W. Norton & Company, Inc.,
500 Fifth Avenue, New York, NY 10110

The text of this book is composed in Trump Medieval with
the display set in Stencil
Composition by Sue Carlson
Manufacturing by Maple-Vail Book Manufacturing Group
Book design by Charlotte Staub

Library of Congress Cataloging-in-Publication Data

Fraser, Jill Andresky.
White-collar sweatshop : the deterioration of work and its
rewards in corporate America / Jill Andresky Fraser.
p. cm.
Includes bibliographical references and index.
ISBN 0-393-04829-2
1. White collar workers—United States. 2. Work
environment—United States. I. Title.
HD8039.M39 U563 2001
331.7'92'0973—dc21   00-046079

W. W. Norton & Company, Inc., 500 Fifth Avenue, New York, N.Y. 10110
www.wwnorton.com

W. W. Norton & Company Ltd., 10 Coptic Street, London WC1A 1PU

1 2 3 4 5 6 7 8 9 0

With much love and many thanks,
for
Steve
Max
Emma

CONTENTS

ACKNOWLEDGMENTS

I wish that I could thank by name all the men and women who shared their work-life experiences and insights with me. Their contributions made this book possible.

Daniel Levine, the editor of www.disgruntled.com, and Ken Hamidi, the founder of FACEIntel, aided me in many ways, including by publicizing my research efforts through the Internet and elsewhere. I am grateful for their assistance.

Sloan Harris of ICM is a rarity among agents: kind, gentle, and supportive. I enjoy working with him.

Although the book-publishing industry has gone through many changes in recent years, W. W. Norton & Company—one of the few remaining independents—still does business "the old-fashioned way." I'm pleased to be associated with the house, and want to thank Gerry Howard, who signed my book and helped me formulate my early research, and Starling Lawrence, who edited the manuscript and shepherded me through the production process.

Phoebe Hoss, Jeff Seglin, and Chris Miles—three dear friends who are also enormously talented editors—helped me revise early drafts and publicize the final product. I'm deeply grateful for their efforts.

Andrea Burtman has given me her lifelong friendship and many great photographs (including the one on the book jacket). I thank her for both.

White-Collar Sweatshop would not exist without the involvement of my husband, Steve Fraser. His support and encouragement kept me going over the four difficult and exhausting years during which I researched and wrote this book while continuing my life as a financial journalist. At a time when other spouses might have confined themselves to occasional dinner-table conversations about a book project, he devoted incalculable hours as well as his extraordinary skills as a nonfiction editor, historian, and writer to helping me produce the best book possible. I cannot fully express my gratitude.

Lori Andresky and Kitty Newhouse Bermudez inspire me always with the memory of their remarkable talents, enthusiasm, and commitment to their crafts. I think of them as I conclude this project.

WHITE-COLLAR SWEATSHOP

INTRODUCTION

The Best of All Possible Worlds of Work?

The 5:29 P.M. commuter train to Scarsdale is jammed: usually it's standing-room-only for the half hour it takes to reach the upscale suburb from New York City's Grand Central Station.

During the ride, Gemma,[1] a marketing executive, phones her office for messages not once but twice, returning as many calls as possible in quick succession from her cellular phone. She keeps her voice low, tries to conclude the calls quickly; too many of them, after all, and her seatmates are apt to send irritated looks her way. But she makes them anyway, despite a longing to doze off: "It's the only way I can leave my office most days at five o'clock and get home to have dinner with my family." Her fellow commuters share the strategy, it seems, judging from the frequency with which they too pull out their cell phones, laptop computers, or yellow lined legal pads.

Despite the crowds and the phone calls, the ride passes fairly quickly. Most evenings, Gemma makes it to her home by a quarter past six. But her workday is not over. By seven-thirty or so, once dinner is done, it's back to those phone calls.

While her children wrap up the last pages of their homework or settle down to watch some television sitcoms, Gemma again checks her voice mail, taking the time to respond to as many calls as necessary. Sometimes there are faxes to handle: sent from clients or colleagues to a home machine perched in a spare room that doubles as an office. Her husband, an investment banker, works there as well during the evenings, usually at the family's personal computer, where he sits, sometimes for hours, writing or amending documents relating to one of his prospective deals. As the evening winds to a close, clients may phone too: his and hers each have the family's home telephone numbers as a matter of course. "When a client needs you, they need you," she sighed, in an early conversation with me.

If boundaries exist between Gemma's home and work lives, they're hard to detect. "I never relax. I honestly feel that I never relax," she confessed. "When I'm at the office, I never go out to lunch. All that I'm aimed at, when I'm at the office, is getting work done. I don't have time for anything else. If I need a pair of stockings, I don't have time to get it. I don't have time for anything, period."

She and I were sitting in a crowded Manhattan restaurant, eating quickly, talking quickly. She was doing me a favor by squeezing me into her chock-full workday, taking the time to talk about all the time she didn't have. "It's gotten worse and worse." She gestured with her fork to emphasize her words. "I fantasize every day about doing more things for myself. I want to work out. I can't. I need physical therapy. I can't get it. You work so hard, rush home to be with the family. Then you're short with them. Even though that's where you want to be, you're too tired at night. You get testy, exhausted."

Like many of the men and women I interviewed during four years of research for *White-Collar Sweatshop*, Gemma inhabits a stress-ridden and precarious universe. By most traditional measures, her career is a smashing success, encompassing as it has a steady string of promotions, salary increases, a big-ticket move to the suburbs. Yet she lives her life feeling like a member of the walking wounded. "The neck," she almost moaned the words, massaging her neck, unconsciously, at various points in our conversation. "I live with pain in my neck from all the stress *and* the phone." Again she motioned with her fork. "I'm on the phone all day—very stressed out. I have no memory. It's the stress." She paused as she carefully chose her words. "The thing is, I still like what I do."

Nick does not know Gemma. They don't work in the same industry, nor do they live in the same state. Yet they share many of the same feelings about their work lives, as they struggle to cope with a corporate world increasingly defined by overwork, stress, and—at more and more companies like Nick's—patterns of underreward.

Like Gemma, Nick also still "likes" what he does, although he is quick to admit that he is no longer certain how much that's worth. "My job *is* extremely challenging—that's not the problem." A mid-level financial executive at one of the country's most successful telecommunications companies, he has held on to his post through more than a decade's worth of corporate acquisitions and divestitures, layoffs and mergers. "I am who I am. I *have* made a significant contribution to this company. I feel proud of that." He paused, then added, his smile a wry one, "It's very hard to say that it was all for nothing."

Nick and I have spoken on numerous occasions, while he has attempted to steer his career along a steady path, despite the tumultuousness and unpredictability of the corporate environment he inhabits. His sense of humor was quick; his observations bleak: "People are to the point where they're keeping their lists, keeping journals of things they can use against the company when their time comes," he told me once, over burgers at a diner near his office. "There's no loyalty, no faith." Perhaps the biggest surprise for him was that he could fall into this same category. "When I started out, I thought I could stay forever. This seemed like such a great place to be."

How things change. He and his wife recently put their four-bedroom Colonial, complete with two lushly landscaped acres in Westport, Connecticut, on the market: not because they plan to move even further upscale but because Nick has come to the conclusion that his career and financial prospects basically have dead-ended—although he is still only in his forties.

"I recently concluded a project that had tremendous bottom-line value for the company and its shareholders," he recalled. "I really made an impact on the company's profitability. But when it came time for my annual review, I got a completely pathetic raise, which I had to be thankful for because it was zero point six percent higher than everyone else got." Maintaining what was basically the status quo was scarcely an option for Nick and his wife, since they had been meeting their monthly expenses by dipping into the family's savings for more than a year now. But even more painful than the decision to downscale their lifestyle was the behavior he felt compelled to adopt at the office: "I had to swallow my pride and say, *thank you.*" His voice dripped with sarcasm. "Just suck it in and say thank you, while management sits and watches the stock price and exercises another fifty thousand stock options."

Year after year of cost-cutting, lagging raises, declining benefits, and increased workloads have taken their toll on Nick, as they have on white-collar workers throughout corporate America. Think of him—indeed, it's the way he views himself—as the victim of a kind of corporate water torture, which has slowly and painfully consumed much of the energy and enthusiasm he once brought to his work life. "You have no control. It's ultimately a humbling experience to realize that you could move mountains and it wouldn't make any difference."

Although the newspapers he reads during his hour-long commute are full of reports about the United States' booming job market,[2] Nick has yet to apply for a position elsewhere. "Why move somewhere else? I figure all these companies are the same. You hear stories from people like me all the time. Everyone on the train has got his or her own story to tell." He sat silently for a moment, then added, "I went home the day I got that raise and made the decision then and there that it was time for our family to start downsizing too."

And then there's Leonard.

Leonard isn't downsizing. He is simply counting the days— although there *are* still thousands of them—until he can finally retire and leave the emotional and ethical stresses of his work life far behind him. Like Nick and Gemma (neither of whom he knows), he too is a corporate success, with a career that has spanned important positions at three major high-technology companies. His six-figure salary and benefits are all that he ever could have wanted. But for some time now, the pressures accompanying his twelve-hour workdays and managerial responsibilities—which have included supervising numerous rounds of layoffs during the past decade— have left him feeling more like a survivor than a star.

"The philosophy now is you have to squeeze more and more out of people. I have to do more and more with less." An ex-marine, he isn't one to complain, but he made it clear to me that he has given up on any hope of a better end in sight. "Earlier this year, they laid off a hundred people in my division. The philosophy was, you *probably* have a hundred people who probably aren't up to par."

He chuckled, the kind of laugh that conveyed just how unfunny the situation at his office has become. "I had a phone call one day telling me, you have to lay ten people off. There was no discussion. It wasn't appropriate for me to say no or yes." Again the chuckle. "We laid those people off, so now I'm in litigation with some of them. They're mad. I understand that. But here's the reality." He paused. "If I don't do it, *I'm* gone. That's clear."

Early on, Leonard himself was a staunch supporter of his company's restructuring efforts. In the first of several conversations between us, he emphasized that he was still proud of the part he had played in his employer's initial efforts to redefine and even eliminate jobs, all in the interests of strengthening a once-weak business and raising the standards of the workforce. But now, he noted, "We do this year after year. We squeeze. We squeeze. People are starting to feel expendable. But if you try to argue, then you're not stepping up."

Another conversation, still the themes were the same. Although Leonard had called me from his car phone, I could hear the disgust in his voice along with the static. "Layoffs are not good. People keep telling me, 'Len, there's a contradiction here. You tell us that things are better than ever. But the layoffs and cost-cutting keep happening. Does this mean that at any time, no matter what, it could happen to me? Anything could happen to me?'" Leonard acknowledged that he was at a loss as to how to answer the men and women who report to him. "Look," he told me, "the last time, I was blindsided myself."

Again, that humorless laugh. "In a way, I feel too old to start again, but too young to hang it up. The only way I can protect myself is by trying to outperform everybody else. That means working harder and harder. I do it for one thing—the money. And

if I can just hold on long enough, I'll be able to retire early and be
finished."

Has there never been a better time to work in corporate America?

A new business-world order exists, spawned and nurtured by
tumultuous changes during the 1980s and 1990s. By the dawn of the
twenty-first century, the United States could boast of remarkably
low unemployment, high corporate profits, and labor markets so
tight that signing bonuses were reported to be almost common for
everyone from new college graduates to teachers and even civil ser-
vants.[3] "In some parts of the country, just about anyone who can
breathe and is ambulatory has a job—and in some cases, they'll
make exceptions," was the way one Conference Board economist
put it.[4]

Although wild stock swings suggested that the extraordinary bull
market of the past two decades might finally be exhausted, the prolonged years of buoyant equity growth had yielded enormous sums
of capital, ripe for investment in America's business future. By the
turn of the millennium, the United States' economy was in
uncharted heady waters, with venture capital investments, initial
public offerings, and stock price-to-earnings ratios all at record levels, and almost every week, it seemed, another off-the-charts corporate merger guaranteed to create a new global superpower.
Although some industries were experiencing painful contractions,
many others were thriving.

Within this environment, one might assume that the rewards
and challenges of work would likewise be unparalleled, especially
for the United States' skilled and experienced white-collar workforce, nearly 80 million men and women strong.[5] Yet behind the
era's high-flying statistics are dismal workplace realities that many
readers of this book will recognize all too well from their own lives.

Overwork is epidemic, for men and women whose job demands
keep increasing, not because of career advances but because of a corporate environment that has depended upon *squeezing*, as Leonard
would say, more and more work out of fewer people with fewer
resources. For today's white-collar staffers, the balanced and secure

nine-to-five work lives of their parents' generation belongs to a utopian past, as they struggle to fulfill job demands that require them to work after dinner and during lunch hours, the way Gemma does, or on Saturdays and Sundays, in between the innings of their children's Little League games, during summer or winter vacations, while waiting on line at movie theaters, driving their cars virtually anywhere, or on countless other occasions as well. Signs of round-the-clock overwork are inescapable; during a late August afternoon ride in a rented pedal boat, after a game of miniature golf, my family and I shared a Long Island pond with a woman who was peddling her two young daughters around, all the while speaking to her office via cell phone.

The new corporate era has depended in large part upon tighter and tighter cost controls, layoffs, efficiency-driven mergers, and endless workplace cutbacks. And so, many of today's overburdened white-collar jobs carry with them diminishing financial rewards—whether these take the form of raises that fail to keep up with growing workloads and inflation, or eroding health care benefits, or shrinking pensions, or disappearing vacation days and holidays.

Long-term financial stability has disappeared, within a business world in which layoffs and other cuts have been as rampant during periods of economic prosperity as during downturns.[6] And the corporate ax keeps falling faster and faster: by the first quarter of the year 2000—yet another in a long line of robust seasons for layoffs—one of every five "downsized" Americans had spent less than twenty-four months in their jobs before getting fired.[7]

Faced with the harsh new realities of the contemporary workplace, men and women find themselves squeezed at all ages and stages of their career paths: during their twenties, as many are forced to choose between the growing pool of temporary jobs and permanent posts that offer little upward mobility in companies committed to churning their workforces; during their thirties and forties, as they struggle to balance the voracious demands of corporate employers with those of children and aging parents; and during their later years, as—despite expectations that they will be rewarded for all their years of hard work—men and women often learn instead that their higher salary levels and extended tenure in the workforce leave them increasingly vulnerable to job loss, with few options except self-employment or contingent labor. In some especially brutal industries, such as Wall Street and the high-tech sector, this career "kiss of death" now hits people as young as in their forties.

The overwork, stress, and insecurity of today's workplaces has been exacerbated, not relieved, by the proliferation of high-tech equipment—laptop computers, cell phones, electronic desk calendars, beepers, portable fax machines, Palm Pilots, and more—that help people try to keep up with growing workloads while also making it impossible for them to fully escape their jobs and relax. New technologies, meanwhile, facilitate intrusive efforts by employers to monitor everything from their staffers' comings and goings to computerized keystrokes and mouse taps, e-mails sent and received, and personal productivity on a weekly, daily, or even hour-by-hour basis.

Work life was not always this demanding and unrewarding. Once, the nation's largest corporations were viewed by white-collar Americans as the source of jobs worth dreaming about: offering security, comfortable working conditions, the prospect of a balanced work and home life, and a wide range of financial benefits. During the early decades following World War II, successful companies and their staffers shared the fruits of economic prosperity as new, relatively paternalistic practices governed workplace relations and helped create long-term bonds between employer and employee.

These early postwar employment strategies fell into disrepute after a variety of economic problems threatened the global preeminence of the U.S. economy during the 1970s. Thanks to compliant government policies and aggressive intervention by Wall Street, the 1980s ushered in a tumultuous era of corporate reinvention accompanied by workplace decline. Along the way, the rules and rewards of the business world changed: although people's job demands and stress loads kept ratcheting ever upward, the only way they could share prosperity's rewards was through the stock market, rather than their paychecks and benefit packages.

Throughout the 1990s, thriving companies like Intel and Microsoft, corporate giants like Citigroup, AT&T, and IBM, and struggling companies like Levi Strauss and Disney were among a long list of those committed to harsh new management strategies. Public relations campaigns conducted inside and outside the corporate workplace aimed to convince Americans that deteriorating job conditions were essential in order to fuel the nation's thriving economy and soaring equity markets.

Yet evidence abounded that "sweatshop" practices demoralized employees and destabilized workforces, and may well have weakened many businesses as they faced ever tougher global challenges. By the turn of the millennium, it also seemed clear that—in its preoccupation with short-term profits and ephemeral stock market gains—the culture of overwork and underreward had exacted a painful toll not only upon the men and women employed by the United States' largest companies but upon their families, vital civic structures, and the nation's society as a whole.

As a financial writer, I have spent much of the past two decades reporting on the corporate trends that underlie workplace change: the downsizings and productivity drives, the megamergers, public policy adjustments, globalization campaigns, increasing emphasis on shareholder rewards, investor activism, and much more. Yet when I first embarked upon this project, back in 1996, one paradox kept nagging away at me: how to reconcile the buoyant optimism of the chief executives, business leaders, and management consultants I interviewed regularly—as well as the widespread confidence embodied in what then seemed to be an inevitably rising stock market—with the often bleak workplace stories and comments I was hearing from my other sources, all those men and women *outside* the executive suite?

They told me about ever-increasing workloads, time pressures, and other job stresses; unrealistic employer expectations; declining levels of career and financial security. Less emotional attachment to the workplace. Less time and energy for the family. Although times were good, attitudes like these reflected a pervasive pessimism about the workplace: a sense that its daily norms and long-term prospects had changed in a host of negative ways that were not going to disappear anytime soon.

Were these tales of overwork and exhaustion, mistrust and despair, simply the ramblings and complaints of small numbers of disgruntled workers, those who just could not keep up with the fast-paced program, as American businesses continued to reinvent and reposition themselves to thrive within the twenty-first-century global economy? And even if they were indicative of larger trends— a darker side, if you will, of the new and invigorated U.S. economy— did these personal costs matter much at all, so long as our corporations themselves kept getting stronger?

To answer these questions, I have spent four years trying to understand the ways in which the demands and rewards of work have been changing within corporate America; why these changes occurred; and what their effects have been, and will continue to be, upon the work and home lives of people employed by large corporations, as well as upon those companies themselves and the greater U.S. economy.

During my research, I conducted in-depth interviews, often on repeated occasions, with men and women of all ages on various rungs of the corporate ladder. Their jobs ranged all the way from entry-level through management positions, and their areas of expertise ran the gamut from finance to marketing and sales, engineering, administrative support services, and everything in between. They represented all the major industries upon which the U.S. economy is based, including computer technologies, banking, publishing, Wall Street, retailing, telecommunications, and much more.

These men and women constitute a broad spectrum of white-collar workers across corporate America: new college graduates, Generation Xers, baby boomers, and others who are older still. Most hold a full-time job, but others juggle more than one job, or work as contract employees or short-term temporary staffers. Some were out of work (or, as many liked to say, currently "consulting"). Some opted for early retirement.

My confidential conversations with these men and women took place in coffee shops, fine restaurants, and family kitchens; during after-hour, weekend, and early morning telephone calls; and via electronic communications. With the help of various business organizations, employee networks, and self-help groups, I hosted roundtable discussions and workshops organized around the themes of my research, all with the goal of broadening my interview and knowledge base to include the broadest possible range of people, jobs, corporations, and industries.

The course of my research coincided with the growing involvement of more people (and more *different* kinds of people) with the Internet, and I expanded my activities accordingly. Besides regularly visiting a host of websites and chat rooms that focus on work-related issues, I posted descriptions of my project in a variety of Internet sites, complete with "hyperlinks" that could connect interested people directly to my e-mail address. Eventually, I hosted my own discussion groups on the Internet as well. In some cases, these electronic sites hooked me up with cranks and kooks: no surprise, I'm sure, to anyone who regularly "surfs the Net." In far more instances, however, the Internet put me in touch with men and women whose work experiences had raised for them many of the same questions I was asking. A few were so anxious about possible leaks to their employers that they insisted our conversations be confined to electronic letters, often remarkably long ones. In the vast majority of cases, however, we followed up our initial Internet contacts with in-depth conversations either in person or by telephone.

These conversations ranged far afield. I spoke to working men and women about the course of their careers; their goals, key achievements, and disappointments; the ways that their work and personal lives had intertwined; and about the evolutions and revolutions they had witnessed within their companies and industries. Above all, I have been interested in *change:* how people's work lives differ from what they used to be, or what people expected them to be, or wanted them to be. When did the rules and rewards of their workplaces shift, I'd ask them, and what corporate decisions or actions were responsible? How do they feel about their work lives *today*, and how have those feelings changed, along with their work environments, over the years?

The past two decades have been a period of great transformation for corporate America: change that takes on a far different cast when looked at, not from the floor of the New York Stock Exchange or a chief executive's suite, but from the wide ranks of a company's white-collar workforce. My sources and I discussed their lives "before and after" the seismic changes that rocked IBM, AT&T, and the Baby Bells, the big U.S. banks, the publishing industry, retailers, all manner of high-tech companies, and more. Since few people's careers have remained static in our rapidly shifting economy, I have been able to track some *as* they changed jobs or employers, and have followed others while they coped with corporate mergers or downsizings. Perhaps also inevitably, some of my sources lost jobs, sometimes high-powered ones, during the years in which I interviewed them.

Their recollections were illuminating. I heard about "the B.U.M. from hell," a notorious "business-update meeting" at semiconductor manufacturer Intel. That was when staffers learned about a formal quota that had been instituted per department to single out layoff candidates. (In Intel-speak, they're sometimes known as the "slower-thans.") It was a manager himself who gave this "B.U.M." its ominous nickname, according to one engineer who attended the meeting, and it was a manager "who came right out and told us that Intel is not going to be a place where you can work until retirement."

Sometimes, in my sources' recollections, a single moment, a comment, a sentence in an otherwise insignificant office memorandum provided an unforgettable glimpse into the dismal workplace realities that many white-collar workers have grown to take for granted.

An executive vice president who managed to survive numerous rounds of layoffs at Lehman Brothers surprised me when she described her most painful memory of the experience. It wasn't the difficulty of maintaining an upbeat facade before potential clients, all the while waiting for an ax to fall on her own neck each time new cuts were announced. Nor was it the way she felt as she walked past all those empty cubicles and offices in a midtown Manhattan skyscraper that increasingly came to resemble a ghost town. No, for her, the lowest—and most personally intrusive—moment came in a hallway conversation with the managing director who was her supervisor. He instructed her to "smile more often so that people would know just how grateful she was to still have her job."

One woman, a manager at one of the nation's largest and most successful financial services firms, told me about how she had been so overloaded and understaffed that she had been forced to work through the entire night before her wedding. The image that stayed with her, years later, was of the company's escalator, which was moving up during the early morning hour in which she was finally heading down. She wasn't complaining, she emphasized; she just could not shake the memory. Sometimes, in retrospect, she could not even believe it had happened.

If, as I will argue, the personal costs have been vast during this period of business and economic tumult, there have also been parallel business costs that the corporate community does not yet fully grasp: costs that may eventually handicap America's large companies in their quest to achieve profitability and competitive preeminence. Despite the gorgeous glow cast by a long-lasting bull market upon much of the nation's economy, there are already, as I will demonstrate, incipient signs of trouble in many of the companies and industries that have based recent growth strategies on harsh new management techniques. Absenteeism, stress-related medical costs, high employee turnover rates, and poor morale are widespread; the flight of capital and manpower to smaller entrepreneurial ventures has also become apparent. In intensified global competition—or in an economic downturn in which American corporations must turn to their employees for the competitive edge that will enable them to survive and thrive—many will find that they have alienated and exhausted the human capital that was once one of their greatest resources.

Does the notion of a white-collar "sweatshop" seem incongruous, implausible—perhaps even offensive—when linked with the image of work life within America's largest and best-respected corporations?

Sweatshop workers are exploited, often illiterate, impoverished, powerless. The United States' white-collar workers are certainly anything but. They're educated, sometimes very well educated. They enjoy comfortable lifestyles, often extremely comfortable lifestyles. They've got plenty of options. Could they really have anything to complain about, especially during an economic period as vibrant as these past years have been?

Then again, for many of the readers of this book, especially those who work in large and demanding corporate environments, the term "sweatshop" may not seem so surprising at all. For them, the more pressing question may be, is there a way out of our contemporary business culture of overwork, stress, insecurity, and under-reward—both for themselves as individuals and for the nation at large?

ONE

"The Pace Was Insane":
Less Time, More Stress

"The whole theme of your book is my life," one IBM veteran in her early forties told me during the first of a series of conversations we shared.

Catherine described to me her steady progression from a junior position at "Big Blue" back in the early 1980s through a fairly continual string of promotions into the ranks of management during the next decade. Early on, she had been identified as a strong performer and, as she put it, "placed on the management fast track." While still in her twenties, she worked twenty-hour days. "It was pretty unbelievable" is the way she recalls it now.

One two-year assignment kept her on the road, visiting IBM's customers, five days a week. "I'd only go home on the weekends. That was just accepted. It was part of the culture. You just did it— kept working and traveling at that kind of pace." Since her husband also worked for the company, he didn't complain; fortunately, his travel schedule was lighter than hers, which allowed them to maintain a semblance of a home life.

Then she was promoted into a line-management position. The good news was, she was on her way up and no longer needed to maintain that relentless travel schedule. The bad news was, her responsibilities included a regular rotation during which she was placed "on call" twenty-four hours a day, on a shift that lasted a week at a time.

To an outsider looking in, what was perhaps most remarkable about Catherine's work and home life was just how unremarkable it all seemed to her and her colleagues. "A customer could get in touch with me anytime. If you were on call, that meant you were their first point of contact." She paused, then added, "At two o'clock in the morning, you would get calls from a customer. But you were still expected to be in the office by 8 A.M. I did it for two years. I'd come home at eight or nine at night. In the midst of that, I had my first back operation. The pace was insane. When you'd get home, you'd go for the wine. And then, pretty much crash and go to sleep."

Although the working conditions were brutal, Catherine never contemplated complaining or switching to another employer. "This was known as a job you had to do to 'get your ticket punched,'" she explained. Little wonder she wanted it punched: this was still the 1980s, when a management job at IBM was the pot of gold at the end of many a white-collar rainbow, thanks to the company's longtime domination of the mainframe computer business, unflaggingly powerful stock performance, and well-earned reputation as a blue-chip provider of employee benefits and incentives.

Then the competitive arena shifted, and IBM's market preeminence (as well as the dominance of mainframes) was challenged by the growing popularity of personal computers. Its stock price began a long downhill slide, various corporate reorganizations were announced, and finally, in 1993, Louis Gerstner, a veteran of the RJR Nabisco restructuring, took the helm with a mandate for change.

For Catherine and her colleagues, the demands of their already difficult jobs were notched up several levels as the company gradually entered a crisis management mode. As they worked harder and harder, many of the benefits they had prized most dearly during their days at Big Blue started slipping away. For one thing, "we used to get one hundred percent medical coverage," she recalled. "Then they switched married couples to coordinated benefits, then they switched us to an HMO. It was just, holy s——!" Worst of all was the damage done by the company's falling stock price, which went from a high around 170 to a low in the 40s; that downward trajectory drastically reduced, among other things, the value of many employees' retirement savings, traditionally one of the biggest benefits of life as one of IBM's "blue suits."

Workloads kept increasing, as the company announced numerous early-retirement initiatives and then layoffs, driving its workforce down from a high of over four hundred thousand to the low two hundred thousands. "It began to trickle down that you had this pace of work and meetings during the day. You couldn't get to your e-mails during the day, so you'd do them at night." Catherine's laugh was bitter. "It was like you didn't have a home life. IBM gave you a computer at home. That made it easy to work." Again the laugh. "I used to pride myself on thinking, I'm not going to complain. I can take it all on. I can do anything."

In the hours Catherine spent describing her grueling working conditions to me—as I came to understand the ways that work had enveloped just about every aspect of her personal life since she first entered the corporate arena back in her early twenties—I kept asking her, and myself, why she had stayed on at IBM, especially as the company began shedding its paternalistic practices and cutting back on the once-traditional rewards for all that hard labor.

Our conversations illuminated several points. She accepted her workload in large part because it was the norm within the corporation: as it increased for her, it increased for her colleagues, too, which meant that it still seemed within the bounds of the acceptable. Also, Catherine was emotionally attached to her employer, identifying with both its successes and failures, in a way that encouraged her to hang on, despite the difficulties of her position.[1] Finally, although certainly not of least importance, she was a success at IBM and had been for some years now. As she continued to rise within the corporate hierarchy, to build her own network of mentors, colleagues, and friends within the organization—to spend most of her waking hours thinking about IBM, working for IBM, *being* at IBM—it was tough to imagine turning her back on so many years of accumulated experiences and ties.

The demands of her job still took their toll. There were two more back operations for Catherine, and more and more problems with her husband, during those few hours they managed to spend together away from the office. By this time, the couple had been trying unsuccessfully to get pregnant for years. Catherine blamed their failure on her chronic exhaustion and job-related stress: the cause also, she was convinced, of her incessant back ailment.

Bt this time, she was working sixteen-hour days *at* the office, then going home to check—among other tasks—her e-mails and voice-mail messages. Her travel pace had picked up again as well. "My husband was traveling then, too. We'd do what we called 'calendar coordination' every two weeks," she told me. "We'd sit down at dinner and plan for every single day. Where would he be and where would I be?" Worn out by a pace of work that she had been maintaining for more than a decade, she decided a few years ago to join a health club, naturally choosing one that was open twenty-four hours a day. "I'd try to go at ten o'clock at night, after I left the office."

Longer Workdays

Experiences like Catherine's reflect seismic changes that have taken place within corporate America during the past two decades, most especially during the 1990s, in respect to the rules, the rewards, and the demands of work. This shift is equivalent to an industrial revolution for white-collar workers who, by necessity, have learned to adjust to (and often successfully function within) whatever versions of the white-collar "sweatshop" have evolved within their own companies and industries.

People are working longer and harder, the kind of hours one once might have expected to see logged in only by chief executives or would-be CEOs (or sweatshop workers!). There may be no greater testament to this reality than the best-selling success of Juliet Schor's *The Overworked American,* which argued, "If present trends continue, by the end of the century Americans will be spending as much time at their jobs as they did back in the nineteen twenties."[2]

Currently, over 25 million Americans work more than forty-nine hours each week, some a good bit more. Here's how those numbers break down: Nearly 12 percent of the workforce, about 15 million people, report spending forty-nine to fifty-nine hours weekly at the office; another 11 million, or 8.5 percent, say they spend sixty hours or more there.[3] Most of these people are white-collar professionals: among them, corporate managers, marketing staffers, investment bankers, office administrators, software designers, lawyers, editors, engineers, accountants, business consultants, and the secretaries, word processors, computer programmers, and back-office clerks who support their activities.

Most people, of course, don't spend sixteen or so hours a day at their offices, at least not on a regular basis, year after year. They might not be able to relate to all the career successes Catherine has had along the way. Odds are pretty strong as well that they haven't lived through the painful medical procedures she has; indeed, it might not be so simple to draw a straight line between their work-related stresses and whatever problems have emerged within their personal lives.

But Catherine is far from unique when it comes to the back-breaking pace of her work life. "Men and women come in all the time, begging for help, more and more stressed out," Zoe confided. A mid-level manager at Levi Strauss, she had worked her way through layoffs and cutbacks during the 1990s. She told me, as she laughed, that she had been with the company so long that she remembered a time when it was still thought of as a good place to work. But no longer, she emphasized, adding, "I'd say the average person is now doing the job of two and a half people."

At workplaces across the nation, most people working more than forty hours each week are between twenty-five and forty-four years old.[4] A good many of them are likely to be juggling the intense demands of these job schedules with the also intense demands of a family, which may include responsibilities for aging parents, as well as spouses and children.

Manny is a good example. He was a technical writer at Intel and, also, the single father of two elementary-school-age girls. "Nominally, Intel has work hours, usually eight to five," he told me. But "life at Intel is intense . . . incredibly hard work." So he evolved his own strategy to cope: "I'd get the kids up, give them breakfast, then I'd take off. Get there about seven in the morning. Usually I'd leave right at five." He'd come home to prepare dinner and eat it with his daughters. "Then I'd put them to bed at eight," leaving them at home alone, he explained, "and come back to the office until about 1 A.M."

In some industries, among them the technology and financial services sectors, the norms—everyday expectations about just how much time people should spend at the office each day—have become so extreme that a twelve-hour workday can seem positively lightweight. As the culture of overwork spread across the United States, inflexibly high demands like these began to seem like a badge of honor, at least from the business world's perspective. Lexus, the car manufacturer, ran advertisements that boasted, "Sure, We Take Vacations. They're Called Lunch Breaks," and "We Don't Have a Company Softball Team. It Would Lower Productivity by .56%."[5]

Newcomers who try to leave such workplaces early, maybe to get home in time to have dinner with their families, must either adapt to the rigors of the daily routine or risk the loss of their jobs. "I see a lot of people who have a hard time understanding families and family pressures," one public relations executive in his mid-thirties confided to me. With a career that has already encompassed three different mergers at three financial corporations and one merger-related layoff, Marc has drawn a drastic, if perhaps understandable, conclusion from his workplace observations: "I personally feel that having a family is not necessarily a good thing."

In industries like his, where white-collar workers can typically spend seventy, eighty, ninety hours a week, or even more, in their offices, machismo attitudes surface—especially in group situations—when people describe just how long and how hard they work. (Remember Catherine's sense of pride about "never complaining"?) When Harvard Business School professor Rosabeth Moss Kanter ran focus groups with about three hundred professionals working in the software industry, she was told about an "ethic that is far and above 8-to-5." Black humor abounded: "Only a half-day?" "That's 8 p.m. to 5 p.m." "This is like a poker game. I'll see you your hours and raise you." Another person explained, "The long hours aren't because we want to outshine everybody; we want to keep up with everybody."[6]

This pace of work is physically and emotionally draining, however, whether or not people choose to complain about it to their friends, relatives, or colleagues. Robert, a thirty-two-year-old financial executive at American Express, described his working conditions to me this way: "I don't get home until nine-thirty some nights. I'm dead tired ninety percent of the time. I think it's slowly sinking in with my wife about the idea that we're going to have to do something with Robert's life."

Two paychecks means twice as much potential for overwork and exhaustion, with just that much less time left over for child-rearing and other priorities. One recent study of multidecade work patterns among two-career couples concluded, in the words of Marin Clarkberg, a Cornell University sociologist, "People are working longer hours, and it's not because they want to." Among the study's findings: 43 percent of husbands and 34 percent of wives reported working more hours than they would like.[7]

What keeps people in their offices all these hours? One would assume—especially in a tight labor market—that the big difference between today's educated and empowered white-collar workers and the sweatshop seamstress would be the former's freedom to "just say no": to refuse to punch these round-the-clock time cards and instead insist upon a humane pace of work.

The explanation is as complex as the corporate world. Some people don't have the clout or the outside options to permit them to strive for more balanced schedules and workloads. Some industries effectively squash resistance early on by expecting their managers to train early recruits to accept (and even expect) excessive demands upon their time. On Wall Street, for example, it is common for a supervisor to instruct new hires to keep a spare set of clothes and toothbrush in the office for all those late night work episodes when it just won't make sense to head home for a quick snooze. Managers like these quickly impose their company's demanding work schedules upon their staffers' psyches and work habits, since they themselves put in extra long hours and can easily identify "slackers."

There are other ways, of course, to make certain that white-collar men and women meet their employers' tough standards. Legal, consulting, and accounting firms track numbers of billable hours, which has always made it simple for them to identify those professionals who fail to work long enough and bring in whatever levels of revenue currently seem adequate. With the development of new software products, other companies have the option—whether they choose to take advantage of it or not—of using personal computers to track the in-office productivity of all kinds of staffers.

As many people rise within their organizations, there's no need for the corporation to *impose* work-hour guidelines or track time spent at their desks. Their workloads are so heavy that they have no choice but to spend long hours there. If they want to hold on to their paychecks and benefit packages, if they want to keep rising within the corporate hierarchy, if they still care about their careers, they will put in whatever hours are necessary to handle their workloads. And they require neither timekeepers nor shop-floor supervisors to crack the whip, since they will *self-impose* whatever work schedule—nine-to-nine, six-to-eight (meaning A.M. to P.M., of course), or well into the morning hours—is necessary to get the job done.

Job Spill

One of the most insidious features of today's white-collar "sweatshop" is the way that increased work time and job demands get disguised, since many work-related activities take place in the ever more blurry terrain between life inside and outside the office.

Remember lunch hours? The very term has become an anachronism for many inhabitants of the corporate world. Thirty-nine percent of workers surveyed by the National Restaurant Association report that they are too busy to take a lunch break . . . they just work through it. Another 45 percent complain that they have less time for lunch than they used to have. While it's tough to tell exactly *how much less*—two recent surveys concluded that the sixty-minute lunch break has shrunk to either thirty-six or twenty-nine minutes—one conclusion is clear: we're gulping down our sandwiches quicker so that we can speed our way back to work.[8]

In Manhattan, for example, where "power lunches" have traditionally been a way of life (and integral to the publishing, entertainment, fashion, legal, and other industries), tony restaurants such as Le Bernardin now offer thirty-minute quickies for working men and women who are too pressed for time to ingest their gourmet meals at a leisurely pace. The latest trend among rising professionals? They schedule two or more mini-meals, with one set of business guests arriving at the table as another departs: "There's no foreplay to lunch anymore," one confided.[9]

The daily commute has also changed. For many men and women, the hours they spend in their cars or on trains getting to and from their offices used to include precious and uninterrupted moments of quiet which they now use, not for personal relaxation, but to return work-related phone calls they were too busy to respond to during the workday. When they get a free moment, or maybe get stalled in traffic, they check voice mail back at the office for new messages. Odds are, they don't even think of this activity as work; for many, it's just catch-up time. They might even blame themselves for being too disorganized or inefficient at the office to get done everything they need to do.

All those people in all those cars, however, with one hand on the steering wheel and the other on the cell phone, are part of a larger trend that has little to do with their personal efficiency. In most cases, after all, they'll have just as many phone calls to return during tomorrow's commute as they do today, even if they manage to catch up on all of them now. For lack of a better term, think of the cause as job "spill," like an oil spill. Then imagine job tasks seeping from the office to the home in much the same way as oil can invade a body of water and a beach. The seepage is just as difficult to block. And it's the dirty secret behind many a corporation's thriving bottom line.

Job spill encroaches upon far more than commuting time. Like Catherine, many of the people who write memos during their train rides home or return phone calls from the highway are the same ones who then proceed to check their e-mails and voice-mail messages after dinner: sometimes several times after dinner and sometimes for quite a long time after dinner. Their nighttime reading material might well be a project update or a stack of memos from colleagues, or a book they're editing, or an investment prospectus they're writing. As with commuting, they usually don't tote this up as additional time spent after an already long workday, although of course it is.

People try to minimize the disruption of their home life by playing their own equivalent of the commuter "catch-up" game: they tell themselves that by working at home during the evening, they're making their lives "easier" at the office tomorrow. Of course, they need to tell themselves the same thing when faced with tomorrow's job spill. Or, they can try not to think too much about it; after all, that's just "the way things are."

Job spill also seeps into the weekend. Although there always were some people—mainly go-getters on the rise and plain old workaholics—who brought office work home with them to do on Saturday and Sunday, the weekend has typically been an inviolate private space, a chance to unwind and get together with relatives or friends or simply relax. As Witold Rybczynski put it in *Waiting for the Weekend*, "It's a time apart from the world of mundane problems and mundane concerns, from the world of making a living. On weekends time stands still, and not only because we take off our watches."[10]

No longer. For many men and women, the pace of work is so intense and unrelenting that they simply cannot squirrel away the time to take off their watches and forget about their offices all weekend long. "I had no hobbies, no outside interests," recalled Patricia, one of a small group of female engineers at one of the nation's most prestigious (and demanding) high-tech giants. "I believe that the divorce rate at these very aggressive companies must be higher than the norm. If you make the choice to have a home life, your career will suffer. You've got to be willing to work the endless hours, come in on weekends, travel to the ends of the earth."

Weekend work is now just unavoidable for a good number of white-collar staffers. Electronic mail has fueled the trend in making it both easier for people to contact their colleagues and more difficult for colleagues to fail to respond (and respond quickly). People are fortunate who can squeeze their weekend work in along with other activities, confine it to *only* Saturday or Sunday, or limit it to a couple of weekends each month.

There are countless subtle, but significant, signs of the invasion of the office into the once-inviolate weekend. FedEx, for example, launched a Sunday delivery service to a series of select U.S. zip code destinations in order to serve a customer base in which "more and more businesses were operating on Sunday . . . [or] were faced with either the occasional situation or the demanding customer who needed things on what was once an impossible deadline."[11]

Bill, a longtime public relations executive, pointed out to me that more and more press conferences and news releases are being scheduled for Sunday. "It's a subtle breakdown of the old rules," he commented. "Maybe next we'll see these announcements coming out on Christmas. Hell, that's only another Wednesday or Thursday or whatever!"

Weekend work can take many different forms, running the gamut from a briefcase full of papers that will demand hours of reading and response time at one's home "office," to cell phone calls that interrupt a Sunday jitney ride back from the Hamptons, to beeper alerts that summon a mother or father away from a child's baseball game. The low point, at least with regard to weekend work, came for Marc one Saturday morning when he was wheeling his toddler daughter in a stroller to a local delicatessen for a breakfast alone.

"There we were in the mall and my beeper goes off." He paused in anger, as if he were still hearing it ring. "Here I am. My daughter deserves my attention, *but* all of a sudden Marc is a husband, a father, and a manager, all at the same time." He paused again, then added, "But that's not right, because when I'm at the office, they don't want to hear that I'm also Marc a father and Marc a husband."

Whether weekend work takes place at a shopping mall (or some other extension of one's home turf) or at the office generally depends upon the norms for each person's industry and particular company. Parking lots may be as much as half full at a high-tech company like Microsoft on a Saturday or Sunday, and it's easy to tell what that signifies: more people working more hours. (Manny reported to me that he used to "sneak [his] daughters in below the security cameras," when he worked weekends at Intel, because he was so desperate to spend time with them, even if only at the office.)

On the other hand, the cubicles and hallways may be empty at a publishing company like HarperCollins during the weekend. But that doesn't mean its editors aren't blue-lining manuscripts from their desks or dining room tables at home, or performing other tasks they are simply too busy to handle during their workweek.

Less Time to Unwind

"You *are* being asked to work weekends," complained Robert, the financial executive from American Express. "You *have* to travel. People don't consider it an acceptable excuse to say, 'I'm burned out and I need to spend time with my family.' People *do* keep mental notes. You see it in their faces."

Few people possess the valuable ability to shut work out of their personal lives, at least for a long enough period to unwind from the intense job schedules they must cope with seven days a week. Since weekends scarcely provide relief for many overloaded men and women, vacations and holidays loom ever more important as an opportunity to restore balance. Yet these too are under siege in the white-collar "sweatshop," both from cost-cutting corporations and from the ever-present job spill.

In *The Overworked American,* Juliet Schor concluded that during the 1980s "U.S. workers have gotten *less* time off—on the order of three and a half fewer days each year of vacation time, holidays, sick pay, and other paid absences." She added, "This decline is even more striking in that it reverses thirty years of progress in terms of paid time off." Symptomatic of the corporate trend was DuPont's decision to reduce the highest-paid vacation level for employees from seven to four weeks, while also eliminating three company-wide holidays from its annual calendar.[12]

With less time off (and jobs whose demands may be such that getting-away-from-it-all for two weeks is virtually impossible), quickie vacations have become increasingly popular. According to the Travel Industry Association of America, weekend vacations now represent more than half of all U.S. travel.

Even a weekend off is more time than some people can now steal away from their workplaces. So a new trend has evolved: twenty-four-hour vacations, which may take the form of overnights at a nearby hotel or spa. (Others manage to cram in round-trip airline flights, boat cruises, or some other type of long-distance conveyance that provides at least the illusion of a full-scale respite from work.) The *Wall Street Journal* termed such vacationers "deadline tourists,"[13] suggesting a heart-pounding compression of time that merely mirrors the intensity of their work and home lives.

Most people still cling to the more traditional forms of vacation (including enough time to work on a suntan or overcome jetlag). But a fair number bring along with them their laptops, portable fax machines, or electronic organizers, no matter how far from the office they go. They're the ones we all see who are speaking to their offices or their clients from cellular phones on the beach or the fishing boat. Intrusions like these from the workplace can even seem funny, so long as they're not happening to you or me. That was the way I felt when one thirty-something Wall Streeter described the time her cellular phone rang during a crowded train ride to her rented beach house in the Hamptons. Everyone within her sight range on the train checked his or her own phone; all were carrying them, in briefcases or handbags, as a matter of course.

Like all those men and women who squeeze work time into their commutes or evenings with the family, working vacationers may tell themselves that a little (or a lot) of work isn't really too bad, so long as it can be done *during* a stay at the beach or a trendy resort. How painful can it be to check one's voice mail, after all, if one can do it while watching the kids play beach volleyball or perfecting a suntan?

People who pacify themselves this way fail to appreciate that any work at all defeats the goal of a vacation, which is to restore one's sense of personal balance, enjoyment in life, and independence from the office. They cannot unwind, not really. The sad thing is, many people have basically accepted that this, too, is "the way things are."

Too Much Stress

Corporate America has always been a demanding place. For large numbers of men and women, however, the traditional demand-and-reward equation that has governed work life within the nation's largest companies no longer adds up. And that's true whether they're earning $30,000 a year or multiples more.

What's tipped the balance for many corporate staffers is the way that increased work time and job spill (with reduced opportunities to relax and recover) has contributed to stress loads so overwhelming that "job stress" and "personal stress" seem inextricably connected and inescapable. The personal toll can be overwhelming. Manny, the single father from Intel, confided to me, "Sometimes I would crash. A crash would mean I'd sit there and stare at the computer—couldn't move, couldn't hear anything. One time, I got a warning from my supervisor."

Many people find themselves pushed close to their own versions of Manny's "crash." International Survey Research Corporation, a Chicago-based opinion research firm, found that 44 percent of employees surveyed from a variety of corporations believe that their workloads are "excessive." (That percentage rose in six of the seven years surveyed, from a low of 37 percent in 1988.) Nearly as many people report that they are often bothered by excessive job pressures.[14]

Just think about it for a moment. People are working ten or twelve or more hours a day. They're working through their lunch hours, during their commutes to and from the office, in squeezed-in spare moments during their evening hours, and whenever else they absolutely need to on weekends and holidays. And many of them still feel that they cannot keep up, that their workloads are excessive.

When the American Management Association conducted an overnight fax survey of its members to explore what it called "the emotionally charged workplace," its results were disturbing. Fifty-one percent of those surveyed cited "frustration" and 49.4 percent "stress" in response to a question about which emotions best described their feelings throughout the workday. The problem of "having more to do than time to do it" ranked highest on a five-point scale that measured respondents' intensity of feelings.[15]

The National Center for Health Statistics, a division of the U.S. Department of Health and Human Services, tracked forty thousand workers to learn that more than half reported feeling either a lot or a moderate amount of stress during the two weeks prior to the survey. In the majority of instances, that stress was work-related.[16] Clearly, the problem abounds. More than 40 percent of professional and clerical workers surveyed by Gallup complained about stress on a daily or almost daily level. Business and sales staffers reported comparable loads.[17]

Unlike hours spent in the office or productivity demands, stress is difficult to quantify. But a person knows it when he or she feels it—and, as I came to discover during my research, one also knows it when one hears it. I heard it in Jerome's voice when he and I met for a rushed lunch on Wall Street to discuss his career.

During more than twenty years in the marketing departments of major banks, including Citibank and Marine Midland, Jerome had worked his way through numerous corporate reorganizations and mergers, surviving some and losing his job after another. In his current position, he was earning less than he had earned five years earlier but was working harder, without any promotion opportunities in sight.

Jerome was plagued by the memory of the time, a few years ago, when he had failed to follow up on a headhunter's telephone call: after all, that job *might* have taken him to a better place and position than the spot where he has ended up. With a son graduating from high school that coming June, he confessed that worries about college tuition were never far from his mind. It would be difficult enough to handle those bills at his current salary, but what if he somehow lost his job again? He had learned the hard way that you couldn't count on anything in the corporate world.

All this added up to stress: stress that was apparent in the angry, clipped tones he used during our conversation and the way that his fingers kept banging the table to punctuate his points. "How long can they tighten the screws on people?" he asked me. Then he answered his own question. "As long as people take it. But they take it. They take it. They accept that this is what's happening to them. And it happened to their friends." He paused, then added in a tone laced with sarcasm. "They can commiserate with each other. If every company's doing it, the norm has just changed forever."

It has. These days stress is a way of life for many white-collar workers, regardless of their particular employer, age, or position on the corporate ladder. Today's pumped-up, high-pressure corporations thrive on stress, which helps motivate people to meet inflated and sometimes unrealistic short-term goals, regardless of the long-term toll it takes on their employees. Within the white-collar "sweatshop," there is little effort to disguise stressing techniques: in fact, the practice has been elevated to the level of business "philosophy." As one management consultant expressed his version, "The workplace is never free of fear—and it shouldn't be. Indeed, fear can be a powerful management tool."[18]

Fear, insecurity, and exhaustion all contribute to rising stress levels in today's large corporations. And these pressures reinforce each other as overworked, stressed-out colleagues take their anxieties and resentments out on their fellow workers. "You should check out workplace bullying," Maureen, a thirty-year-old marketing representative at Simon and Schuster, advised me.

The problem, in Maureen's assessment, was not so much outright confrontation between professional colleagues: it was a "subtle" hostility between them that often manifested itself in rude behavior, angry or dismissive conversational tones, or short fuses. In her own office, she complained, people were quick to blame others for anything that ever went wrong. "The underlying thing is the sense of fear. They're feeling very insecure about their jobs," she commented.

A tour through the vast body of work-related websites on the Internet reveals "The Work Doctor," a site started up in 1998 by two self-described employee advocates and psychologists by training, who promise to "listen unconditionally . . . support the hurting." Calling itself the "U.S. Campaign Against Workplace Bullying Headquarters," the site attracts an average of nearly thirty-five thousand visitors per month, ranging in age from seventeen to fifty-eight—a strong indicator that others agree with Maureen's assessment of the significance of this problem. (The site's demographic surveys suggest that about 30 percent of its visitors are "professionals" and another 40 percent work in some type of management position. The majority of these have been female so far.)

According to the "Work Doctors," "the American workplace's 'dirty little habit' is that harassment, abuse, cheating, power plays, denial of simple rights, and other forms of mistreatment occur regularly. Rarely is the wrongdoing illegal. It is bullying." Among the classic workplace types they describe is the "opportunistic bully" who has "learned well the lessons of contemporary workplace dealings. He is only copying what he sees the parent [corporation] do," which includes "seizing the opportunity" to compete with and "obliterate" coworkers.[19]

"The backbiting and politicking that you see at big companies these days is unbelievable," noted Zoe, the veteran of Levi Strauss's downsizing campaigns. "People become territorial because they're so scared. They're vying for power. If you know that cutbacks are coming, you'll do anything to position yourself so that you'll survive, even if nobody else does. There's lots of nastiness. All kinds of false accusations."

Along with verbal abuse and bullying, physical violence can surface in today's stressed-out offices. The phrase "going postal" has entered the lexicon of today's high-pressure, lean-and-mean workplaces: shorthand for people who crack under the strain of working conditions too tough for them to handle. But although few of us even give a thought to the risk of office violence, some studies suggest that it may be more common than many people imagine. According to a survey conducted by the Society for Human Resource Management, nearly 10 percent of employers can expect some type of violent altercation to break out in their offices each year.[20]

Direct links clearly exist between corporate developments and the personal problems facing many workers. In Maureen's office, relationships between coworkers deteriorated during the period when Simon and Schuster's corporate parent, Viacom, began to publicize its intention to sell part or all of the publishing company as soon as an acceptable bid came along.

I spoke to her during that period of complete instability (while she and her colleagues were, as she reported, plagued by anxieties about whether they could expect good severance packages if and when they got laid off, if and when the company got sold). "The fear level *is* pretty high," she concluded, then added that for a lot of people, including herself, these kinds of stress "also delay what seems like the passage to adulthood. Things like buying a house. Because people feel like even if they're employed, they don't know if they can hold on to their jobs long enough to live with a mortgage."

White-collar men and women also move in the opposite direction—fueling credit card binges and other forms of risky overextension that thrived during the 1990s—as they seek to alleviate their anxieties about the future of their careers or their feelings of personal inadequacy (because they haven't managed to get their hands on stock options or some of the other corporate goodies they keep reading about in the newspapers).

To make matters worse, with cost control a major priority at most large corporations, workplace conditions have deteriorated in ways that may even seem, at first glance, to be too petty to notice. But they quickly add up for stressed-out workers whose tempers are frayed and whose patience is short. "Did you hear about the water yet?" is a question I was asked by three different white-collar employees whose company, NYNEX, had merged with Bell Atlantic in the course of the many months I spoke with each of them.

They were different types of people, and each one had his or her own perspective on what had gone wrong with the company during many years of employment. But all three were preoccupied with water—or, to be more specific, with the *lack* of drinkable water at the company's office on Manhattan's Avenue of the Americas.

"The quality of water in our building is rather poor," one told me, his voice positively dripping with understatement. He explained that NYNEX had made it a practice to provide employees at this facility with bottled water: scarcely the most decadent of perquisites (especially when one considers the time it took people to ride the elevator downstairs and walk to a nearby grocery or coffee shop, inevitably crowded, instead). But after the merger, "in the interests of cost reduction," this manager said, drawing out every word, "they eliminated the bottled water."

He wanted to make certain I understood just how discomforting this decision had proven to be. (In fact, all three NYNEX veterans spent considerable time describing the water situation.) "No water means no coffee either." From her vantage point at Simon and Schuster, Maureen would not have been surprised to learn that heated confrontations soon broke out between departments that decided to ante up for their own water so as to be able to make their own coffee in the office, and those coworkers from other departments who occasionally crept in during a busy morning or afternoon to sneak a spare cup to which they were not entitled.

Annoyances of all scales abound. For all the jokes Scott Adams pokes at cubicles in his Dilbert cartoons, life in a cubicle is far from funny for most of the estimated 35 million white-collar workers who reside in one during eight-, ten-, twelve-, or longer-hour workdays. For one thing, cubicles keep getting smaller: Facility Performance Group Inc., an Ann Arbor, Michigan-based organization that tracks office trends at seventy large corporations, has reported that work spaces have shrunk by 25 to 50 percent over the past ten years for most workers.[21]

Far from creating the collaborative, open environments that many top executives boast of when describing their "bullpen" designs (often from their own, multiwindowed and lushly furnished offices), cubicles foster all kinds of negative feelings. As one workplace observer aptly described, cubicles (whether of the relatively larger or relatively smaller variety) remain "mechanisms of constant surveillance."[22] Their ticky-tacky, one-size-fits-all, institutional-gray designs demean white-collar professionals just as surely as do the lack of a door and any illusion of privacy. Meanwhile, their very air of impermanence—since most can be set up, moved, or reconfigured at will—is a not-so-subtle daily reminder of the lack of stability and security in the corporate workplace. If there is any lesson that the 1980s and 1990s have taught white-collar workers, it is that they can be replaced easily.

Other new arrangements convey similar, unspoken messages. With the virtual office or "hoteling" trend, employees are stripped of anything resembling a workspace and become "floaters" who may claim a desk or an office only on an as-needed basis. Despite the impact on people's day-to-day work lives, the strategy has its appeal for companies looking for ways to cut real estate and operating costs.

Cubicles, "hoteling" offices, and other arrangements like these help ratchet up job pressures by creating corporate atmospheres that are anything but comfortable, secure, and permanent. Most people understand the subtext. For cubicle dwellers: Work harder, because we can all see, smell, and hear what you're doing . . . or not doing. For hotelers: Be productive, or your "stay" at this company will soon be over.

The Toll

Unpleasant working conditions, difficult job demands, and rising career insecurities have combined to make stress the constant companion of many of today's white-collar men and women. It is a complaint so common as to seem banal, boring, perhaps the most hackneyed cliché of our age. But the reality of it is the very opposite: a heart-pounding, anxiety-ridden emotional state that regularly plagues men and women at work and outside of work, leading to migraines, ulcers, pinched nerves, insomnia, clammy palms, skipped heartbeats, and any number of other symptoms of our stressed-out age.

One estimate pegged the annual cost to the U.S. economy of such work-related stress at $200 billion.[23] Talk to enough corporate staffers these days and that seems quite believable. "I've started getting heart palpitations. I just went through stress tests. I'm trying now to detach myself, to focus on my own health," Donald told me.

Just forty years old, he was a marketing staffer who had spent more than a decade at NYNEX, where he managed to hold on to his post through a number of layoffs and, eventually, the company's merger with Bell Atlantic. But between the years of cutbacks, the career uncertainty, the increasing workload, he was bitter. "I don't have any pride in this company. I don't feel any attachment. I don't feel any loyalty. It's only money. That's all I care about—the money." His father had been a blue-collar worker, employed by a municipal agency. Donald recalled, "He hated his job. He was powerless. He pushed me to become a professional. But even though I'm a professional, it doesn't mean anything. We're all just trying to survive."

The long-term toll of job-related stress appears to include all kinds of health risks. One ten-year study, which tracked about one thousand Swedes and was conducted by UCLA and the Karolinska Institute in Stockholm, found that serious work-related problems made a person "five times more likely to develop colorectal cancer." Meanwhile, "unemployment of more than six months doubled the cancer risk."[24]

A University of California at Davis research team that tracked female lawyers found that those who worked long hours were "five times as likely to experience great stress at work and three times as likely to suffer miscarriages as [were] female lawyers who work fewer than 35 hours a week."[25] A University of Michigan study of nearly fifteen hundred nurses found that women who worked more than forty hours during the week or experienced high job stress were 70 to 80 percent more likely to deliver premature, underweight babies.[26]

I discussed job stress with Ida, a sociologist by training, whose career path had taken her through a series of human resources jobs at large corporations. "What helps people who are living through life at a lot of these companies is that there's the mortgage to pay and all those bills. Their outlet is sports, the Internet," she told me, adding, "The fact is that for many people, they have no choice."

Ida started working in corporate America during the 1960s, when she believed that the nation's prosperity would help make people's work lives more challenging, secure, *and* rewarding. But she lost those illusions after participating in a huge round of cutbacks at a big-name manufacturing firm. "People were literally dying. There were heart attacks, all kinds of medical responses." Now, she believes something very different: that job stress is responsible for "the decline of the civil society, the increase in traffic, in rage."

Damaging as they may be, however, recent increases in stress and work loads are only part of the problem for the inhabitants of today's white-collar "sweatshops." Despite nearly two decades of economic prosperity, many people have found themselves working harder within a business world whose reward structure has deteriorated in a variety of important ways.

TWO

"Working Three Times Harder and Earning Less": The Shrinking Paycheck and Other Squeezes

Not only are today's corporations demanding more work from their white-collar employees, they are also scaling back on financial rewards. Despite all the economic good tidings that rang in throughout most of the past decade, many men and women had salary increases that were modest at best. Most people employed by large corporations watched workplace benefits and bonuses diminish or disappear.

As the new millennium began, studies by the Center on Budget and Policy Priorities and the Economic Policy Institute demonstrated just how few middle-class Americans actually shared the fruits of recent prosperity. During the decade from 1988 through 1998, family incomes for the nation's middle 20 percent rose by $780, compared with a gain of $50,760 for the nation's wealthiest, those in the top 5 percent income tier.[1]

Other white-collar men and women found themselves somewhere in between, with their salaries rising (although not as fast as their job and stress loads). If they felt better off, it usually had more to do with rising home prices and retirement-account values than with the size of their paychecks and other, more liquid household assets. For countless people, the only way to obtain what seemed a fair reward for all their hard work was to push household borrowing to dangerous and unparalleled heights. Along the way, personal-savings rates dropped to a historic low.[2] At a time when most working people were already stressed out by the voracious demands of their workplaces, financial pressures like these raised anxiety levels higher still.

Early on, as corporate America initiated an era of cutbacks and layoffs during the 1980s, General Electric's chief executive, Jack Welch, popularized the notion that there was "unlimited juice" to be squeezed from the lemon, so long as companies pursued a relentless campaign to achieve greater operating efficiencies.[3] That struck other CEOs as inspirational. As corporations aimed to achieve these efficiencies, white-collar staffers often found themselves confronted by the prospect of wage freezes or even reductions, job loss, or contingent employment. By the end of the nineties, the more-work/less-reward approach to corporate management left many feeling as though they themselves had been squeezed nearly dry.

Salary Stagnation

"What used to be an 8:00 A.M. to 5:00 P.M. job is now a 7:00 to 6:30 job. It's crazy," complained Danny, a public relations executive at one of the nation's largest financial services firms, with headquarters in Manhattan. "Some people get co-opted into this attitude that the payoff is going to come to them from the stock price." The thirty-two-year-old himself owned a tiny stake in the company for which he worked, obtained through annual stock grants to his pension plan. Still, he remained convinced that he and his colleagues were worse off each year, no matter how much stock they received, as their job demands continued to increase even faster.

"You might have to put in twelve hours a day, seven days a week, in order to actually get the stock payoff." Danny referred to the company's vesting schedule, which required its employees to work for a prolonged period of time after each stock grant was made in order to fully own the shares within their retirement accounts. Even after that point, he concluded, "the payoff translates into a very small number for most people. I've always said that if you add up all the hours I work and divide that by how much I get paid—even including my stock gains—I probably earn less per hour than half the secretaries on the floor."

Danny is scarcely alone. The business boom of the 1990s has owed its success, in large part, to employers' ability to keep operating expenses—and most especially payroll expenses—under control.

Their cost-cutting techniques have included layoffs, early-retirement programs, and reengineering campaigns to redesign job flow. No matter how good times have gotten, companies like these have continued looking for ways to eliminate staffers deemed unnecessary or inefficient, while pushing others to work at paces that once might have seemed unfair or unsustainable. Some corporations maintained robust hiring schedules after, or even during, layoff phases.[4] This gave them the option of replacing higher-paid, older workers with less expensive junior staffers and part-timers or consultants who would not qualify for costly benefit packages.

"Seeing all this is making a big impact on me," Danny told me as our conversation drew to a close. "As I have progressed in my career, my wife and I have made a big decision not to keep our expenses up to our income. I drive my little clunker of a Nissan to the train station each day and I see all those big cars in the parking lot. But I don't want to be desperate if something happens to me one day. If my income really went up," he added, "we would stay in the same house and finally start socking it away. I think there are a lot of people who have been lured into a false sense of security. They don't realize that the almighty dollar is driving every single decision their bosses make."

The business world held fast to the cost-cutting strategies of the eighties and nineties even when reporting impressive levels of revenue growth, profits, and cash flow. One might have expected, as during previous periods of corporate prosperity, that a rising economic tide would carry people's salaries along with it. But this failed to happen during the recent boom for several reasons: the anti-inflationary rationale for fiscal discipline (since low wages can help keep price growth under control); the lack of unified resistance from white-collar staffers; and strong encouragement by Wall Street (which views payroll-related savings as a source of either higher profits or increased growth capital).

Pressures on white-collar wages only increased as the boom took hold. A report by the Economic Policy Institute revealed that while corporate profit rates were higher in 1997 than at any previous busi-

ness-cycle peak going back forty years, "labor's share" of rising business income had declined.[5] Put simply, as the corporate pie got bigger during the past decade, working men and women took home a
smaller slice of it all the same.

When viewed from a financial perspective, a variety of trends
throughout the 1980s and 1990s all converged to keep the lid on
payroll costs, no matter how much harder the United States' white-
collar men and women were working. Most of this past decade's job
growth took place at smaller companies and start-ups, where
salaries and benefits were typically lower than at large corporations.
Some fortunate men and women received stock options that more
than compensated for this shortfall; the vast majority of Americans
just read about them in newspapers and came to rely more heavily
upon their credit cards.

At large companies, the reengineering craze provided a philosophical justification for shrinking-reward strategies. In reengineered companies, internal reorganizations usually produced
large-scale layoffs; these resulted in lower payroll costs while also
motivating existing workers—who were afraid of losing their own
jobs—to take on greater loads without demanding additional pay. In
some cases, scared staffers even accepted reduced salaries when
their jobs were "redefined" and workloads increased. The management consulting guru Michael Hammer, the creator of the movement, acknowledged at one point that he had been "insufficiently
appreciative of the human dimension."[6] But most employers were
not complaining.

Also fueling salary cuts and controls was the merger trend, which
led to deals of increasingly grand scope as the 1990s progressed. But
although many large corporations got bigger, *much* bigger, few people's paychecks expanded accordingly. Corporate couplings often
tended to reinforce the preoccupation with cost control, since payroll savings from anticipated layoffs and cutbacks were typically an
essential ingredient in merger strategies for success.

Even without the rubric of a trendy management style or the
impetus from a merger, other companies managed to accomplish
similar cost-control goals by placing such high productivity and
work-hour demands upon their staffers that longer-tenured workers

almost inevitably burned out. Or they got fired for failing to meet ever tougher performance standards. Silicon Valley and Wall Street became notorious as places where only the young (which has meant, mainly, *men* ranging in age from their twenties through their early forties) could thrive.

In workforces like these, employee burnout was essentially viewed as a positive, if Darwinian, trend: it helped ensure the maintenance of a younger workforce, whose selling points could include its technological up-to-dateness, lower salary demands, and, presumably, good health. Younger workers also tended to lack the family responsibilities that weighed down many older colleagues. That meant less of a strain on the corporation's medical-benefit costs as well as fewer distractions for employees when called upon, as they all too often were, to work longer hours.

Here's what the decade's shrinking-reward structure has actually meant in terms of the paychecks of full-time white-collar employees. (These are people nominally working thirty-five- to forty-hour workweeks, a description that does not include all the evening, weekend, and commuting-time job tasks they might perform outside the office.) White-collar males earned an average hourly wage of $19.24 in 1997. When expressed in 1997 dollars (which takes inflation into account), that is an increase of *six cents*—just three tenths of one percent—from the average hourly wage they earned twenty-five years earlier, in 1973.[7] For white-collar women, the picture was slightly more complicated. Thanks to efforts to close the wage gap between the sexes, as well as other factors such as increases in job tenure and hours worked, white-collar women did manage to earn more in 1997 than in 1973.[8] Still, in the 1990s, women's wages increased at a far slower rate than they had during the previous decade.

As corporate cutbacks proliferated, both sexes got hit hard during the prosperity boom by salary erosion within certain job categories. Between 1990 and 1997, male managers watched their paychecks shrink, as did men working in sales, administrative, and clerical posts. The most vulnerable women, at least on the salary front, were those who held service, technical, clerical, or administrative jobs.

Even Christmas bonuses have been fading fast, with employers believing that these send a message of entitlement and benevolence that does not fit in today's competitive marketplace. Back in 1950, just about half of corporate employers boasted some type of year-end bonus. According to a recent survey by Hewitt Associates, a management consulting firm, only 36 percent of companies now do. Most decided to drop the bonus during the past decade.[9]

All these changes are a far cry, the economist Lester Thurow noted, from typical compensation patterns throughout much of the post-World War II period. During this earlier era, he explained, wages "rose even when there were unemployed qualified American workers who would have been glad to do those jobs for less. This anomaly was explained by arguing that firms deliberately paid incumbent workers above-market wages to secure a high degree of cooperation, commitment, and effort that they could not have gotten if their workforces could have quit and easily gotten equal wages elsewhere."

Thurow went on to observe, "But in a world where there are always millions of unemployed and underemployed workers"—which was certainly the case during much of the late 1980s and early-to-mid-1990s—"the same degree of cooperation, commitment, and effort can be achieved by using the motivation factor called 'fear' . . . [E]xamples abound of profitable firms that simply marched in and dramatically lowered the wages of the existing workforces by 20 to 40 percent. Workers complain but they don't quit."[10]

In recent years, the shrinking-reward trend has spread far beyond the world of America's largest corporations, playing out according to the dynamics of different workplaces and fields. "Architectural firms always have had a basic level of inequality built into their structure," Martin, a fifty-year-old architect, commented, "because they're set up as partnerships and, if you're not a partner, you never really share the profits, no matter how hard you work." People in the industry would swap jokes, he told me, such as "I. M. Pei doesn't pay."

Still, he added, his workplace conditions became much worse during the nineties, when the corporate cutback mentality penetrated the large northeastern architectural design firm that employed him. "I was working on a project that was profitable, but there were other projects that the company was involved in that were not. We were all brought into a room and asked to take a rather significant pay cut," he recalled. "It was mandatory. But management promised us that the cut would be restored and that we would all be taken care of."

At the time, Martin was regularly working at least ten hours each day, as well as weekends and some evenings at home. "I'd never gotten a bonus in my life, no matter how much money the firm was making. Now that times were bad, I was supposed to share the pain. But I was a professional, which meant that I'd work as long as I had to in order to get the job done."

He and his colleagues went along with the mandatory cut and kept putting in as many hours as they always had. After some time, conditions got better for their employer, but, as Martin put it, "the joke was on us—that salary cut was never restored. And we were never reimbursed for all the money we had given up." The next time the construction industry went into one of its inevitable downswings, many of the people in that room wound up losing their jobs.

At universities and colleges across the country, cost-control pressures have resulted in the transfer of more and more of the classroom-teaching load to low-paid adjunct professors and graduate students: the academic world's equivalent of temp workers (typically lacking as they do any type of job security, employee benefits, or professional status). The number of professors getting hired at full-time salaries keeps shrinking. And along the way, many schools have also reduced the rates at which they award the employment guarantee known as tenure to their senior professors.[11]

Even those symbols of white-collar success and security—doctors, lawyers, and accountants—have suffered during at least some phase of the lean-and-mean 1990s.[12] Within the medical profession, the impetus has come from managed care, which imposes corporate cost controls and bureaucracies upon physicians, therapists, lab technicians, and other health care professionals. Although many work longer hours than ever (often, in part, because of the additional paperwork requirements connected with managed-care systems), many have seen their earnings affected as a result.[13]

Lawyers and accountants have been hit by their own versions of corporate cost control. Business clients either might conduct billing audits in search of fee savings or hire lower-paid in-house or junior professionals rather than partners from pricey consulting firms. "Bills must give precise descriptions of even the most mundane tasks. Lawyers find themselves spending otherwise billable time haggling with outside auditors," reported the *Wall Street Journal*.[14]

After stagnating for most of the past two decades, white-collar paychecks only began responding to pressures from the tight labor market and to show some upward movement as the nineties drew to a close.[15] Yet according to an analysis by Dismal Sciences, an economic consulting firm that tracked salary patterns for 129 common job categories, nearly 20 percent of them—including aircraft pilots, teachers, and salespeople—failed to keep up with inflation during the past decade. Others, such as real estate brokers, therapists, journalists, and secretaries, made only modest paycheck gains.[16]

The only segment of the white-collar community that has truly seemed exempt from salary pressures these days is the American chief executive officer, a rare breed whose median salary plus bonuses grew by a whopping 44.6 percent during those otherwise cost-conscious years of 1989 through 1997. When his (and occasionally her) additional forms of compensation are factored in—gains from exercised options, gifts of restricted stock, and other forms of long-term incentive awards—that increase looked even higher: 71 percent during the years from 1992 to 1997 alone.[17] And as the stock market continued to boom, their skyrocketing earnings set one record after another.

Declining Financial Realities for Young Workers

During the 1990s, there was a lot of media hype about the fabulous financial prospects available to young men and women. "In this economy the people with leverage are knowledge workers of a certain [young] age, so-called gold-collar workers: Anyone who's educated, smart, creative, computer literate, equipped with portable skills—and demanding," enthused one reporter.[18] But unless they were seeking jobs on a short list of hot industries—among them business consulting and high technology—earning prospects were in fact far less promising for many young people.

Entry-level wages for male college graduates actually declined by 6.5 percent between 1989 and 1997—the second consecutive decade during which their starting wages declined. A new college graduate back in 1973 could have expected to earn $14.82 per hour (in inflation-adjusted 1997 dollars), which adds up to *$1.17 more per hour* than his "gold"-collared counterpart was paid in the high-pressure corporate world twenty-five years later.[19]

For entry-level female graduates during the recent economic boom, the salary situation was also dismal: their paychecks fell by 7.4 percent during the nineties. By 1997, newly minted women were earning seventy-five cents per hour less, when adjusted for inflation, than their counterparts had earned in 1973.[20]

A study by two Labor Department economists, Geoffrey Paulin and Brian Riordon, found that unmarried men and women between the ages of eighteen and twenty-nine were significantly worse off economically during the 1990s than they had been in the 1970s or 1980s. During this roughly twenty-five-year period, this group "suffered a real average income drop of about 11%, with more than 80% of the decline occurring in the past decade."[21]

Although the business world has been thriving, it remains tough for many young people to get a toehold in entry-level jobs that will pay decent salaries and offer them real prospects for advancement. Michael, a twenty-something who graduated with an undergraduate business degree, internship experience, and a 3.5 average from one of New York's better universities, spent nearly a year trying to get hired by a Wall Street firm, bank, or other financial services company.

"First, I went on all kinds of interviews with on-campus recruiters and I came close, but I never got any job offers," he recalled. "After graduating, I sent my résumé everywhere. I responded to all kinds of job listings. And I wouldn't even get letters of rejection. I'd just send my résumé and it would be nothing, nothing. I felt almost abandoned."

When he finally found a Wall Street job, it was far from perfect. (In fact, it once might have been described as indentured servitude.)

He was expected to work full-time for three months as an apprentice, without earning any compensation at all. During the next three months, he would take home commissions based upon whatever income he could earn as a novice investment trader, but would receive no salary at all. "It's ironic," he noted. "I will have earned more money during the summers that I spent working as a waiter than I'll take home during this whole year after graduating from college."

Michael's new bosses did not make any bones about the financial sacrifices they expected him, and his young colleagues, to make in return for the opportunity to get started. "They come right out and tell you that if you can't support yourself from other sources of income during your first six months on the job, don't take it," he confided. "It's very difficult to know what to do. If they would even give me a small base salary, it would make my life so much easier, since I don't have savings and will have to earn money some other way, while I'm starting out at this job, in order to pay my bills."

It's a harsh new work world for almost everyone. But younger men and women have little leverage with which to resist the work-harder-for-less syndrome because they must compete for an ever-shrinking pool of starter jobs that offer true upward momentum. "It seems as though everyone I know has been taking salary cuts in the hope that their next job will lead someplace," observed Mariah, a twenty-six-year-old assistant in one of the divisions of Calvin Klein. "You know how hard that is?" she asked me. "New York City is so ridiculously expensive. It's impossible to find someplace you can afford to live."

Five years after graduating from college, she told me that she finally felt as though she had landed a job offering her the potential to rise. "But it's frustrating," she added. "I take work home all the time. So do all the people I work with. I stay at the office after the cleaning women come in at night." She paused. "I'm working three times harder than I did at my last job and I'm earning less. But at least I've got the chance to move up—so long as I'm willing to go back to graduate school and spend tons more money getting the right kind of degree."

Rising Contingency Rates

Compounding their financial pressures, large numbers of newly minted college graduates cannot find full-time posts, and thus have been forced to accept part-time jobs, temporary posts, and other forms of so-called contingent employment. During the late 1990s, about 30 percent of the 5.6 million Americans working in contingent jobs were under the age of twenty-five.[22] Nearly half of those surveyed told the Bureau of Labor Statistics that they would have preferred noncontingent work *if* they could have found it.

Getting to the root of this problem raises the chicken-versus-the-egg dilemma: Are many of today's young people unable to find full-time jobs *despite* the recent period of business prosperity or *because* of a boom that has depended upon extreme measures of cost control (among them, many corporations' decision to transform full-time jobs with benefits into lower-paid part-time or temporary jobs without them)?

This visitor to www.disgruntled.com, a work-related magazine on the Internet, might not care about such subtleties. He wrote, "If you'd asked me three years ago if I thought that today I'd be working part-time as a temp slave for Smelly Temporary Services . . . I would've said, 'No way.' Who me? White college graduate on the dean's list, hard worker all his life, son of successful middle class Jewish parents? No way a change in our economy would affect me, I would have replied. Yet after faxing 234 résumés in the last three months for positions as an administrative assistant, interviewing for seven of them and receiving no offers . . . I reluctantly accepted a temporary part-time administrative assistant position at $9.80 an hour for 15–20 hours a week so I could pay my rent and pay off student loans."[23]

This trend will likely accelerate, to the detriment of many young people like this one, as more large corporations opt to cap or reduce their salary and benefit costs by relying upon contingent employees as much as possible. According to one survey, three quarters of the nearly five hundred companies questioned made use of contingent workers: of this group, the majority had increased their usage levels during the five prior years.[24]

For most businesses, contingent staffing extends far beyond the occasional hiring of a temporary secretary or file clerk as a fill-in for sick or vacationing staffers. According to a Conference Board survey of more than ninety large U.S. corporations, more than one third expected temporary hires, part-timers, freelancers, and independent contractors to account for at least 10 percent of their workforces by the year 2000.[25]

Avid users of contingent labor included Gannett Company, Dow Corning, and Mary Kay Cosmetics. Their motivations varied, but the survey noted that "where benefit packages for core employees are very rich, as at Mary Kay Cosmetics, avoiding such expenses can be a very attractive feature of a contingent work force." The practice also, according to the Conference Board study, was "closely identified with continued downsizing, since headcount restrictions are often imposed on managers to keep the core employment down once the job cuts have been made."[26]

In today's business world, almost any technique that yields target levels of work from staffers in return for lower corporate costs and commitments is viewed as a win-win strategy. Contingent employment helps boost the corporate bottom line, while also creating a "just-in-time" workforce that can be increased or decreased as rapidly and impersonally as when manufacturers order raw supplies or otherwise regulate their inventory levels.

Despite the corporate world's enthusiasm, however, contingent employment imposes a harsh financial penalty upon younger workers who might like but cannot find full-time positions within today's economy. Full-time contingent workers aged twenty to twenty-four years old now earn about $300 each week, which is nearly 10 percent less than their noncontingent counterparts, according to the Bureau of Labor Statistics. For slightly older men and women, those aged twenty-five to thirty-four years of age, the financial toll is harsher still: the weekly median salary for full-time contingent workers adds up to $421, 13 percent less than for their full-time counterparts.[27]

With such wage pressure, it's little wonder that contingent workers of all ages tend to hold multiple jobs more frequently than the rest of the U.S. workforce.[28] After all, as the self-styled employee of

"Smelly Temporary Services" went on to emphasize in his e-mail diatribe, many young people can barely get by on the cut-rate salaries available to them as contingent workers in the new and prosperous corporate world.

"The money I make ($700–$800)," he explained, "is barely enough to live on. Thus, I now qualify to pay $10 a month for health insurance. The remainder of my bill is paid by the state. I also get food stamps, energy assistance, telephone credit and subsidized housing. None of these 'benefits' are paid for by either 'employer.'" (He is referring to both the temporary-employment agency that places him at job sites and the corporations that actually employ his services.) His conclusion? These benefits are "paid for by the rest of us, the taxpayers[,] in the amount of $5,800 plus a year. . . . So, if you're an employer using one of the temp slave companies or reducing your workers' hours to save cost . . . you might want to ask yourself in a rare moral moment why taxpayers ought to pay for your 'money-saving' efforts."

Although these jobs may be temporary, their financial consequences are often anything but short-lived. Since contingent jobs tend to offer less training, opportunity for advancement, and networking prospects, a significant portion of those young people who are relegated to these posts may find themselves stuck in a white-collar black hole they cannot escape because it simply is not possible for them to cross over into the traditional, full-time jobs their parents once took for granted. Fewer and fewer of these exist in a downsized corporate world whose sights are firmly set on the bottom line.

Thanks to corporate America's preoccupation with controlling compensation costs (everywhere outside the executive suite), increases in contingent employment rates bounce across industry lines and job categories. Upscale "professional specialty" jobs currently log the same high percentage of contingent employment—6.0 percent—as the presumably less skilled positions that are lumped within the Bureau of Labor Statistics' "administrative support, including clerical," category.[29]

Even scientists, "who[,] by virtue of their expertise, are widely thought to be immune to job insecurity in the high-tech knowledge economy[,] are being reduced to temp work," observed Jeremy Rifkin in his *The End of Work*. One national temp agency, which specializes in placing high-end technical workers in companies that range from Johnson & Johnson to Miller Brewing Company, has a roster of more than one thousand chemists, microbiologists, and lab technicians on call.[30]

For older, more experienced men and women who might find themselves forced to accept contingent positions after years of working (and rising) within a corporate hierarchy, the transition to casual "contract" status can be shocking. "There is absolutely nothing—or very little—written about what I'm going through. It's an unprecedented time: the economy at its best, yet the toll is unbelievable on individuals. It is beyond belief," complained Graham, a forty-year-old who had lost his mid-management job as part of a widespread layoff that followed a merger at his regional bank.

"A friend of ours was laid off at Chase. She's working temp jobs," he told me. "At one point, she went through three interviews for the same position. Then, at the end of the conversation, the interviewer mentioned, by the way, it's not even a full-time job—it's just another temp."

Although Graham was also job-hunting, his age and salary level seemed to be strikes against him with potential new employers. He found himself interviewing for jobs at much lower pay levels. Along the way, he drifted into the world of independent contracting. "I just finished up a temporary job," he confided. "It was a senior-level position—spec'd out as a temp. It paid very well, actually. I was identifying acquisition opportunities for a company. And I did the job very well—identified some targets, very much what they were looking for. Then they decided to bring the project in-house, which effectively cut me out of the loop. It just ended one day. One week I was working, the next week I was not. No notice."

For a man who had been drawn to the banking industry in part because it once seemed to offer a secure corporate existence, the stresses associated with contingent work life were overwhelming. "It's a very precarious existence. You're not on the top of everybody's Rolodex. It's anybody's guess whether you'll ever even get another call. All my adult life," he concluded, "I was in a decision-making position, a control position. As a consultant, you have no control. I don't view this as something I want to keep doing."

Neither did Martin, the architect, who eventually found himself forced to accept a contingent position, too. But there was one unexpected advantage, he told me: "My payment level was much lower as a contract employee than it had been at my last job. But I wasn't under any obligation to work longer than forty hours each week—and if I did, I got paid overtime."

There were tradeoffs, of course. "I had to pay for my own medical insurance. And I didn't have any other kind of benefits or vacations. If I stayed home because I was sick, I wouldn't get paid." But that overtime could add up. "In my old job," he recalled, "I was paid for a forty-hour week but regularly used to work fifty or sixty hours. So it wasn't completely clear which way I was worse off."

Job Loss and Downward Mobility

Like Martin and Graham, many other long-successful white-collar men and women have eventually found themselves suffering the unwanted financial consequences of the nation's recent economic boom. In technical terms, they are the "displaced": those who have lost jobs as part of layoffs or downsizing campaigns.[31]

Since layoffs have increasingly become part of the management norm, it is likely that many people will find themselves in this category at some point during their working careers—and that they will suffer financially because of it. The health of the nation's economy has provided little buffer against this risk: during the prosperous years 1995–97, six and a half million men and women were displaced; millions of them took years to restabilize their careers and their finances. In all, more than 45 million Americans have been laid off from jobs, many of long tenure, during the past two decades.

Since the Department of Labor first began surveying this trend in 1984, a disturbing and consistent pattern has revealed itself: displaced workers often fail to find new work at salary levels comparable to those they have earned in the past. Countless men and women never manage to find their way back to traditional, full-time jobs and wind up consulting, temping, or starting their own businesses for lack of any other real choice. Although some people manage to overcome the obstacle, for many others getting laid off is a career bump that permanently disrupts their lives and downgrades their earning potential.

The risk of job displacement has shifted in recent years, with white-collar staffers becoming increasingly vulnerable. Back in the early eighties, blue-collar workers faced nearly three times as great a chance of losing their jobs. But today their risks are nearly the same; and in some primarily white-collar industries, among them finance, insurance, and real estate, the odds of getting laid off have more than tripled during the last decade and a half.

Many families never recover from the financial hit of a job loss. Part of the problem is simply how long it can take someone to get rehired, especially if one's industry or region has already experienced heavy cutbacks or the job seeker is older (meaning, in his or her forties or fifties). According to the eight DOL surveys that have been conducted since January 1984, only about half of all displaced workers have managed to find new full-time positions in anything resembling a prompt fashion.[32] For many people, there's no alternative but to dip into their personal savings or borrow against the value of their homes in order to make it through the ordeal.

After Peter, a financial manager, was laid off by one of the nation's largest credit-reporting companies, he spent more than four years looking for another post. "I did everything from delivering newspapers to taking in foster kids to keep bringing in money," he confided. "I applied for at least one hundred jobs. I tried everything."

He was in his late forties when he lost his job, as part of a widespread cutback within the company. "It was awful. I had three kids in college," he told me. "I started looking everywhere. I was absolutely qualified." Yet no one offered him a position. "I went to one interview for an out-of-state job and the guy told me, 'I could lose my job for telling you this. But there's no way they're going to hire you because you're over forty-five.' It was a stroke of luck," he added, "when I finally found the job I'm at now. I'm on the road a lot, but I can live with that. It beats being unemployed. It beats delivering newspapers."

Since Peter lived in a relatively small midwestern city, I was curious about the kind of community-support networks he had been able to tap into during his prolonged period of unemployment. But he quickly dispelled my illusions. "They say there's support," he said. "I went to some of those groups. They tell you, 'You're too old. There's no way we can help you.' You just get to the point where you want to kill someone. It was very tough."

His brother, meanwhile, lived through his own variation on the displacement theme. "He worked for one of the big food manufacturers," Peter described. "They told him, we're closing down this office. The only thing you can do is to move. He decided he had no choice." He accepted a transfer, sold his house, and relocated his family to Pittsburgh. "He wasn't even there a month. They came to him and said, we're closing down this operation, too. He wound up losing a lot of money selling that house in Pittsburgh. But he wanted to move back to the area he knew best and to start looking for work there."

The financial toll persists even after displaced workers get rehired, as most people eventually do, especially in a tight labor market like that of the late nineties. Unemployed job hunters are scarcely in a strong negotiating position; most companies will take any advantage they can when it comes to keeping salary costs low. Of the group that lost jobs during the years 1995 through 1997, about 40 percent earned less once they were reemployed than they had at their previous jobs. In many cases, the pay cuts they took were big ones: one of every four people surveyed got paid *at least 20 percent less* by their new employers than by their former ones.

As often happens in our harsh new economy, the more experienced (and presumably older) people were the ones who took the biggest financial hits. In every single period that the DOL surveyed, earnings declined for those displaced workers who had spent more than three years with their last employer: Their pay cuts averaged 9.5 percent.[33] That adds up to a lot of unhappy households.

For Donald, a onetime resident of Cleveland, Ohio, the financial cost of job displacement proved far worse than any statistic can convey. Confiding his recent career path to faceless companions in an

Internet chat room, he reported, "I was a fifty-one-year-old sales executive with a national heating and air conditioning company. I had worked for that company for twenty-eight years . . . earning one hundred and fifty thousand dollars a year. Then in 1993, my company downsized, and I was simply told I 'was no longer necessary to the company's future.' . . . I sent out almost 2,000 résumés and got two responses. No one wanted to hire me. I was overqualified (I think that means too old) or they were looking for someone with a different background (I think that means younger). . . . Today, our life is quite different. Now we live in a small rented apartment in Florida. My wife works cleaning condominium rentals, and I work as a salesclerk at Sears, earning eight-fifty an hour."[34]

A downward financial slide often follows a job displacement. Thus, strong hiring demand and low unemployment rates, both key elements of the 1990s business boom, failed to compensate for the financial havoc corporate layoffs wreaked upon the white-collar community. Employers may have been earning record revenues and profits during this decade, while their stock prices soared to new highs. But many people were simply earning less, no matter how hard they were working. For some, like Donald, their new and reduced incomes scarcely compensated for all the savings they had cashed in and money they'd borrowed during prolonged periods of unemployment.

Lurking behind the various financial risks many white-collar workers now face is another serious hazard. According to a research team from York University in Ontario, middle-income men and women have a three times greater likelihood of dying than high-income people do during any five-year period that follows an income drop of 50 percent or more. This heightened risk of fatality exists even for people whose income drops are temporary.[35]

One can only speculate about the health, as well as financial, prospects of those seventy thousand or so men and women whose layoffs were announced or projected by just ten large corporations—among them, Eastman Kodak, Citicorp, and Apple Computer—during the brutal autumn of 1997. Then again, *their* futures might look positively benign compared with those of all the people who were laid off a year later, by a roster of once-desirable employers that included Merrill Lynch, Metropolitan Life, Raytheon, Boeing, and Johnson and Johnson.[36] Although there was plenty of publicity about just how difficult it was to recruit and retain qualified workers in a tight labor market, cost-conscious companies managed to lay off a whopping 10 percent *more* men and women during 1998 than at any point during the previous ten years.[37] And the trend continued.

Yet today's corporate "sweatshops" have taken a financial toll upon men and women that goes beyond stagnating salaries and the increased risks associated with unexpected job loss or contingency. A wide range of benefit cutbacks have reduced the rewards of the workplace while leaving many people without health care or retirement protections that white-collar workers have come to take for granted.

THREE

"This Is the Way of the World": The Disappearing Benefit Blanket

Before the 1980s, employee benefits—health care coverage, pensions, vacations and holidays, profit-sharing plans—were a big part of the security blanket white-collar workers sought when they decided to pursue a career in corporate America.

"I've always played it very safe with a very safe company, but things are in so much flux now," confided Billie, a mid-level manager with a publishing company that had completed a series of mergers during her ten-plus years on the job. Along the way, her once-impressive package of benefits had worsened steadily even while, as she put it, she and her colleagues juggled such heavy workloads that they were often too busy to even take a vacation. "I say to myself, maybe it's time to roll the dice and try something very different. Why am I working here?"

Many people find themselves asking the same question as most businesses, despite having thrived during the past decade, have cut away at their benefit packages even more than at white-collar compensation levels. Health care insurance has declined in both quality and scope of coverage; pensions have drastically deteriorated; vacations, holidays, sick days, and personal days have all been reduced.

It's another facet of the work-harder-for-less mind-set that drives today's cost-conscious business leaders (many of whom are sheltered from the pain by supplementary benefit packages reserved for chief executives and top corporate officers). Any dollars saved from benefit plans can, at least in theory, go toward bottom-line results or growth-oriented activities, both of which could boost stock prices. Why waste funds on employees instead?

Once benefits were viewed as part of the cement strengthening the ties between white-collar men and women and their employers. There seemed a compelling logic to the notion that hardworking employees deserve the short- and long-term rewards that a comprehensive plan can provide: the better a company's package of non-wage rewards, the easier to attract high-quality people and to retain them. Rising costs (which averaged over 6 percent annually during the golden years of corporate benefits, the 1960s and early 1970s) were considered a trade-off well worth making.

As these costs kept going up throughout the rest of the seventies, however, attitudes about them began to shift. Increasingly, benefit expenses were seen as one of the business world's big problems: a threat to the nation's economic well-being, because they helped push corporate prices too high to compete in the global marketplace. From the early eighties on, most large companies have aggressively been looking for ways to contain or curtail their packages. And most have succeeded. Since 1979 the value of nonwage corporate benefits has increased by just pennies, or a fraction of a percentage point, each year.[1] Even after the economy rebounded dramatically during the nineties, employers failed to loosen the purse strings.

"There's something so unfair about all this," Margot told me. A marketing manager with a large corporation that owned a number of major retail chains, she noted, "Everybody's got their cell phones and their beepers and their laptop computers, because we've all got to be accessible all the time, even when we're away on vacation. Every time there's a layoff, we all have to take on even more responsibilities. And we suspect that more layoffs are coming, which means our jobs are just going to keep getting worse." She took a deep breath, then added, "But the reward structure doesn't begin to keep up. Our benefits have been getting worse for years now. And the company's attitude is, This is the way of the world. If you don't like it, go someplace else."

Health Insurance Cutbacks

Benefit reductions of all kinds have made many working people's lives more difficult, stressful, and financially precarious. Yet on a day-to-day basis, it's the declining quality of health care coverage that has exacted the greatest toll on most white-collar workers, especially those with families.

As health care costs have spiraled upward in the United States during the past two decades, cost-conscious companies have looked for ways to reduce these expenses, with an intensity of effort that comes close to rivaling their preoccupation with capping payroll costs. Cutbacks have assumed a variety of forms, some of them once unthinkable before corporate America became obsessed with the bottom line.

Health insurance coverage was virtually universal in the world of big business by the end of the 1970s. During the next two decades, however, growing numbers of companies axed or decimated their plans. The impact on the psyches, as well as financial well-being, of many white-collar Americans was shocking. By 1995, one of every four people working full-time for the nation's larger employers no longer had medical coverage. And countless more worried that they, too, could soon lose it.[2]

Most white-collar Americans can remember a time when health care benefits were a good thing, rather than a source of endless anxiety. As recently as 1991, two thirds of all the people working full-time for big companies were covered by traditional fee-for-service plans (which gave them flexibility about which medical professionals they could consult and what type of medical care and procedures could be provided). By 1997, only 27 percent of the people working for big companies were covered by these plans. Within less than a decade, most had been switched to some type of managed care.[3]

Controlling health care costs—like any kind of fiscal responsibility—makes good business sense. But many companies have taken such extreme measures on this front that it has become increasingly difficult for their staffers to view insurance as anything resembling a "benefit." Rather, it's just another sign of how much worse work life keeps getting, boom or no boom, in corporate America.

"My company changes its insurance carrier every year or so," complained Beatrice, who runs a small marketing division for a financial services firm based in suburban Connecticut. "It's always the same thing: you get that whole big book and you look through it to see which of your family's doctors the new plan will cover. Of course, it never covers any of them. Or, you have a choice of two plans, but the kids' doctors are covered by one of them and your own doctor is covered by the other and there's no way to split the family's coverage so that you all can continue seeing the doctors who know you. So you've got to start switching the family's doctors one more time. Or you make a decision that you're going to forget about the coverage and just pay the bills yourself. That's what my husband keeps saying we should do. But it's very hard to make that decision."

The hassles abound, making life just a little tougher for a woman who already spends several evenings each week working late at the office or entertaining business clients. "Every time the company changes plans, you've got to figure out how to handle the new prescription-drug coverage, which means going to the drugstore and changing all that information in its computer one more time. Forget about dental coverage—we haven't seen that in years. But with the rest of it, you've got to figure out what kind of office visits you're entitled to and which ones you're not," she noted. "One of the insurance companies would only pay for children's checkups every two years—that was ridiculous. But then the company changed that plan, too."

Beatrice paused, then added, "I called up the company's contact person in our human resources office and asked him, 'Why do you have to keep making all these changes so frequently just to save a few dollars? Do you really think you're doing us any favor by changing plans *so often*"—she dragged out the words—"that you barely have time to figure things out before you've got to move on to the next one?'"

Companies pass more health care costs along to their employees in a variety of ways. Most large corporations now force staffers to pay a portion of their policy fees themselves, especially when they sign up for family coverage; twenty years ago, that was far less common.[4] Dental benefits have disappeared entirely at many workplaces; those that remain are usually so limited in scope and costly for participants that they scarcely matter.[5] Employee copayment charges, meanwhile, have been rising consistently, whether in the form of higher charges for HMO doctor visits or of lower insurance reimbursement levels and larger deductibles with traditional fee-for-service plans. Charges connected with prescription-drug coverage have often gone up by a factor of five or ten from the once-typical two-dollar charge.

Margot felt grateful, she told me, that she had a way out of her company's increasingly unattractive health care plan, since she could pay to be covered through her husband's employer, which offered better and less expensive coverage. "But I look at the option here every year and can't believe how tremendous the costs have become for employees. There are some women in my office who sign up because they don't have any other health care choice, and they're the ones I really feel sorry for."

For men and women in workplaces across the nation, other financial stresses arise from cost-containment practices that never get written about in corporate benefit manuals. Still, people recognize them when insurance carriers routinely seem to deny claims or frequently lose paperwork in what appear to be efforts to keep reimbursements low. When I interviewed Billie, the publishing manager, she was at home on maternity leave, during which she had spent much of her time battling her employer's insurance carrier for medical reimbursements to which she and her husband were entitled.

"There's one large denied claim that's just ridiculous," she told me. But she felt conflicted about challenging it, because she hated to waste precious time during her leave. "You get into the mind-set of, I'm just so happy to have my baby. Maybe I shouldn't make myself crazy if I end up having to pay an extra couple of thousand dollars."

As with the negative salary trends that have whipsawed American workers for much of the past two decades, some portions of the workforce have been more affected by benefits erosion than others. Insurance coverage for part-time, temporary, and other contingent workers is sparse, with only about one third of these men and women even eligible to participate in employer-sponsored health plans. Younger workers yet again suffer the most. Only one of every four young people working in a contingent job is covered by some type of company plan.[6]

Also hard hit are people who work for those large companies that have conducted mergers or acquisitions (an increasingly common occurrence during the nineties). Their benefit packages tend to deteriorate because of the same business dynamic that produces layoffs and other human-resources-related cutbacks: after spending enormous amounts on the deal, companies want to reduce their operating expenses, boost bottom-line results, and justify the merger to Wall Street. Thus, on the day that Exxon's acquisition of Mobil was finalized in 1999, at a point when future layoffs already seemed inevitable, the new company ended Mobil's practice of providing health care coverage to the partners of newly hired gay employees. The oil giant became the second large U.S. company to take this step, following Perot Systems a year earlier.[7]

When Citicorp merged with Travelers, the havoc on the benefit front was worse still. "No matter how much people's workloads increased at Citi over the years, I give John Reed [Citicorp's long-time chief executive] credit for a paternalistic and humane view," confided Zachary, a financial manager who had been with the firm for nearly twenty years. "He felt that these were the people who had gotten this company through hell during the 1980s—the company wasn't going to touch their benefits."

All that changed in 1998, when Citi merged with a company well known for slashing costs and benefits after megamergers: Travelers. "They've got a real reputation for all the 'killing' they do when it comes to benefits," Zachary added. "When the merger hit the press, which was the first time most people heard about it, we all dreaded the layoffs and cutbacks we presumed would be coming."

By the time I interviewed Zachary more than a year and a half later, the company's benefit package had already deteriorated (although he and his colleagues were convinced that things were not yet as bad as they would eventually get). "In the U.S. Citi used to budget in the low 30 percent range of people's salaries to cover benefit costs," he told me. "Now it's down in the low twenties. For many employees, their own costs connected with insurance coverage have risen and they receive smaller insurance reimbursements. What's particularly offensive," he emphasized, "was the way they kicked off the cutbacks, with a video presentation in which John Reed and Sandy Weill [Travelers' chief executive, who with Reed became cochairman of the new company] told us about how good the new benefits were, because they were going to help make the new firm more competitive."

The Wide Range of Benefit Cutbacks

Benefit erosion has gone far beyond insurance cutbacks at most large companies. It's both demoralizing and anxiety-producing to have benefits shrink while job demands are increasing. "You get to the point where you don't even want to read anything that comes out of the human resources department, because you know it's only going to be bad news," confided Margot, the marketing manager in the retail industry.

When her company eliminated a group of paid holidays, she added, "nobody even bothered to tell us. It was just, here's the new calendar—and when you compared it to last year's, you could see that some days, like Martin Luther King's birthday, were gone." As often happens with benefit cutbacks, the people at the top were sheltered from the blow: they received a comparable number of floating "personal" days in return for those disappearing holidays. "How's that supposed to make you feel," she asked me, "if you're working hard and you didn't receive them?"

At the newly merged Citigroup, benefit cutbacks came in all shapes and sizes. "It wasn't subtle. It was a bludgeoning" was the way Zachary described the process to me. "The company no longer matches employees' charitable donations, which Citi always used to do. The next thing we're waiting for is for prices to rise in the company cafeteria. It's like a whole process of water torture as you watch the benefits shrink away."

Some hard-driving corporations keep family-friendly benefit policies on their books: these might include opportunities to apply for flextime work schedules or "personal" leaves of absence. But they place such heavy productivity demands upon their employees that few can take advantage of them.

Arlie Russell Hochschild examined the phenomenon in *The Time Bind*. Although many of the employees she interviewed at the company she called "Amerco" complained about their difficulties coping with job and family pressures, almost no one (except new mothers) took advantage of the company's leave policy; its "flex-place" benefit, which allowed people to work from home or some other location, was used even less. "In fact, during the years that I was studying Amerco, parents and nonparents alike began to work *longer* hours," she reported, adding, "[M]ost agreed that Amerco was 'a pretty workaholic place.'" Eventually, before Hochschild's book was published, the company's "Work-Life Balance" program was dismantled, amid a "reengineering" campaign that included widespread layoffs and other cutbacks.[8]

Other companies penalize staffers in clear, if indirect, ways when they make the mistake of signing up for leaves or reduced work schedules. According to one study of the career paths of more than five hundred managers at a large financial services firm, those men and women who took short leaves (lasting on average less than two months) found themselves 18 percent less likely to be promoted than non-leave-takers. They also typically received low performance ratings during the year in which their absences occurred, which helped translate into slower salary advancements than those of their peers.[9]

Sybil, a vice president who spent more than a decade at Merrill Lynch, bemoaned a similar disjunction between benefit policy and reality. "The corporation is in this incredible drive to be politically correct. So they'll send you these communications telling you it's okay to stay home to take care of your sick parents or your kids. It's incredible cynicism on people's parts," she commented. "For management to tell you that it's okay is B.S. It's not okay. It doesn't work. For the people who don't avail themselves, there's just more work."

Normally a soft-spoken woman who prided herself on her refusal to complain about anything, she waited for a moment as she tried to gain control of her emotions. "This cynicism leads to incredible anger at the office. I felt it. Employees at the company just want to turn to these people and strangle them. Yet when you're recruiting, you're instructed to make sure to talk about our policy on family leave and all this B.S."

Demoralization and resentment are often strongest at those companies whose work-harder-for-less practices have been stepped up in the wake of mergers or acquisitions. In these situations, shrinking benefit packages only exacerbate the emotional and financial stresses that arise from heightened layoff risks, tighter corporate cost controls, and a general sense of uncertainty about one's long-term future.

"Intellectually, you can even know that it's going to happen, but emotionally it's just impossible to prepare yourself for the impact of these kind of take-aways," Zachary commented. "You feel like an interchangeable part, like a commodity. There are so many different kinds of disenchantment that you feel."

Countless men and women experienced similar downward transitions during the 1980s and 1990s. But although the statistics reflect the phenomenon, they cannot begin to describe what it feels like to live through it. "We were always lean-and-mean, but in the old days, management cared about making life lucrative, if nothing else, for the people who worked here," recalled Simon, a production staffer who got his first career break twenty-five years ago on *Women's Wear Daily*.

Over the years he switched to other posts within Capital Cities, the newspaper's corporate parent; the company, meanwhile, acquired ABC, then sold itself to Disney. After another period of uncertainty, his division got sold to Condé Nast, the magazine publishing empire, in 1999. In the course of all those corporate maneuvers, Simon watched some of the most lucrative of his benefits disappear, while others got leaner and leaner.

He was bitter. "Cap Cities used to have a wonderful discounted-stock plan. The best piece of advice anyone ever gave me early on was to buy whatever shares I could afford, anytime I could afford it," he recalled. "People made a lot of money that way—and they stayed with the company for years, because they felt all their hard work was rewarded."

Then, during the period Simon called the Disney era, all that changed. The stock incentives were basically gone. "I would say to my wife, 'This is such an incredible blow to the people who work for this company. Why aren't I reading articles about it anywhere?'"

Meanwhile, the company had "one big perk that was laughable," he told me. "You could get a 30 percent discount on Disney merchandise and a certain number of free passes to the theme parks. Even *that* wasn't unlimited."

Other benefits included what Simon called "this convoluted health insurance plan, where you had various choices but it was very difficult to tell how bad some of them really were. There was a couple I knew that was going through infertility treatments—the woman needed to spend a month on the phone, calling possible doctors and researching the different coverage options, to try to figure out what would be best for them."

Vacations shrank, predictably. "In the old days, once you worked for the company for more than twenty years, you had five weeks of vacation. After thirty years, you'd get six weeks," he noted, "and there were plenty of people who stayed with the company long enough to get that. When Disney came in, they capped vacations at four weeks. And they took away some of our personal days."

His voice deepened with anger as he asked me, "Does Michael Eisner [Disney's chief executive officer] know how dumb that was? People worked so hard for this company. Didn't they deserve even that little reward?" He took a deep breath, then added, "Does it really make a difference to a company this big when they do stupid little things like that? But it really mattered to us."

Benefit cutbacks like these were especially painful, Simon emphasized, because workloads and demands at his company had always been fierce—and had only increased since the merger. "We were so lean it was unbelievable. We were always under pressure. And the ironic thing was, even if we met our goals, maybe even exceeded them, we never earned any brownie points. There was never any alleviation from the stress," he emphasized. "You *knew* the money was there. But no matter how well we did, we never got the money to hire an assistant or get any extra help."

After having been burned by one merger, Simon told me how much he dreaded the unfolding impact from his division's sale to Condé Nast. "On the one hand, the company knows about the world of publishing, and that's good. But it's a private company, so there's not going to be any stock benefits. And it's got a reputation for taking care of people at the top, so that's not going to do much for me." The first sign of trouble, he said, had arrived with end-of-the-year bonuses that were distributed soon after the merger, when "a lot of people didn't get what they expected. I nearly cried," he added. "Who knows what's going to happen next?"

Just as paycheck erosion has been a key element in the 1990s business boom, benefit cutbacks have likewise helped fuel corporate prosperity because they squeeze more out of workers for less. Although few people bother to complain (after all, health care and other benefit cuts have become a way of life in corporate America), this trend has been far from inevitable. The 1990s combination of low inflation, a booming stock market, and abundant capital resources created a growth-oriented economic environment in which many corporations *could*, without loss, have halted or even reversed their assault on their employees' benefits if they had wanted to.

Instead, the trend has continued just as layoffs, downsizings, and other human-resources-related cutbacks have thrived, all within a healthy business world. That's because the "sweatshop" economy is insatiable and its ultimate arbiter is Wall Street. Its goals are governed by a single overriding assumption: the only bottom line that matters is the corporate bottom line.

Breaking the Pension Promise

Salaries, benefits, and pensions were once the triumvirate of rewards that attracted white-collar men and women to large companies. And just as the first two have decreased, so too have pension prospects declined for many people working in corporate America.

Most large employers simply spend less now than they used to on their pension plans. Back in 1979, companies paid 63 cents per hour for pension costs related to each employee. By 1996 that was down to 45 cents.[10] Given the extent of that cutback, it's a fairly good bet that employees will suffer, if only when their retirements come around. But this trend has been easier to overlook than salary or benefit erosion, since the bull market of the nineties convinced many baby boomers and others that their futures were secure because of the paper value of their investment savings.

If and when the stock market weakens, families will confront the financial reality of long retirement years without the corporate pension blankets that cushioned earlier generations of white-collar staffers. Before benefit erosion set in during the 1980s, most people working full-time for larger companies could count on "defined benefit" pensions (the cream of the crop, since they eliminated all uncertainties by guaranteeing employees a certain level of benefit, tied to one's age, seniority, job tenure, and salary level at the time of retirement). By 1995, only about half of those men and women working for big business were covered by such a guarantee, and their ranks were shrinking fast.[11]

A variety of corporate trends conspired to set defined-benefit pensions on what appears to be a path to extinction. During the 1980s, the Pension Benefit Guaranty Corporation (which provided the equivalent of FDIC insurance for guaranteed pensions) was forced to bail out a group of high-flying companies that had either dangerously depleted their pension funds or ended up in bankruptcy court. Their staffers usually wound up with a cut-rate version of the pensions that had been promised to them, and a pattern of declining benefits was set in motion.

Plenty of healthier companies also managed to find ways to wriggle out of defined-benefit obligations during the past two decades. Sometimes—as when Montgomery Ward shuttered its $1.1 billion plan during the late nineties—they took advantage of the bull-market-inflated value of their pension funds to help pay government tax penalties attached to dissolution. Or they merged with other companies, which gave them the option of redefining or eliminating their pension plans along with their corporate structures. After Ronald Perelman took over Revlon during the mid-eighties, he shut down its pension plan and gained control of more than $100 million in so-called surplus assets.[12]

As older corporate workers were laid off or retired throughout the nation, their younger counterparts found themselves getting hired with less attractive pension options or none at all. Some companies offered "defined contribution" pensions instead: not as desirable from an employee's vantage point because they offered less financial certainty for one's retirement years. (With these plans, corporations agreed to a fixed level of annual contribution, generally tied to a person's salary level, seniority, and job tenure, but made no guarantees about how much he or she would actually receive upon retirement.) Yet even these pensions have experienced cutbacks: back in 1986, 60 percent of full-timers at larger companies were covered by such plans. Ten years later, that level was nearly 10 percent lower.[13]

The one type of pension plan that has shown a significant increase in corporate America is the tax-deferred savings plan, which most typically means the 401K. From the business world's perspective, these are preferable to traditional pensions, since they combine low corporate cost with flexibility. Back in 1986, only about a third of people working full-time for larger companies participated in this type of plan. Now, more than half of them do.[14]

While certainly better than nothing for working men and women, these pensions cannot hold a candle to once-common defined-benefit plans. With 401Ks, most or all of the retirement-savings contributions come from employees themselves. Despite tax incentives, participation in them actually lowers most families' disposable income, so that these plans create financial stress in the short run, even while helping to alleviate long-term anxieties. That's why a considerable number of people choose not to sign up, although 401Ks and comparable plans may represent their only real opportunity to supplement Social Security benefits.

Margot's experience within the retail industry was fairly typical. "We used to have a very good defined-benefit pension plan, but that's been cut back over recent years to the point where you could never possibly count on it," she said. "The shame of it is," she added, "when the company introduced a 401K plan, people didn't understand that if they didn't do this, they weren't going to have much of anything. They wouldn't be able to afford to retire. But a lot of people said, 'No way am I going to put my own money into a retirement fund.' They didn't understand how bad things were."

Some miss out on the chance to get much benefit from 401Ks because of the tortuous rules that often govern plans. The biggest culprits are so-called vesting requirements, which force employees to work for a long period, perhaps as long as seven years, in order to gain ownership of whatever small contributions their employers may make to their retirement accounts.

Businesses have a strong incentive to set their vesting requirements high. That's because they get to recapture funds that employees lose if they leave the company before getting vested, an increasingly likely scenario in these days of downsizings and job turnover. Corporate savings can add up: at Dayton Hudson, where the job-tenure requirement has ranged between three and five years, nearly 25 percent of the people who participated in the company's 401K left without ever becoming fully vested. At Limited, where tenure is pegged at seven years, the rate of so-called forfeitures was greater still, at nearly 35 percent.[15]

If some men and women will not or cannot jump aboard the 401K life raft, however, others have deluded themselves into believing that it's a luxury ocean liner, capable of carrying them to a cushier retirement than their predecessors ever achieved. The prolonged stock market boom of the 1990s has cast a rosy, if misleading, glow over many people's pension prospects. Those who believe that the United States' bull market can last forever feel that employer cutbacks on the pension front just cannot hurt them.

Some people see through the delusion. "We used to have a defined-benefit pension. That's largely gone now for a lot of employees. The company used to make very generous 401K contributions—that's been cut back or eliminated for many people, based upon their salary level," noted Zachary of Citigroup. "There are people who think that it all doesn't matter, so long as the stock price keeps rising. But they're wrong."

There are already warning signs for those willing to look more closely. Stock market volatility during the late spring and summer of 1998 offered a short-lived reminder that retirement funds could shrink as well as increase. For some men and women, they already have: thanks to the growing risk of job displacement and salary reduction, higher college tuition costs, ever-shrinking employee benefits, and a host of other financial pressures, more people have found themselves raiding their retirement savings simply to make ends meet. A revealing 1998 study by the Federal Reserve Board of New York determined that nearly half of those families making early cash withdrawals from their 401Ks had spent the money on something other than retirement, including buying a home, reducing debt loads, or coping with current household costs.[16]

Even without a major stock market downturn, the investment risks that underlie many 401K plans—and therefore many people's retirement savings—have come to light in the aftermath of some major corporate collapses. Morrison Knudsen, the manufacturing firm, and the retailer Carter Hawley Hale both had 401K plans that permitted their employees to invest retirement savings in company stock; in Carter Hawley Hale's case, that was their *only* investment option. But despite some high-flying years, both companies wound up in bankruptcy court, ravaging many employees' retirement savings.[17]

So far the Pension Benefit Guaranty Corporation has intervened in cases like these to wrest extra money from bankruptcy proceedings in order to supplement employees' depleted retirement accounts. But there's no guarantee that this will continue to happen. Worse still, there's no safety net at all for those people who reduce their long-term financial security by making early withdrawals or investing in an increasingly volatile stock market that may go down as easily as up.

The Impact on White-Collar Workers

Anyone who discounts the worsening effect of pension erosion on the quality of people's lives should stop by "The IBM Pension Club," an Internet chat room that got launched during May 1999 by a disgruntled employee. IBM had just announced plans to switch to a controversial new form of pension known as the cash-balance plan.

CRIME OF THE CENTURY blared one Internet entry, which opened with these apocalyptic words: "IBM is killing the baby boomers. . . ." Another Internet visitor pleaded, "Pass on to everyone you know to wear Black and Blue on Wednesday, June 23, as a subtle, symbolic and united show of our sorrow and anger over being beat out of our pension by our company."

A real page-turner, at least for IBM's current and former staffers, the site managed to attract fifteen thousand "hits" per day within less than three weeks of operation. Many of the visitors were irate:

"Hoping that this message is seen by the IBM human resources folks I would like to ask them one question . . . don't you think there could have been a more equitable way of changing the pension plan? As a 19 year employee I feel that you really stuck it to me this time."[18] Another noted, "American employees are getting screwed—Why? Because Gerstner [Louis Gerstner, IBM's chief executive] and his bandits can get away with it here and they CANNOT get away with it elsewhere."[19]

The plan IBM had decided to adopt for most of its 140,000-plus employees had already won converts at large corporations across the nation, since it offered companies the opportunity to achieve major savings in pension costs. These were usually achieved at the expense of older and longer-tenured employees, whose benefits under cash-balance plans tended to be far inferior to those they could have expected to receive from their former pensions. BankAmerica, Xerox, and Bell Atlantic helped lead the way.[20] But with huge savings projected—at IBM alone they were pegged at $200 million annually—benefit experts predicted that most of big business would follow suit.

All this was proof yet again that pensions were deteriorating across corporate America. Cash-balance plans had a couple of advantages, including the fact that—like 401Ks—their accumulated savings were "portable" and could be taken with employees when they change jobs; they also allowed workers to start amassing pensions from the earliest years of their full-time employment, which does not happen with traditional plans.

There were significant downsides, though, which were easy to overlook given the complexities of these new models. (Confusion and deception were major topics of conversation among the visitors to the IBM Pension Club. As one put it, "There is no fog, just a thick blanket of bullshit. They are shafting us, the numbers speak for themselves. Wake up everyone, we should be angry.")[21] Many plans included greater vesting risks than 401Ks; some firms set additional restrictions governing even those holdings that did become the vested property of employees.

The biggest problem associated with these plans, however, centers on the way their benefits get assessed. Old-style pension formulas favor seniority and job tenure (thus most of their rewards get calculated near the end of people's careers). Cash-balance plans assess rewards at a slow-but-steady pace in the course of a person's entire work life. That means they're not too bad for people who have a lifetime to build pension value; but for those in their forties, fifties, and sixties there's just not enough time to make up for lost ground.

At IBM, resistance from older employees (both on the Internet and through more traditional means, such as legal threats and government lobbying) persuaded the company to offer some compromises with its new plan, primarily by doubling to more than sixty-five thousand the number of people who would be permitted to keep their old pensions if they chose to.[22] The IBMers were so successful, in fact, that www.disgruntled.com awarded them the Web magazine's "Disgruntled Employees of the Year" accolade for "using the Internet to get their message out. . . ."[23] The larger significance of this victory remains to be seen, though, since many big companies continue to make the switch.

For job-changers and younger entrants into the workforce, less desirable retirement plans like these will increasingly become the norm. Meanwhile, the growing use of contingent labor by large corporations should only exacerbate pension declines. Five of every six men and women working in contingent jobs as of 1997 lacked any coverage at all.[24]

As with other benefits, most roads lead downhill on the pension front. Business cost-containment policies of the past two decades have exacted a painful and far from fully recognized toll on working men and women when it comes to their retirement security—or ultimate lack of it. Thus, between deteriorating salaries and benefits, mounting workloads, time pressures, and other stresses, many white-collar workers now find themselves in corporate "sweatshops" that offer few rewards and make far too many demands.

FOUR

"They Used to Use a Ball and Chain": Technology's Impact upon the Workplace

We've all got the cell phones, the beepers, the laptops. I bring mine back and forth between my home and office every day," commented Phyllis, a finance officer with one of the nation's large retail chains. "Everybody does it—you feel like you always need to be accessible. Even when you're on vacation, you've got to be accessible. You've got to be prepared to check in all the time." She sighed, then concluded, "All those pieces of equipment are a big reason we're working harder."

Today's new technologies, for all their ability to lighten routine job tasks, lower business costs, and boost performance levels, are inextricably linked to contemporary overwork patterns. As many people's work lives seem to be moving inexorably toward a "24/7" vision of round-the-clock, ever-increasing productivity, they could hardly meet their employers' rising expectations without a ready arsenal of workplace tools—Internet-linked computers, personal digital assistants, cell phones, pagers, laptops, and even e-mail-receptive watches—at home as well as at the office.

Technology has done more than simply *facilitate* the current trend of working longer and harder. It may, indeed, have exacerbated patterns of overwork and job stress by broadening many white-collar staffers' (and their employers') definitions of "on the job" to include areas far beyond the traditional confines of their office space.

Technological developments, meanwhile, have permitted corporations to extend their control over employees to an oppressive degree: all in the interest of keeping men and women at maximum productive efficiency, whether they find themselves in their cars or commuter trains, hotel rooms, or even master bedrooms. White-collar staffers themselves have responded by using the Internet to vent their hostilities and anxieties about deteriorating conditions, as well as, increasingly, to mobilize resistance to "sweatshop" trends.

Technology Encourages Job Spill

When I set up an Internet discussion site to explore issues like these relating to work and technology, here's how "tickler" responded: "I had two phone lines (local and toll free) at home, 2 voicemails, email, and the rest . . . [and] was besieged with the usual crap of being assaulted during the evening, nights, weekends, and the like."[1] Those images of "siege" and "assault" are apt, since many people feel as though the office is invading their home front—an invasion facilitated by the introduction of at least some of these pieces of electronic equipment into the house, the car, or another personal space.

White-collar workers increasingly find themselves somewhere in the vast space that looms between "just checking in with the office" and "just having one or two things to finish up," whether it's during their after-dinner hours, commuting time, weekends with the family, sick days, vacations, or holidays. Workloads inevitably increase: according to a study of people who spent five hours or more each week on the Internet, 25 percent of them reported that they were working harder at home without any reduction at the office.[2]

Despite workers' complaints about excessive job demands, however, more and more workplace gadgets keep showing up outside the office. As they do, they blur the old lines between home and office. In 1997 more than one quarter of American families owned pagers—twice as high as the year earlier—and more than one third of U.S. households owned cellular telephones.[3] That same year, 3.6 million households purchased fax machines, 14 million bought notebook computers, and a whopping 31 million bought personal computers.[4]

The trend only accelerated. By the year 1998, two thirds of all households had cellular phones; just about half of them had pagers.[5] Market researchers projected "home market" sales of personal computers and related consumer electronic appliances at about 35 million units during that same year.[6]

Many, if not all, of these tools can be used by families for personal matters, too, as when children swap homework assignments by fax or surf the Internet for fun. But for large numbers of people, one significant result of having these workplace technologies at home was greater access to work, clients, colleagues, the office. The flip side was that the business world now had greater, round-the-clock access to its workers.

By the late nineties, it was estimated that 7 million Americans regularly checked their business e-mails from outside the office.[7] At more and more workplaces, such checking became an unspoken requirement of many people's jobs. America Online, for example, "occasionally announces e-mail-free weekends, usually around a holiday, when employees are not expected to check e-mail. On all other weekends, of course, they are expected to check their e-mail."[8]

What about when they're on the road? The many Americans who find themselves traveling for their jobs—and 32 percent do, at least occasionally[9]—have been robbed by high-tech equipment of whatever personal downtime they once might have cherished: in the quiet of an airplane (where, now able to plug their laptop computers into new "EmPower" jacks, they never run out of battery power and so can never doze off or idly leaf through a magazine); in airport lobbies (where Internet-access kiosks allow them to check e-mail accounts, while frequent flier clubs provide faxes, copiers, dataports, and the like); in rental cars (where rental cell phones and beepers are usually available, along with cars and adapters that can turn cigarette lighters into sources of power for portable computers); or in hotel rooms (which increasingly provide the same range of office-electronics comforts that their customers have come to rely upon in their homes and workplaces).[10]

One could say, simply, that all this new technology has increased the capabilities and outputs of business travelers. Or an observer of the current corporate scene could view new workplace gadgets from a different, darker perspective: as instruments designed to eliminate human inefficiency or "personal downtime," all in the interest of creating an optimally productive white-collar work machine. Whether these work machines (that is, business travelers) return home more stressed out than they were when they left the office scarcely matters in this new business-world order.

Here's how "technoid," another visitor to my Internet chat room, described the way technology had ratcheted up the demands on his travel time. "When I travel to another country, someone from a local office always escorts me with a cell phone. This means I'd have problems to fix at the customer site, problems they'd call in on the phone, and problems in e-mail when I got back to the hotel."[11] All those mobile pieces of electronics allowed "technoid"'s employer to keep him working at what the company deemed an appropriate level of efficiency, "10–12 hour days, and they'll always ask you to work seven days a week." He added, "If a customer canceled meetings or I finished early, they'd always have more meetings lined up to replace the time so that I couldn't go home early."

Perhaps business travelers should expect to perform business tasks whether they're in the air or on the ground; after all, they are on their employers' payroll. But until recently, most vacationers were freed from similar constraints, unless they were such high-level executives that their companies simply could not function without them, even for a few days.

Thanks to the democratization of workplace technologies, however, that's no longer the case. One recent survey of "messaging technology" found that 53 percent of all those who owned pagers *had* been paged during a vacation. Meanwhile, 41 percent of those who owned cell phones had used them to call their offices while on vacation; another 32 percent who had access to the Internet while on vacation had checked their e-mail; and 34 percent had checked their office answering machine or voice-mail account while on vacation.[12]

"Yes, people feel good about the stock market going up. Yes, some people are taking better vacations and they've got more money to spend on them," Zachary, a longtime employee of Citicorp told me. But the trade-off wasn't worth it, he explained. "If you've got to be on call during the whole vacation—if you've got to check in with the office through the voice mail and the e-mail, and everyone out there can reach you if they need you—then you're worse off." He quipped, "It's kind of like, people have the money to buy toys, but they're so busy with work that they don't have the time to play with them."

Anecdotal evidence including observations at restaurants, movie theaters, beaches, and the like suggest that workplace gadgets have become even more intrusive for weekend vacationers. Cellular telephone calls have became so frequent (and annoying), for example, on Hampton jitney rides between New York City and the upscale Long Island beachfront communities known collectively as the Hamptons that the bus line now posts signs asking its riders to limit their calls to three minutes.

Whether vacationers keep themselves plugged into their jobs because their employers demand it or because their workloads are so heavy that they effectively have no other choice scarcely makes a difference: the bottom line is, they never get a break from work. "With this technology there are no rules about when to stop. And that may make the whole idea of vacation a misnomer," commented Kelly Moore, a Columbia University sociologist who has studied the effect of technology on social relations.[13]

The boundaries between work space and personal space keep getting fuzzier all the time, thanks at least in part to a seemingly endless stream of new equipment. While many of these help people perform practical tasks, others amount to breakthroughs that would seem to border on the absurd (were it not for the insidious work-all-the-time message they convey to an already overstressed white-collar population).

According to the *Wall Street Journal*, "all kinds of gadgets, from laptops to phones, can now work not just by the pool, but in it." Among the aquatic-office developments highlighted was a battery-

operated cordless telephone complete with water-resistant handset;
and a new type of floating lounge chair capable of supporting people
who want to combine a swim with work on their laptop computers.
Fortunately, pens that can write underwater are also available. On
the lower-tech end of the overwork spectrum, the *Journal* also
described the pool scene at Miami's ritzy Delano Hotel, where a
desk and chair are permanently set up in the shallow end of the
water and, according to a hotel spokesperson, "people work there all
the time."[14]

Elsewhere, signs of the "you can't get away from it all" times
abound, often tied to some type of technology. One was a recent
advertising campaign from Sheraton Hotels of New York that boasted "everything you've always wanted in an office. In a hotel room."
The traveler's fantasy list that appeared in this ad included "HP
fax/copier/printers, data ports and more." Also noteworthy was an
article that appeared in *Gourmet* magazine's typically pleasure-ori-
ented "Travel Journal." It focused on such devices to stay "linked-
up, logged-on and tuned-in" as "OFFICE Pro by Kluge," a portable
mini-office/computer center masquerading as a piece of luggage
which enables travelers to carry their laptops, batteries, diskettes,
power cords, personal digital assistants, cell phones, papers, and
files, along with their clothing.[15]

Does hitting the road armed with equipment like this sound like
a way to control or *create* work-related stress? Consider "technoid"'s description: "Lugging a heavy laptop from country to country is a big hassle. . . . It's like a boat anchor when you have to scuttle
from one end of a huge airport to another to catch a connecting
flight. . . . You can never relax or get away from it."

Others would agree. "I think the worst thing that has happened
to the workplace is the laptop," noted "WallyK" in another e-mail
to my chat room. "Now I am, literally, physically carrying around
the heavy burden of work on the train, the plane or the subway, back
and forth to work." Tech advancements may have made it simpler
for "WallyK" to perform job tasks, but life in general has become
much more difficult, as this e-mail went on to explain. "It wasn't
very long ago when, if you did take work home, it was infinitely
more transportable on a sheet of paper. Now, unfortunately, I can

read my office email wherever I go. The problem is, I don't want to carry around a machine and I don't want to read my email outside of the office."[16]

If we can, as we increasingly do, take our offices and workloads along with us wherever we go, this is clearly a mixed blessing at best. As one business observer, writing in the *Harvard Business Review,* put it: "What those tools have done . . . is help to extend the working day: in effect, they have created a portable assembly line for the 1990s that 'allows' white-collar workers to remain on-line in planes, trains, cars and at home. So much for the liberating technologies of the Information Age."[17]

The Negative Impact on Work Conditions

Physical discomforts tied to inescapable office technologies abound. Eye strain, wrist strain, and back strain are all common complaints among those who spend long hours at their computers, whether at the office or at home. So are stress-related headaches, especially for corporate staffers who carry pagers, beepers, or cell phones in their pockets, handbags, or briefcases which enable them to stay "on call" at the office virtually twenty-four hours each day.

Some white-collar staffers have already rebelled. "I finally just threw out my beeper," Isaac confessed, with a smile that was proud as well as embarrassed. As a mid-level manager with Virgin Atlantic, he recalled, "I had a cell phone and a beeper. I canceled two three-day weekends with my wife because the office was able to find me by beeper and get me to go back to work."

Once he got started talking about that beeper, it was hard to stop him. "I remember one time, I was on a train to go home. Somewhere in the middle of New Jersey, I got beeped. My cell phone had burned out during the ride because I was using it so much. So I had to get off the train at a station much closer in than where I lived, so that I could start returning those phone calls. I made the decision after I left that station and got back on the train to go home that I would never do that again."

Since then he has maintained his no-beeper policy. "The attitude that most people have is, if the technology allows it, it just happens. If the technology allows it, you're not supposed to have a choice."

But he had learned his lesson the hard way. "If someone eventually says to me, 'Isaac, you need to get a beeper because we're having too much trouble reaching you,' then I'm going to quit, because I'm never again going to be tethered to technology."

If new technologies have contributed to workers' stress by changing the settings in which white-collar employees perform their jobs (and the conditions under which they perform them), these tools have also, for many people, changed the *pace* of work.

Electronic mail, currently used by an estimated 82 million American workers, has played a key role in the corporate speedup. Since e-mails are frequently slapdash and ungrammatical, one might expect them to be taken less seriously than other forms of business communication. Yet perhaps because of the involvement of the computer in their transmittance (or because their very sloppiness conveys the impression that their authors were too busy to worry about dotting every *i* and crossing their *t*'s), they seem to carry much more weight than the same messages would if conveyed via telephone or some other method.

They're a huge source of job stress in corporate America. Remember "tickler"'s description of feeling besieged by work? One survey found that 28 percent of today's "message users" feel more pressure to respond quickly to work-related messages than they used to feel five years ago. An estimated 24 million Americans suffer from so-called message overload.[18] And that problem will likely continue to worsen, since market researchers predict that by the year 2001, 135 million Americans will have e-mail access.[19]

The concept of message overload would sound all too familiar to Jimmy, a consultant on international sales, who was interviewed by Arlie Russell Hochschild for her recent book *The Time Bind*. He described the following: "I'm gone for a couple of hours, and I have twenty electronic messages on my computer when I get back. People are working weekends; you can see by the dates. They send things Friday at 10 p.m., Saturday mornings at 9 a.m., Sundays at 9 p.m. Of the twenty messages on my machine, I have to do something about twelve of them. My head spins."[20]

Within many corporations, there seems no electronic end in sight. A Silicon Valley executive complained that he received about one hundred e-mails every single day. "On average, it takes one minute per e-mail to answer. I don't have 100 minutes a day, however." Another added, "There will be ten e-mails between the time you pack your briefcase and lock the door" to head home from the office.[21]

When one looks beyond e-mails, the problem only intensifies. A 1998 survey by Pitney Bowes found that the average office employee sent or received 190 messages *every single day*, including faxes, traditional letters, telephone calls, and electronic messages. By 1999 this volume had spiraled even higher, to 201 messages daily.[22] Nearly half of the people surveyed reported being interrupted by six or more messages every single hour they spent in their offices. One of every four people complained about being "distracted" or "very distracted" by these various interruptions.

No wonder white-collar workers complain about job stress.

It's also not too hard to figure out why people frequently check in with their voice-mail and e-mail accounts when they're not at the office: they're just trying to keep the message landslide from burying them alive. The analogy to an assembly line seems all too apt. At the same time that corporate men and women feel *more* pressure to respond—and more quickly than ever—to office communications, their work pace has picked up as well, in part because they keep receiving increasing numbers of communiqués that demand prompt attention.

Craig Brod, a clinical psychologist, coined the term "technostress" back in 1984 to describe these and other experiences he observed in people adapting to new technologies at the workplace and elsewhere. "For the manager, as for the clerical worker," he wrote, "a key element of technostress is a distorted sense of time. Days, hours and minutes take on new meaning as time is compressed and accelerated. Recognition of what is humanly possible fades." Among the many results, he argued, was people's "tendency to push themselves harder than ever to match the efficiency and tirelessness of the computer."[23]

Technological innovations are speeding up the work pace in other, even more fundamental ways as well. In her provocative study *The Electronic Sweatshop*, Barbara Garson explored how corporate employers had begun using what she called "a combination of twentieth-century technology and nineteenth-century scientific management . . . [to turn] the Office of the Future into the factory of the past." At first, she added, "this affected clerks and switchboard operators, then secretaries, bank tellers and service workers. The primary targets now are professionals and managers." To Garson, the objective of these changes was simply "to make white-collar workers cheaper to train, easier to replace, less skilled, less expensive and less special."[24]

Garson examined the ways that new technologies had begun to affect a wide range of white-collar professionals, including investment advisers and social workers. Her study of airline reservation clerks illustrates the patterns she uncovered: "American Airlines had divided the two-minute reservation conversation into segments—opening, sales pitch, probe and close—and provided a set of interchangeable conversation modules for each segment. An acceptable conversation could now be put together like a mix-and-match outfit or a Chinese dinner—one from column A, two from column B. On one level, it's obvious why this is considered efficient," she explained. "In industry, production is routinely arranged so that the bulk of the work can be done with a minimum of skill. The more an airline can standardize the reservation conversation, the less they need to depend on the agents' experience and judgment. This should make the agents cheaper and more interchangeable."[25]

For the many white-collar workers whose jobs are susceptible to some variant of technology-based reengineering, the impact of these changes can be shattering. Work becomes simultaneously duller and more routinized yet increasingly stressful, as employees must continually update their skills and employers find new ways to monitor and speed up productivity.

"Employers look at something like 'mail merge' and think that office work has gotten so much easier," Joan, an office administrator on Wall Street, told me, "because a secretary can now press a button on her computer and send the same letter to twenty people. But because of reorganizations and layoffs, that secretary is now working for four or five people, instead of one person, which means that—even with the new technology—she's working harder than ever. And she's usually lost whatever meaningful connection she once had to the people she works with or the end result of her work."

Marnie, a paralegal I interviewed who was employed by one of Boston's top corporate law firms, argued a point I heard from others as well: workloads often seem to increase with each new technological advancement within the workplace. This occurs not only, she explained, because of the difficulties and stresses involved in learning to use these tools but because key executives themselves often fail to understand their limitations. The result is unreasonable job demands.

As she put it, "We've got this great new computer in our office. And now we can do even more. But it turns out that the new technology only helps me handle seventy-five percent of my workload. Still, my managers keep dumping more work on me, and they don't care about my problems." She paused, then added, "There isn't enough help, and they expect perfection. I feel as though I'm on one of those treadmills in a little rat cage at work."

From a vantage point ten years after Garson's study, it now appears that white-collar workers can be sorted into three basic categories: those whose jobs have been "reengineered" by technology, somewhat along the lines described above; those who are increasingly being replaced by technology (as when nearly 180,000 bank tellers were replaced by ATMs between 1983 and 1993);[26] and those whose work lives appear—at least for now—to be resistant to such changes, typically because of the high levels of skill, experience, or creativity their jobs require.

That third category is small and shrinking, seemingly before our eyes. That's because new technological advances have pushed computer and other electronic capabilities far beyond the realm most people would have imagined possible even a decade ago. At the same time, the business world has displayed an insatiable appetite for all those advances that can be translated into productivity measures (often by facilitating human resources cutbacks).

In his book *The End of Work*, Jeremy Rifkin warns of the unprecedented problems the United States will increasingly come to face as the result of "technological displacement." Rifkin predicts that the trend, now seen in all three traditional sectors of the economy (agriculture, manufacturing, and service), will eventually affect hundreds of millions of people. Already, he argues, "most Americans feel trapped by the new lean-production practices and sophisticated new automation technologies, not knowing if or when the re-engineering drive will reach into their own office or workstation, plucking them from what they once thought was a secure job and casting them into the reserve army of contingent workers, or, worse yet, the unemployment line.[27]

All kinds of careers that once might have seemed immune to technology-driven obsolescence (perhaps because they depended upon interpersonal relations or the so-called human touch) have started showing signs of vulnerability. Many corporations are experimenting with electronic commerce operations that should help them reduce their sales and marketing staffs as well as cut back on business-travel costs. Accountants, financial planners, and financial consultants are increasingly getting replaced by sophisticated software packages; stockbrokers are losing customers to electronic trading programs; and robots have even begun to plug in for pharmacists.

While trends like these took root during the late 1990s, the threat of technological displacement was masked somewhat by the strength of a national unemployment rate that hovered around a thirty-year low. The risks were still apparent, though, in the downwardly mobile earnings and employment patterns displayed by ever more vulnerable white-collar men and women.

Despite the United States' tight job market and booming economy during the latter years of the 1990s, unemployment stints tended to last longer than during any other period since the 1950s. The culprit, according to a recent study by two New York University economists, William J. Baumol and Edward N. Wolff, was the speedup in technological change that had occurred during the past two decades. The pair detected a positive correlation between lengthening jobless spells and increases in nationwide productivity rates, research and development expenditures, and spending on computers per employee. Changes in computer spending had the greatest impact on joblessness. The economists concluded that "changing technology tends to raise skill requirements. And because training and retraining costs are high, employers tend to shun poorly educated workers and especially older workers."[28] For a working population that is aging along with the baby boomers and already burdened by patterns of longer work hours, greater job demands, and decreasing financial rewards, trends like these can only intensify stress loads.

Monitoring and Controlling the Workforce

The *New York Times*, Xerox Corporation, and Edward Jones & Company, the brokerage firm, do not appear at first glance to have much in common.

But all three captured headlines in 1999 for firing groups of employees after catching them in the act of some type of electronic no-no. At the *Times*, "inappropriate and offensive" e-mails led to the termination of more than twenty employees from its Norfolk, Virginia, payroll-processing center; at Xerox, Web surfing nailed forty staffers (some of whom had used office access to the Internet to visit pornography sites).[29]

Here's another way that technology has helped worsen work life: by providing corporations with an arsenal of new, and continually improving, tools with which to supervise their employees' activity and output. For white-collar workers, who have traditionally enjoyed greater latitude than their blue-collar brethren (themselves regulated by tools such as time cards and assembly-line monitors), this is yet another feature of the corporate "sweatshop."

Two business-software packages gained popularity during the late 1990s. The "Investigator" program, sold by WinWhatWhere Corporation, can be installed by a company in any or all of its desktop computers in order to record how many keys are stroked, mouses clicked, and commands entered by each employee during a day. Its users include Exxon Mobil Corporation, Delta Air Lines, and Ernst & Young LLP. "Desktop Surveillance," which marketed itself as the "software equivalent of a video surveillance camera on the desktop," allows employers to view, in real time or playback, whatever tasks their staffers are performing on the computer.[30]

While some people might argue that these monitors are not all that different from the time records long maintained by high-end professionals such as lawyers and accountants, the comparison is anything but apt. These software packages were designed to be installed and operated within someone's computer without him or her being aware of that fact. "Investigator" can do far more than indicate productivity: its corporate users can adjust the software program so that anytime a staffer types an "alert" word (such as boss or union), the document in which it appears is automatically e-mailed to the appropriate supervisor. Some so-called keystroke loggers keep such comprehensive records of computer activity that an employer can read every single thing a person types at the office— whether or not he actually stores it in his desktop computer's hard drive, prints it out, sends it to someone via e-mail, or decides to discard it instead.[31]

And software packages like these represented only one part of a trend. "Back in the fifteenth century, they used to use a ball and chain, and now they use technology," one public relations executive complained to me. Some corporations have programmed their internal computer networks and security systems to make it possible for anyone within their organization to track the movements of anyone else at any time. That can include the exact moment each person starts work, leaves the office, or vacates his or her desk for a trip out to lunch or to the rest room.

One manager who begged me not to mention her company (or even her industry) told me about a time when supervisors had figured out that two of her colleagues were having an affair, because they could track electronically the exact timing of each of their movements into and out of the building in which they worked. One of the pair was eventually fired—not, she assured me, because of the affair, but because of his lack of productivity.

The justification for electronic monitoring is as old as the industrial age itself: greater efficiency. After all, business operations can be much more productive when coworkers and supervisors know how to track people down at any point in the workday. What's unusual about today's monitors, though, is their target: initiatives like these strip white-collar workers of their traditional perquisites (most importantly, a degree of independence). The message not so subtly being conveyed by their employers is this: We need everyone to work harder and longer but can't trust *you* to do it unless we start watching more closely . . . and if we find out that you're not working as we expect, we'll replace you.

In a disturbing article written for *PC Week,* Bill Machrone, then the vice president of technology for Ziff-Davis, compared many of today's corporate employers to Santa Claus ("he knows when you are sleeping, he knows . . ."). As Machrone explained, "He or she may not be able to pry into your personal life, but when you're at work, there's little you can do in the office that can't be monitored." One machine "records the destination and duration of every one of your phone calls. With Caller ID services, it can know who's calling you, too. . . . [T]he times you log in and log off are all dutifully recorded in a log file. The network operating system also records your use of central databases and other network services."[32]

Employee monitoring, like other deteriorating-workplace trends, continues to pick up steam, owing to the business world's seemingly endless quest to raise productivity regardless of the toll exacted upon working men and women. Back in 1993, for example, a survey by *Macworld* magazine found that nearly 22 percent of the companies surveyed engaged in electronic monitoring of their workforce. (Less than one third of those companies bothered to inform their staffers.) Nearly 30 percent of them justified the practice by citing a desire to "monitor work flow."[33] The American Management Association estimated that by 1999 45 percent of American corporations were monitoring their employees' e-mails. But that's not all. When video surveillance, phone-call tracking, electronic monitoring of computer work, and other types of supervision were counted in as well, a whopping 67 percent of companies acknowledged the practice. *BusinessWeek* termed it "Big Brother at Work."[34]

Meanwhile, state-of-the-art technology increasingly equips corporations with new and different tools that (presumably) cut costs while (certainly) degrading the status and power of working men and women. Software-based résumé scanners add, in the words of one observer, "another hefty dollop of uncertainty into a process already chock-full of anxiety." Large employers such as Sony, Coca-Cola, IBM, PaineWebber, and Microsoft now shortcut their hiring processes through techniques such as word searches for target "skill sets" on résumés and computerized percentage rankings that eliminate candidates for consideration when they fail to "scan" high enough.[35]

At the other end of the spectrum, computers have also started playing a role in large-scale firings. When Commercial Financial Services fired nearly fifteen hundred employees during the early summer of 1999, it chose to do so via e-mail. "Is the pink slip history?" asked the CEO of Challenger, Gray & Christmas, an international outplacement firm.[36]

In an evolving business world in which the culture of overwork has been fueled by a wide range of technological advances, stressed-out workers often reach out to the world of machines for terms and images that can accurately describe their personal problems, whether emotional or physical. Big Brother would certainly applaud the trend.

In this, white-collar workers are following a blue-collar pattern. Jeremy Rifkin noted, "In the industrial era, workers became so enmeshed in the rhythms of mechanical machinery that they often described their own fatigue in machine terms—complaining of being 'worn out' or experiencing a 'breakdown.' Now," he added, "a growing number of workers are becoming so integrated with the rhythms of the new computer culture that when they become stressed, they experience 'overload' and when they feel unable to cope they 'burn out' and 'shut down,' euphemisms that reflect how closely workers have come to identify with the pace set by computer technology."[37]

The most recent linguistic blurring of man and machine? Some people have started complaining about their lack of personal "bandwidths." As the *Wall Street Journal* reported, "[S]trictly speaking, bandwidth is the size of the 'pipe' through which Internet and e-mail traffic travels. There seems to never be enough bandwidth. . . . To the 'technoscenti,' though, the word 'bandwidth' is evolving to mean anything that is overburdened—particularly time, but also nerves. In California's workaholic, hyperambitious Silicon Valley, it has become an acceptable way of acknowledging one's personal limitations."[38]

White-Collar Protests in Cyberspace

Ah yes, those limitations. At a time when many working men and women find themselves bumping up against their own shrinking "bandwidths" (even when they wouldn't characterize the problem in exactly this way), technology has surfaced to play yet another, different role in the business world by providing a much needed release valve: the Internet.

To someone seeking to understand the experience of work, as well as employees' attitudes about it, in today's hard-driving corporations, there may be no better way to begin than by exploring the Internet. Indeed, the Net has surfaced in recent years as a virtual town meeting hall where growing numbers of people interact and share their work-related complaints and anxieties.

The big draw for them, of course, is the cloak of anonymity provided by e-mail addresses and cyber-aliases. It's true that this cloak can be penetrated through extraordinary measures, as when hackers or employers intrude themselves into computer correspondence that once seemed private. But consider the real-world alternatives for those white-collar workers who may fear that layoffs, workload reorganizations, or even their own replacement by temporary staffers are just around the corner, *any corner.* Those conversational venues that are closer to home (the traditional watercooler gripe session, stress management seminars, or a host of mental health services paid for, and potentially monitored, by employers) often seem fraught with far greater risks of personal exposure than anything cyberspace can offer.

Given the variety of forces conspiring against them, today's white-collar workers may indeed be afraid to challenge their employers about their workloads or express their resentments face-to-face. But a tour of work-related Internet sites reveals a working population that is angry, exhausted, sometimes crude, and almost invariably frustrated by conditions on the job. "All jobs are bad," commented one anonymous visitor to www.disgruntled.com, a slick monthly Internet magazine whose focus on the dysfunctional world of work drew on average about three thousand "page views" each day from visitors.[39]

He (or possibly she, since the message was, of course, anonymous) continued, "There is no such thing as a good job—there are only jobs which are less painful, degrading and soul-killing than others. Your readers should be looking for ways to destroy their company from the first day that they sign on. They should be noting what software is illegal, what labor laws are ignored, what cash is a little too fluid and what EPA regs are flaunted."[40]

Some e-mail missives reveal a bitterness that practically drips off the computer screen. "Don't these people realize what us high powered executives have to go through on a daily basis, the pressure we are constantly under?" asked one satirical writer. "First we have to labor through the *Wall Street Journal* while drinking imported but possibly bad tasting coffee. . . . I don't think your readership has the remotest concept of management's contribution. We drive the stock market up by good management and increase profits that benefit the ex-pizza maker's investment portfolio. And it's not relevant that he may only have two shares and I have options on 1.7 million. We're talking principles, principles that have made America great."[41]

The vehemence with which many Internet correspondents rail against their employers can be shocking. But it becomes understandable when one considers the technological context. For those men and women who send these notes or visit antiwork websites during office hours, the very act of using their companies' computers to do so is a small but significant act of rebellion: a way to assert some measure of control over their tech-controlled time schedules and their psyches.

Correspondents often send messages like these from home, perhaps because they fear repercussions from an employer monitoring their activities. The ability to use their personal computers in this way (instead of simply as a tool to help them cope with job spill from the office) can also be empowering. This is one electronic activity conducted *by* personal choice, for no reason other than one's personal satisfaction. That's why people decide to devote their precious moments of relaxation at home to venting pent-up stresses through the Internet's antiwork websites, even after being plugged into their computers all day at the office.

Calls for corporate sabotage abounded at www.disgruntled.com, as elsewhere in cyberspace. "If your readers want to think about revenge . . . they need to think about stealing equipment, destroying or corrupting important files, blowing the whistle on illicit practices, and selling proprietary information to competitors."[42]

It's highly unlikely that most white-collar workers would actually carry out these threats. During my own research, not a single man or woman whom I interviewed acknowledged committing any act, even a petty one, of sabotage. (In fact, the consistency with which people seemed surprised or offended by my questions on this subject demonstrated how closely they still identified with notions such as self-responsibility, personal integrity, and their status within the corporate hierarchy, even when they felt betrayed or otherwise misused by an employer.) Still, the electronic conversations that appear in work-related chat rooms and other websites makes it clear that, if nothing else, these Internet threats provide overstressed workers with a valuable opportunity to play out their collective revenge fantasies.

The growing pool of contingent white-collar workers are among the most vocal workplace critics on the Internet. Most are practically invisible and almost certainly interchangeable within the corporate world. The Internet gives them an opportunity to articulate their resentments in an electronic forum in which their status is the same as everyone else's and their voices can be as easily heard.

"'Temp' is short for 'slave,'" wrote one. "Never forget that and you'll always have a niche in the expendable, American workforce." The author of this entry continued, "More and more companies are abandoning the idea of health benefits and retirement plans, and bear hugging the dream of employees they can instantly fire. . . . Some of the drone bees aren't taking to this treatment lightly, even though they're desperate for a paycheck like the rest of us. I've worked with plenty of temps who coveted the supply closet as though it were the Emerald City populated with free envelopes and paper clips."[43]

Although the wide world of Internet users may generally be a younger one, a tour of work-related websites makes it clear that these also draw heavily from an aging baby-boom population that has notched plenty of its own battle scars in the corporate arena. At www.disgruntled.com, subscriber surveys revealed that the Internet magazine's audience was divided fairly equally among Generation Xers and "mid-level" working people in their thirties and forties. Among this older group, at this site and elsewhere, it's fairly common to find undercurrents of surprise or confusion in their messages: many seem to be surfing the Internet in an effort to make sense out of the unexpected and negative developments in their work lives.

This e-mail anecdote is fairly typical: "My story: Until 1994 I was a salesman . . . it was a great job, and I loved it. I had held that job for 15 years, and received regular merit increases, and was always told I was doing a good job. Then, out of the blue, my boss called me into the office one day and told me the company was downsizing and had decided to consolidate territories. My territory, he explained, would be joined with one that was being covered by a young kid they had just hired. . . ."

Six months later, "while I was still looking for a new job, my wife was downsized by the company she had worked at for 9 years," this man went on to explain in remarkably self-controlled, almost neutral tones. "Suddenly we were both out of work and desperate. This went on for a year and a half without a decent job for either of us. I was forty-eight and she was forty-seven, and nobody wanted us it seemed. My biggest problem now is trying not to feel like a failure. I know I was the victim of a greedy employer but . . ."[44]

Group therapy in cyberspace is a big part of the appeal of work-related websites for such people. In an era in which newspapers and other old-media venues continually trumpet the signs and success stories of economic prosperity, the cynicism that flourishes across the Internet comes as a relief. Net surfers seek comrades who can convince them that they're not the only ones for whom the world of work has become something in between a hassle and hell.

But what they find on the Internet varies. The "greedy" employer, the stupid employer, the abusive employer: hostility to the corporation, or to the top management that many people view as synonymous with the corporation, are basic themes.[45] At one site among many, web visitors can find "Bad Managers" (which describes itself as reporting on "true life horror stories of software development cowboys"), where one message continuously blinks across the right-hand corner of the screen: "You are not alone. Is your boss giving you the Hump? You are not alone."

One reason these sites have quickly gained popularity is because many "hyperlink" their web pages to each other. That enables visitors to identify and travel easily between a vast selection of electronic hot spots that share their antiwork perspectives. Some of these antiemployer or workplace-support messages turn out to be marketing ploys by entrepreneurial individuals or companies. Their goal, fairly simple to identify, is to attract more and more unhappy workers to their websites and thereby lock in revenues from either advertising or merchandising sales. Fairly typical of the genre is www.jobhater.com, which mainly sells T-shirts that enable unhappy workers to broadcast their woes.

At the other end of the spectrum are activist sites that attempt to rally Internet visitors into getting involved with some type of organized group, running the gamut from existing trade unions to self-help groups of, say, downsized employees. And somewhere in between are electronic chat rooms and websites that basically exist to help working people air and share their grievances.

In the late-1990s business boom, accompanied as it has been by ever more difficult and demanding workplace conditions, one trend seems clear: the number of antiwork websites, as well as their legions of visitors, seem to be endlessly proliferating. Current listings, as I write these words, run the gamut from "The Official Anti-Nike Site" and "The Disgruntled Ex-Burger King Employees Page" to "Working Stiff," www.dinosaurclub.com (aimed specifically at downsized, middle-aged executives) and "TempSlave." There's even a site called www.nynexsucks.com, whose allure for unhappy employees (as well as customers) proved so powerful that it continued to receive active electronic postings long after NYNEX had merged with Bell Atlantic.

The long-term implications of this trend remain uncertain. Even electronic communication may, like so many other technological advances, be subtly contributing to the spread of today's white-collar "sweatshops." While cyberspace camaraderie, and all those rants and raves about work that dot the e-waves, may help over-stressed workers release some steam, the Internet may—by pacifying some people and intimidating others through the implicit message that work life is tough for everyone these days—rob many white-collar workers of the strength to resist excessive employer demands.

FIVE

"My Full Intention Was to Be There Forever": Sharing the Rewards of Postwar Prosperity

In a business world in which patterns of overwork, stress, and underreward have become the norm—and perhaps inescapable—for countless men and women, the question of just how much things have changed during the past two decades is important for anyone hoping to understand why they have changed; what the impact of these changes has been, and continues to be, upon American workers; and, finally, whether harmful patterns of change can be reversed.

Today, many companies proudly proclaim the "end" of paternalism as if discarding dusty old traditions that have hampered corporate America for umpteen years. But the paternalistic benefits, career security, and moderate demand-and-reward structure that many baby boomers and their parents once took for granted were themselves modern inventions: mainly the product of huge changes that transformed the U.S. economy and business world after World War II.

The era in which they flourished was relatively short-lived, lasting for just about three decades before economic pressures began to build, ultimately resulting in harsh new changes at one large company after another. Yet the image of the "benign" corporate employer exerted an enormous pull upon the collective psyche of America's rapidly proliferating, increasingly well-educated, modestly ambitious white-collar population. Many people dreamed of nothing more, at least on the career front, than the opportunity to work their way somewhere up the ladder at one of the nation's largest, best-known, and most highly respected corporations.

Despite some relatively mild recessions, the early postwar decades were a period of economic growth, price stability, and corporate prosperity.[1] Perhaps most notably in contrast to current conditions, stock ownership was not a prerequisite in order for the white-collar community to share the business world's rewards. Many people can still recall the satisfactions of this period, when household incomes and their families' standard of living seemed on an inevitable uphill rise, just as corporate fortunes were.

Today, white-collar jobs and large employers seem far less desirable, accompanied as they frequently are by "24/7" job stresses, a host of technological intrusions, and all kinds of financial and career insecurities. But although people may sometimes seem excessively nostalgic about an earlier corporate world of work which could never have been quite as safe and comfortable as it appears in retrospect, the postwar period through the 1960s was indeed a time in which prolonged economic growth improved work and home lives much more than the past two decades of prosperity have.

Employment Security

The very notion of long-term job security now seems hopelessly antiquated: a lose-lose strategy that supposedly saddled corporate America with a bunch of deadbeats and handicapped the best and the brightest from job-hopping their way to success.

But before World War II, to a population that was still reeling from the effects of the Great Depression, such stability and security seemed a fantasy too good to ever come true. The war brought the nation to full employment for the first time since the 1920s; and in its aftermath, amid widespread anxieties about a postwar recession and its possible consequences, Congress passed the Employment Act of 1946, which "committed the federal government to maintain maximum employment and with it a high level of aggregate demand."[2]

This policy benefited working Americans as surely as it did their large employers. The government made huge investments in the business sector, especially through highway construction and defense-related expenditures. Wartime research helped jump-start an era of technological innovation, which included IBM's development during the early 1950s of the first general-purpose computer. Government education initiatives that included the GI Bill, meanwhile, helped upgrade the workforce, providing the business world with the large pool of white-collar staffers upon whom corporations increasingly depended for administrative, management, and other essential skills.

Long-term employment security became a real possibility in the years following World War II as big business thrived in the global marketplace (given a head start because the United States' manufacturing facilities and other infrastructure were largely undamaged by the war, unlike much of Europe's and Asia's). Large companies were viewed by many people as the best of all possible employers within the best of all possible work worlds.

William H. ("Holly") Whyte, Jr., a journalist at *Fortune* magazine, sketched out the impact of this unfolding boom upon the white-collar psyche in his 1956 classic *The Organization Man*. Generalizing from years' worth of interviews with college seniors, he noted, "They have been getting more and more relaxed. . . . In the immediate postwar years they were somewhat nervous about the chances for the good life. They seemed almost psychotic on the subject of a depression, and when they explained a preference for the big corporation, they did so largely on the grounds of security. When I talked to students in 1949, on almost every campus I heard one recurring theme: adventure was all very well, but it was smarter to make a compromise in order to get a depression-proof sanctuary. 'I don't think AT&T is very exciting,' one senior put it, 'but that's the company I'd like to join. If a depression comes, there will always be AT&T.'"

Whyte concluded, "Seven years of continuing prosperity have made a great difference. Students are still interested in security, but they no longer see it as a matter of security *versus* opportunity. Now, when they explain their choice, it is that the corporation is security *and* opportunity both."[3]

Statements like these—as well as the vision of AT&T as an employment bedrock of stability—evoke a sense of just how far the corporate world has turned in half a century. So do business publications from the early postwar period, among them the *Management Record*, produced by the Conference Board as a contemporaneous report on large-corporate trends.

In these pages, business executives often emphasized their commitment (or at least desire) to provide employment security for their workforces. Back in 1962, Earl S. Willis, the manager of employee benefits services at General Electric, wrote an account of his company's policy that makes it abundantly clear just how far he was from the layoff-friendly ethos that would flourish under CEO Jack Welch twenty or so years later. (Welch was slugged "Neutron Jack" by his detractors, especially during the early days of his leadership, when they quipped that the only things left standing, after all the layoffs and cutbacks, were the company's buildings.) According to Willis, "Guarantees of employment cannot be made by businesses whose markets are as unpredictable as General Electric's. Nevertheless, we recognize the desire of employees for job continuity, and we have long striven to provide the greatest measure practicable.

"Maximizing employment security is a prime company goal," Willis concluded in the pages of the *Record*.[4] In another issue, a representative of a large electrical equipment manufacturer explained his company's similar commitment: "The employee who can plan his economic future with reasonable certainty is an employer's most productive asset."[5]

What a contrast to today. Most large corporations have wiped out anything resembling an employment manual for fear that such a booklet might create legal obligations to staffers who interpreted it as a promise of job security. Many require their employees to sign documents acknowledging that they are employed "at will," giving the company the right to terminate them at any point in time, for any or no cause at all (so long as their civil rights are not violated).

Yet even as recently as twenty years ago, IBM's employment handbook boasted, "In nearly 40 years, no person employed on a regular basis by IBM has lost as much as one hour of working time because of a layoff. When recessions come or there is a major product shift, some companies handle the work force imbalances that result by letting people go. IBM hasn't done that, hopes never to have to. . . . It's hardly a surprise that one of the main reasons people like to work for IBM is the company's all-out effort to maintain full employment."[6]

IBM was scarcely alone. In his *White-Collar Blues,* Charles Heckscher noted that "at least through the 1970s, half of the men in the U.S. workforce ended in jobs that effectively offered lifetime security. Amazingly," he concluded, "this percentage is by the best estimates *higher* than the model of loyalty, Japan."[7]

The allure of employment security made the United States' large corporations irresistible to those white-collar staffers fortunate enough to get their feet in the door—as well as to the many more who applied but failed to win entry. "They weren't born entrepreneurs," Amanda Bennett wrote of these workers (from a 1990 perspective) in her book *The Death of the Organization Man.* "They didn't like risk, and they didn't like uncertainty. . . . They wanted the security of a regular paycheck. The security of being a little piece of a big machine. The security of knowing that every day when they woke up, the job would be there."[8]

And indeed it was. During the early decades following World War II, white-collar men and women were largely sheltered from the vagaries of the marketplace by large corporations who made good on their long-term employment commitments. The only exception was the 1969–70 recession, when major cutbacks in federal spending for defense, aerospace, and military-related research led to layoffs among highly skilled professional and technical workers— white-collar groups once thought invulnerable to career misfortune.[9] Yet even this downturn was relatively short-lived.

Throughout the 1970s, although the U.S. economy was roiled by skyrocketing inflation, flagging corporate results, seemingly insurmountable global competition, and a stagnating stock market, the white-collar community still felt confident about the job security that large corporations had to offer. There were so many years, after all, of accumulated proof that "the system" worked for them and their employers; memories of the earlier, far less stable employment scene that had existed before World War II were long distant, if not forgotten.

"When I started to work at W. R. Grace back in the late seventies, I never thought I would leave it. My full intention was to be there forever," William told me twenty years later, with a rueful smile. "My boss had been there for twenty-plus years," he recalled. "Another fellow in the department was there for thirty-some-odd years. When I got my ten-year pin, we all joked that I was the spring chicken." Now that pin is a bittersweet relic for a man who was taught by layoffs, at Grace and elsewhere, that "forever" no longer exists.

The Benefit Blanket

For risk-adverse white-collar workers, comprehensive—and steadily improving—benefit packages were also part of the large-company allure: a major reason why the nation's best-qualified workers typically bypassed smaller companies with their skimpier offerings. But the lavish corporate benefit blanket that many people took for granted before the 1980s was—just as job security was—a by-product of World War II. Wage freezes instituted during the war required employers to make heavy use of fringe benefits to attract employees within *that* tight labor market.[10] After the war ended, there was no going back.

Postwar paternalistic benefits evolved in a variety of ways. Some executives believed that the business world (and the nation's economy) would profit by treating employees better, in part by increasing their sense of security and emotional attachment to their employer.

One 1950s examination of the postwar scene singled out a "wing of business opinion which is anxious to disassociate modern business from the 'socially irresponsible' business of fifty years ago." Among the group was Thomas G. Spates, vice president of General Foods, who "believe[d] the nation [could] be saved from socialism and communism if employers 'start[ed] treating their workers like human beings.'"[11]

But although some executives were so motivated, corporate benefit packages were costly even forty or fifty years ago, which might
have discouraged their widespread adoption except for one factor:
the power of militant unions during this early postwar period.
White-collar workers, who resisted efforts to unionize themselves—usually because they identified more with top management
and the company than with their blue-collar colleagues—nonethe-
less benefited from the continuing success of postwar collective bargaining efforts.

Each union breakthrough during this activist era helped raise the
benefit benchmark for all staffers, since employers feared that a failure to improve packages would prompt dissatisfied men and women
to unionize: typically, any existing white-collar plans were modified
to meet or exceed union achievements. By the mid-1950s, according to Jeremy Rifkin, "an informal accommodation of sorts was
reached which was to last, more or less intact, until the mid-1970s.
Labor was to share, at least in part, in the gains in productivity—
enjoying better wages and benefits—in return for the promise of
labor peace and cooperation."[12]

When people look back upon this era, it is not simply nostalgia
that makes them believe that the large-corporate world once represented a haven of safety and security for its employees. During the
three decades of white-collar prosperity that followed World War II,
all-important medical benefits as well as other lifestyle enhancements, such as paid sick leaves and vacation policies, steadily
improved, in marked contrast to the deterioration of recent years.
By 1960, 40 percent of those workers who had major-medical insurance were covered "free," meaning that their corporate employers
paid full policy costs. Ten years later, the percentage of those entirely covered had risen to 63 percent.[13]

The benefit blanket became bigger and better at one major corporation after another during the early postwar period. In the early
1960s, an employee booklet circulated by the Consolidated Edison
Company of New York boasted of "A Record of Progress" which
included "*protection against loss-of-income benefits* [sick pay, medical coverage, and paid absences] . . . a 143% increase [from 1945 to

1960]; *leisure time benefits* [vacations and paid holidays] . . . a 172% increase; *retirement benefits* [pensions] . . . a 562% increase."[14]

Before 1973, which looms in the history books as the rupture point for postwar economic prosperity,[15] a Bureau of Labor Statistics survey reported "substantial" improvements in health and other insurance benefits. At large companies, these typically included special benefit enhancements, such as optional life insurance, long-term disability benefits, and major-medical benefits—all of which, the report noted, were offered more frequently for white-collar than for production workers. New enhancements added during the 1960s included "liberal benefits for convalescent and nursing home care, psychiatric care, and dental care."[16]

Whether the impetus for postwar improvements like these came from union strength or corporate benevolence, the result was undeniable: the big-business world became a more secure, hospitable, and desirable environment for its white-collar inhabitants, sheltered as they increasingly were from the risk of unexpected job loss, financial insecurity, rapidly rising health care costs, or the potential for an impoverished old age. "Not only do the younger people accept the beneficent society as normal," reported "Holly" Whyte, "they accept *improvement*, considerable and constant, as normal too."[17]

The Pension Umbrella

Pensions represent the third essential piece of the corporate safety net that has been shrinking over the past twenty years, before our very eyes.

Unlike long-term employment commitments and other employee benefits, pensions have a history that predates World War II at many of the nation's largest corporations. The Standard Oil Company (New Jersey) launched its pension plan in 1903, and liberalized it about thirty years later; the modest plan at E. I. duPont de Nemours and Company dated back to 1904.[18]

But despite their early roots, private pension plans only truly flourished during the postwar period, as they became increasingly common and lucrative for white-collar workers (again thanks to collective bargaining achievements for union members). The trend became apparent almost immediately after the war's end. In 1946 the IRS reported that nearly seven thousand corporate pension plans and about twenty-five hundred profit-sharing plans existed; just four years later, 50 percent more existed.[19]

The impact of organized labor's achievements was often obvious. In 1950 Ford Motor announced that "salaried men and women, as well as union employees, are to be covered by a pension plan. . . . The basic pension at the retirement age of sixty-five will be the same as under the union-negotiated plan. . . . This basic pension is paid for entirely by the company." Higher-paid workers—presumably those who fell into white-collar categories—were also eligible for other, supplementary benefits.[20]

After nearly thirty-five years of enhancements, the nation's corporate pension fund assets grew to more than $115 billion by the end of the 1960s.[21] That safety net covered a lot of Americans: nearly 25 million, according to a National Bureau of Economic Research report, which represented a 400 percent increase since World War II. "These were the decades of most rapid growth in the creation of promises and expectations for greater security in old age," the study concluded.[22]

There is no more galling contrast for many baby boomers than between their own pension prospects and those of their parents. During the 1980s and 1990s, many large corporations cut back or eliminated pension protections that in some cases had existed for nearly as long as the century. As a result, growing numbers of men and women now lack pensions entirely.

Brian, a software engineer who spent the 1990s scrambling from one contingent assignment to the next, confided to me that he was haunted by the memory of his father's forty years as an engineer with General Dynamics. "I look at my father's career," he mused, "how lucky he was to have a retirement package." Brian and his own family have struggled simply to find health insurance that he can buy, as an independent contractor, at any price. He has no pension and little in retirement savings.

He paused, then acknowledged, "There's a certain outrage. Then again, you have to stay constantly focused. You can't distract yourself. You can't look back. We're all precariously balancing ourselves above a yawning chasm."

Work Time

Employment and financial security aside, there is one other essential way in which white-collar work life differed during the early postwar period from today's norms: the pace and demands of work were simply less intense for the vast majority of working men and women.

Overwork is romanticized and celebrated these days as a kind of live-wire act that fuels corporate growth while somehow fulfilling each individual's potential; it is viewed as exhilarating—if also exhausting—and nothing short of crucial in a business world that runs on speeded-up "Internet time." During the early postwar decades, however, most people had a different and far more balanced set of expectations about the requirements and rewards of economic prosperity.

Sloan Wilson captured the white-collar mood of his times with his 1950s classic *The Man in the Gray Flannel Suit*. Wilson's hero is tempted by the high-demand, high-reward job his boss dangles before him: "We might as well admit that what we want is a big house and a new car and trips to Florida in the winter, and plenty of life insurance." Yet he ultimately resists that temptation, because he simply is not willing to sacrifice his family and the rest of his personal life, including evenings and weekends at home, to the office.

"It's just that if I have to bury myself in a job every minute of my life, I don't see any point to it," is the way he expressed his reservations to his boss.[23] Significantly, his refusal does not brand him as a loser or an uncooperative slacker; the corporation can and does accommodate his lifestyle choice by offering a more moderate career path with its own modest rewards.

Wilson's book was popular because his contemporaries could identify with this vision of a comfortable, balanced life. Throughout the early postwar period, the ranks of the United States' largest companies were staffed by many such people: they had no interest in bringing work home with them and, except on an occasional basis, did not need to do so. They left their offices in plenty of time to eat dinner with the family, and spent weekends relaxing, playing with the kids, or pottering around the house. They were drawn to the large-corporate world not only for its safety and security but because its workloads and schedules seemed more predictable, manageable, and reasonable than anything small businesses could offer.

Two postwar time trends played an important role in making this kind of choice possible. Thanks to collective-bargaining achievements and other benefits of the prolonged business boom, corporate staffers made real gains in leisure time. The five-day-on, two-day-off workweek that most people now take for granted—even if they do overwork their way through it—was, like other paternalistic benefits, a postwar innovation. "After World War II, people weren't willing to return to a six- or even five-and-a-half-day week," Witold Rybczynski reported in *Waiting for the Weekend.* "The five-day week, and the two-day weekend, were now a fixture of American life."[24]

Leisure time improved in other ways for large-corporate staffers, especially through increases in their time off (yet another trend that has reversed itself during the past two decades). By the 1960s, when a thriving stock market and a long string of technology-driven productivity gains convinced many that the postwar era of prosperity could last forever, "lifestyle" benefits became as important to white-collar men and women as insurance and other "security" protections.

The Bureau of Labor Statistics reported that "during the '60s the average increase in workers' paid vacations was close to half a week. . . . In terms of total weeks of vacations, the increase was from 87 million to 129 million, or almost 50%. . . . Some of this, of course, reflects the increase in the workforce," the report acknowledged. "But it doesn't spoil the story, since the number of workers increased by only 18%. . . ."[25]

During the recent period of prosperity, a large company's success has typically translated into less leisure time for its staffers, since excessive workloads regularly intrude upon family and other personal commitments. The split between the corporation's best interests and those of its employees is often unmistakable. But during the early postwar period—when benefits were rising and job demands were more stable—many white-collar workers viewed increased leisure as one of the most significant ways that a benign business world could share its prosperity with them. "Above all, the new capitalism has brought to the average American a leisure that was undreamed of by its pioneer founders," concluded one 1950s examination of the business world.[26]

Hours spent at the office remained fairly steady during the early postwar period, since most large corporations increased the size of their workforces rather than, as today, expecting people to accommodate heavier workloads during periods of growth. Economist Juliet Schor concluded that "[b]etween 1948 and 1969, the most comprehensive measures—hours worked per adult—rose modestly, from 1,069 to 1,124 per year. . . . Surprisingly, weekly hours for non-student men were virtually constant over the period (39.9 to 39.5), even when increases in vacation and holidays are included."[27]

During this period, overwork was largely confined to people at the top of the corporate ladder, or those whose sights were set there. "Common to these men is an average work week that runs between fifty and sixty hours," described Whyte, in terms that today would apply to a far greater portion of the workforce. "Each workday the executive will put in about 9½ hours in the office. Four out of five weekdays he will work nights. One night he will be booked for business entertaining, another he will probably spend at the office or in a protracted conference somewhere else. On two of the other nights he goes home. But it's no sanctuary he retreats to; it's a branch office."[28]

Most corporate staffers led a very different existence from this. Looking at one subset of the white-collar population, the vast once-thriving ranks of corporate America's middle managers, Charles Heckscher noted, "Their jobs, unlike those at the highest levels, were not very stressful: they generally worked 9 to 5 and within clearly delimited boundaries. As a class they expressed great contentment with the state of their lives," he added.[29]

Paul, a marketing manager who worked for Procter & Gamble in the 1950s, explained these distinctions to me, sketching out the differences between his own approach to his career and that of an unusually hardworking colleague. That man rose through the ranks to run the company eventually. "I worked hard. There were a lot of bright and competitive people there and we all worked hard. But *this guy* would work on Christmas Day."

One memory has stayed with Paul during all these years: "Our department had four or five calculators. There was even a time when two guys once had a fistfight over who would use one of them. But that was nothing compared to this guy, who went out and bought one of his own calculators"—an expensive purchase in those days—"so that he could go home and keep punching out numbers."

Today, distinctions like these have fallen by the wayside, since many people—whether they fantasize about one day running a company or simply are running in place to hold on to their jobs—own personal computers, have twenty-four-hour-a-day access to their e-mails and voice mails, and probably perform their own equivalent of "punching out numbers" during evenings, weekends, vacations, commuting time, and plenty of other once-inviolable moments in between.

Yet white-collar staffers once had another choice—not in some idyllic, preindustrial age, but recently enough that some can still remember what it felt like to work under such conditions. Paul, for example, continued to rise up the corporate ladder for many years, first at P&G and then at several other large companies, despite the fact that he confined his "number-punching" activities to the office.

Today, overwork is viewed as the price tag for success. But in the early aftermath of World War II, many people believed that prosperity could raise their standard of living while eventually permitting them to work *less hard*. Talk about visions that date an era! In *The Overworked American,* Schor quoted one postwar expert who predicted to a Senate subcommittee that by the 1990s "we could have either a twenty-two-hour week, a six-month workyear, or a standard retirement age of thirty-eight."[30]

Writing just a couple of years before the OPEC oil crisis helped put an end to all such fantasies, an official of the U.S. Bureau of Labor Statistics, Geoffrey H. Moore, commented that "[t]he drums are beating in the hills for a four-day, forty-hour workweek—not only beating but bringing forth considerable reaction." Moore himself could see the logic of the change: "Anyone who fights through the traffic every day—on the commuter trains, the subway, the freeway—can readily believe it. Four days of this kind of struggling has got to be an improvement over five almost any way you travel it. . . . "[31]

After two decades of workload increases, as well as declines in vacation days, holidays, personal days, and sick days, today's large corporations march to a different drumbeat.

The Corporate Triangle

For some people, a single image or memory embodies all that was different about pre-1980s corporate America and the big-business world today. For Alan Downs, a management consultant who cut his teeth on a series of downsizing campaigns (and then went on to regret the error of his ways in a book called *Corporate Executions*), the defining moment came when, as a young man recently employed by Hewlett-Packard, he heard CEO David Packard describe his management philosophy.

"As the cornerstone of his talk, he drew a triangle with each of the three points accentuated. At each point he wrote one of the following labels: shareholders, management, and employees," Downs recalled. "This, he said, was the fundamental secret to successful management. Any good management decision is based on the best interests of each of these three corporate constituents, keeping the triangle balanced. A decision that undermines any of these ultimately undermines the company's long-term success."[32]

Since few business executives in this stock-market-obsessed age share this view, their employees have received fewer of the rewards of recent corporate prosperity than others did during the early postwar boom. Some of today's business leaders openly revile a philosophy like Packard's, as when "Chainsaw" Al Dunlop, the former chief executive of Scott Paper, commented, "Who or what are stakeholders? They're the company's employees, the community where a business operates, even the company's suppliers. . . . If you see an annual report with the term 'stakeholders,' put it down and run, don't walk away from the company," he advised. "It means the company has its priorities upside down."[33]

The big-business world that flourished during the early postwar decades was far from perfect. Discrimination against women and racial and religious minorities was rampant. Administrative bureaucracies grew fat and lazy, only to handicap the massive corporate operations that depended upon their effectiveness. Many of the United States' best-known companies took their global preeminence for granted and barely survived long enough to learn how to compete in the new world order.

Yet despite these and other flaws, it's not hard to understand why the postwar period of corporate paternalism still exerts such a powerful emotional influence upon baby boomers and their parents, if only as a reminder of how different the conditions and rewards of work can be. Relatively brief though it was, this era permitted white-collar workers to share the benefits of business prosperity, as well as a deep-seated sense of confidence about their own financial future and the economy's.

Those who lived through its disappearance are often bitter about what corporate America has left behind. Paul, the onetime Procter & Gamble manager who followed his own moderate career course, eventually lost his job in a downsizing campaign during the 1990s. After that, he decided to set himself up in business as a consultant. "I knew I could never land another corporate job. I recognized reality. When you're too old and potentially a drain on pension funds and medical bills—you're fairly unemployable," he told me, sounding a common refrain. "Employees feel less loyal to a company—companies feel less loyal to an employee. Attitudes have changed. I don't know anyone who feels anymore, 'I love this place. I'm always going to be here.' Before," he concluded, "it used to be, 'I'm a Procter & Gamble person.' Now, it's 'I'm a Paul person,' or whatever your own name is."

Another source of mine told me about his friend Ron, who had spent his career working up the ladder at Goodyear. "His department at one time had two hundred or so people in it. Now it's down to fourteen. The ones who are left—they don't make waves." My source paused, then added, "You can sense it everywhere. They don't say too much. But when people open up to you, you realize they don't care how they do their jobs. These are people who built these companies. They're going out feeling like losers. It's been very damaging."

The extent of that damage is tough to comprehend without considering it in the context of the corporate world's changes during the past half century. Three snapshots of AT&T illustrate the deterioration in employer-employee relations. Back in the 1940s, a manual written for staffers of the "long lines" department described the company's pension plan, adding, "By means of this and other welfare practices, the Company endeavors to 'take care' of its employees throughout their working careers, and beyond. In return, it naturally expects employees to be genuinely concerned with the welfare of the business and to feel personally responsible for its reputation and continuing success."[34]

Just a few years later, Mr. W. L. Lees, a vice president at another division, noted, "We are convinced that our employees are not Communists. We are convinced that our employees are not Socialists. . . . So we are beaming our educational material at the moment to answer the question: What do I, the employee, get from working for the Bell Telephone Company of Pennsylvania?" Lee explained, adding, "As far back as 1928, our company sensed the need and the desire of our people to know something more about the company for which they work . . . 22,000 of our employees and 6,800 of their families participated in these meetings last year."[35]

Hard to believe that before the end of the century, a very different type of employee-education initiative would be attempted at AT&T. At a moment of organizational crisis, when about forty thousand employees were targeted for layoffs, this campaign aimed to convince staffers that their jobs weren't really jobs—or at least what they had always thought of as jobs: they were "projects" or "fields of work," carried out by employees who were really "self-employed vendors," whatever they once might have deluded themselves into believing (perhaps because of what the company had mistakenly conveyed to them, when they got hired). Mr. Lee's nineties counterpart, vice president for human resources James Meadows, made the message abundantly clear: "In AT&T, we have to promote the whole concept of the work force being contingent, though most of the contingent workers are inside of our walls."[36]

The paternalistic business-world order celebrated in different ways by W. L. Lee, David Packard, and many, many others died a painful death during the 1980s, as the rewards and demands of work began to deteriorate at one large corporation after another. To understand why the decline occurred during this decade, one must examine the investment and regulatory conditions that forced massive change within a troubled national economy.

SIX

"Ma Is Dead": Workplace Change in the 1980s

The early postwar decades faced their own share of financial challenges, including six recessions—most of them mild—through the end of the 1970s. Yet it was only during the 1980s that white-collar conditions seriously deteriorated at large workplaces across the United States as paternalistic practices fell into disrepute.

Why then? Business conditions were ripe for a major transformation, as economic problems and a crisis of confidence reached proportions unparalleled in post-World War II America. Aggressive action by U.S. investors forced gut-wrenching changes upon the nation's largest companies. Yet without the cooperation of white-collar staffers—motivated by a complex set of emotions during this decade of transition and decline—"sweatshop" management practices might never have seized hold of today's workplaces.

The Business World in Crisis

The 1970s ended in recession, during which two of the giants of American industry, Chrysler and Lockheed, managed to survive only thanks to government bailouts. The stock market was in a prolonged slump, the worst the nation had seen since the 1930s. The new decade began with inflation approaching 15 percent, unemployment over 8.5 percent, productivity in a slump, and a pervasive mood of unease, sometimes bordering on panic, about the nation's economic prospects. Gold prices, which tend to rise along with investor pessimism, were skyrocketing.[1]

Amid this general sense of financial crisis, a glaring spotlight was turned upon the U.S. business community. As popular wisdom increasingly began to have it, large corporations had become bloated and inefficient. Business executives were blamed for their current crop of problems, after having supposedly handicapped their organizations with labyrinthine bureaucracies and unrealistic delusions about their unshakable marketplace prowess. Misguided management policies had produced a workforce, so this thinking went, spoiled by excessively cushy financial arrangements, low performance demands, and a false sense of entitlement to their jobs.

To critics, the proof of all this was in corporate America's growing inability to compete with nimble new competitors, largely from Japan and West Germany. By 1981 the nation imported 26 percent of its cars, 25 percent of its steel, 60 percent of its televisions, radios, and tape recorders, and 53 percent of its numerically controlled machine tools. "Twenty years before, imports had accounted for less than 10 percent of the U.S. market for each of these products," noted one business observer, adding ominously, "Foreign-made goods were competing with more than 70 percent of goods produced in the United States."[2]

It seemed time for some harsh medicine for companies and consumers alike. In an effort to drive down inflation, Federal Reserve chairman Paul Volcker pushed interest rates to a punishing 12.4 percent—twice the level they had been at just ten years earlier. By 1982, as the economy slumped in another, yearlong recession, unemployment climbed to 10 percent.[3] Business bankruptcies rose to a post-Depression record. People were scared about their futures. And so were corporate executives, whose problems kept mounting, along with foreign competition, oil prices, industry deregulation, and the impossibly high cost of business borrowing.

By 1982, when management consultant Tom Peters coauthored *In Search of Excellence,* executives were so desperate for new ideas that they kept the book on the *New York Times* best-seller list for half a year. As one business writer put it, Peters' analysis of what worked and what did not work in the new global economy "arrived upon this desolate scene like a Candygram at an intensive care unit."[4]

Investors Intervene

While corporate leaders floundered, Wall Street—mobilized by a relatively small group of high-profile investors—began to pounce upon one opportunity after another in an effort to wring huge, quick profits from undervalued stocks. And there were a lot of profits to be made. Within just a couple of years, what had begun as an era of national confusion, financial anxiety, and more than enough finger-pointing to go around soon evolved into something quite different: the decade of the deal.

Federal and state regulatory changes created an environment in which corporate mergers and takeovers could flourish, to the investment community's seemingly endless delight. During the early 1980s, President Ronald Reagan appointed as head of the Department of Justice's antitrust division an attorney who had previously defended large corporations against antitrust suits, virtually guaranteeing the federal government's noninterference with the growing merger-and-acquisition movement. Once the Supreme Court declared unconstitutional those state laws that aimed to shield local companies from out-of-state suitors, a "merger frenzy" took hold.[5]

Despite the compliance of government regulators, the "greed is good" decade could never have played itself out in one merger-and-acquisition attempt after another without the inventiveness of Wall Street, personified at the time by Michael Milken of the investment house Drexel Burnham. His popular "junk" bonds—high-yield debt instruments—financed many of the riskiest and most aggressive corporate raids: activities that likely could not have found backers in an earlier, more cautious business era. By 1986 corporate America had issued about $125 billion worth of high-yield bonds, up from just $15 billion a decade earlier. It was a sign of these destabilized times that nearly one quarter of the nation's total corporate debt was now "junk."[6]

A flurry of new activity—hostile takeovers, leveraged buyouts, corporate bust-ups, and similar transactions—came to preoccupy the managers of large-corporate America, whose priorities were driven by equity, rather than business, goals. Consumer confidence rebounded following drastic declines in inflation and interest rates.

The result of both trends was a stock market rally that eventually turned into an outright boom, with equities rising by an average of 26 percent annually between 1982 and 1987.[7]

Investment profits aside, though, corporate America remained in crisis throughout much of the 1980s—it was just a different crisis from that of the 1970s. Michael Useem sketched out the extent of the damage in his book *Investor Capitalism*: "Of the country's 500 largest manufacturers in 1980, one in three had ceased to exist as an independent entity by 1990. The *Fortune* 500 employment rolls dropped from 16 million in 1980 to 12 million by 1990. One-third of the *Fortune* 500 had received hostile ownership bids. . . . The 500 largest industrial firms had reduced their product diversity by half."[8]

These statistics only hint at the havoc wreaked by investor assaults upon corporate America and its white-collar staffers. During the decade of the deal, a crisis might get triggered by "green-mailers" like Saul Steinberg or Ivan Boesky—both of whom amassed enormous fortunes by launching hostile bids on companies, with the goal of being paid to go away. Investor-raiders like these inspired terror in management suites, often prompting executives to resort to questionable self-defensive strategies. Some preserved their companies' independence, but at a cost so high—often tied to buying back their own stock at inflated prices—that long-term survival remained in doubt.

White-collar working conditions deteriorated because of these maneuvers. Huge rounds of cost-cutting, layoffs, and benefit reductions occurred as "target" companies struggled to handle the huge debt loads necessary to fight off raiders. Some companies even cashed in part of their employees' pension savings—$21 billion worth during the eighties and early nineties—in order to finance payments to greenmailers or carry out their own takeover plans.[9]

As the decade unfolded, the lines sometimes blurred between greenmail assaults and other hostile maneuvers as men like Carl Icahn, Ronald Perelman, and Carl Lindner went on junk-bond-financed shopping sprees across corporate America, with the goal of actually taking control of a company and then selling it off, whether in pieces or as a whole. The profits they earned from hostile takeovers were often even greater than those tied to greenmail assaults. Yet regardless of which approach investors took, workplace conditions declined.

From a stock market perspective, the middle years of the 1980s proved intoxicating. The Dow Jones Industrial Average skyrocketed from below 1,000, the level at which it had vacillated since the mid-1960s, to approach 3,000, a once-unimaginable peak. During these heady times, more Americans started getting involved with the stock market, primarily through mutual fund savings and 401K retirement holdings. Back in 1979, the entire mutual fund industry held under $95 billion worth of assets; ten years later, that number had risen to nearly $1 trillion.[10]

The rise of small investors played an unexpected role in the developments of the 1980s. As the mutual fund industry attracted more cash and the stock market continued to boom, the number of funds multiplied. In 1979 there were fewer than three hundred stock-based funds; by 1989 there were nearly eleven hundred. As stock mutual funds became wealthier and greater in number, they became ever more powerful forces in the financial marketplace, controlling large blocks of investor dollars that could swing stock prices up or down.

The people who put their savings in mutual funds were often the same white-collar men and women whose work lives began deteriorating during this period. Few held large enough investments in these funds for their profits ever to compensate for lost jobs, benefit cutbacks, or other workplace insecurities. But that was the trade-off many of them made without knowing it. Their portfolio managers often backed investor-raiders or otherwise supported major corporate changes, all in the interest of achieving short-term profits at any cost. Pension fund managers—whose dollars also came from the corporate workforce—followed a similar path. Funds from IBM, Xerox, Atlantic Richfield, Standard Oil, and General Motors were among those that invested heavily in junk bonds.[11]

Without the heavy backing of mutual funds, pension funds, and other large institutional investors, Wall Street's assault upon corporate America during the 1980s might have fizzled out, if only for lack of financing. Instead these groups "rendered shares to would-be acquirers, they invested funds in takeover and buyout funds, and they gave votes to strategic block investors," in Michael Useem's words.[12] This partnership between Wall Street raiders and the Main Street investment community left many large companies (and their employees) with little hope of survival unless they could reinvent themselves as lean-and-mean profit machines.

Destablized Companies, Deteriorating Job Conditions

The 1980s were a decade of extreme transition. That was certainly true for the companies that overhauled and reinvented themselves, whether they took these actions because of stock market raiders, marketplace competition, government deregulation, or other factors. But it was also true for the white-collar employees who first found their jobs and then often their emotional attitudes about work changing.

In its most unmistakable form, workplace change centered on hours spent at the office. As corporations struggled to survive, overwork patterns among their employees became pronounced. In 1980, 11.2 percent of Americans working at full-time jobs spent forty-nine to fifty-nine hours at the office; another 7.9 percent spent sixty or more hours there. As the decade progressed, people kept putting in more time on the job. By 1989, 14.7 percent of full-timers spent between forty-nine and fifty-nine hours at work—and another 10.3 percent fell into the sixty-plus category.[13]

As investor-raiders forced corporate America to become ever more cost-conscious, a shrinking-reward pattern also became firmly entrenched in the workplace. During the 1980s, family incomes grew at a slower rate than during any other postwar business cycle. According to analysis by the Economic Policy Institute, "What income growth there was over the 1979–89 period was driven primarily by more work at lower wages."[14]

Barry Bluestone and Stephen Rose calculated that during the extended period from 1973 through 1988, "the combined average husband-wife hourly wage increased by only 1.8 percent—the equivalent of a real hourly wage increase of less than 30 cents over the entire period, or 2 cents each year." Most of that paltry increase, they concluded, was "purchased with a 16.3 percent increase in hours worked."[15]

Corporate benefits also deteriorated, both because of investor-provoked cutbacks and the eroding influence of the United States' labor unions. President Ronald Reagan's firing of striking air traffic controllers was symptomatic of the decade's decline: the increasing occurrence of concession bargaining—in which union salaries and benefits were frozen or slashed—reinforced the policy of fiscal austerity at large workplaces across the nation.[16]

At some point during the volatile 1980s, most white-collar staffers found themselves working harder and longer, for less reward, under increasingly insecure conditions. Yet many acquiesced to workplaces changes, remaining loyal to their employers during years of instability and decline. Why?

Seduced by the Go-go Eighties

The first time I met Ben was in a self-help meeting for out-of-work executives. It was the summer of 1997. Ben and about twenty other men and women shared junior-sized desks and cheap telephones (as well as job-search leads) on a first-come, first-served basis in a tiny, somewhat dingy set of offices housed in a downtown Manhattan high-rise. The organization had been around for decades. The members hoped to pass through it in just a couple of weeks, or months if absolutely necessary. They didn't have much in common except the fact that each one had earned $40,000 or more, sometimes a good bit more, in their previous, employed lives.

After our initial conversation that day, I went on to interview Ben, a longtime banker, every couple of months throughout the course of my research: drawn both by his quick intelligence and his efforts to make sense of the way that his work life had evolved—or perhaps I should say devolved—since he had graduated from business school back in the early eighties. We spent dozens of hours in conversation during the year-plus in which he remained, contrary to both of our expectations, unemployed.

Looking at the 1980s through the kaleidoscope of Ben's career helped me understand just how heady a time it had been, not only for Wall Street raiders and top executives but for growing numbers of men and women on all rungs of the job ladder in many industries across the nation. The decade offered them a fast-forwarded version of the American Dream: a new career equation befitting a rapidly changing corporate world. Its underlying premise was an employee's ability and willingness to work not just hard but *really hard*— to do whatever was necessary in order to make the next corporate deal pay off, or to help an employer fight off a hostile takeover bid, or to achieve some pressing bottom-line goal.

If white-collar professionals sometimes felt exhausted by the unparalleled intensity of their jobs, or regretted time that could have been spent with their spouses or children instead of business associates, few focused on the longer-term consequences of their life choices. They expected that there would be a reward for all that hard work, which would be less slow in coming and more ample than their parents had ever dreamed possible. The key to that reward was the stock market, which promised enormous payoffs but imposed a discipline upon employer and employee alike.

After the gloom and doom of the 1970s and early 1980s, people like Ben were convinced that financial prospects for themselves, their employers, and the nation were better than they ever could have been in the safer but stodgier postwar era—and, indeed, his career got off to a great beginning. After a couple of starter jobs, Ben settled himself while still in his mid-twenties in the corporate finance department of a large New York savings and loan institution. What a vantage point it was. While few industries passed through the eighties unchanged, the S&L business positively transmogrified itself during the decade, as one risk-adverse bank after another turned into a highflier hooked on a potent combination of junk bonds, real estate plays, and the like.

In many ways, savings and loan institutions like Ben's embodied everything that was thrilling and chilling about the 1980s. These banks had begun the decade as one of the most beleaguered of U.S. industries, caught between the income they were earning from low fixed-rate mortgages and the skyrocketing interest rates they needed to pay in order to woo savers away from more lucrative money market funds. Congress deregulated the industry in 1982 in order to save it: new regulations permitted these once-stodgy consumer banks to invest in commercial loans, corporate debt, and other higher-risk, higher-reward transactions.

With almost one trillion dollars in assets between them, many S&Ls wound up (along with pension and mutual funds) as central players in the merger-and-acquisition movement that was ransacking corporate America in search of huge, stock-based profits.[17] Before the 1980s ended, many had taken such big gambles that they ended up insolvent. But that crisis took years to develop; and before it did, the savings and loan industry seemed to many to embody the gold-plated potential of aggressive new business strategies.

Although given to understatement, Ben was, if anything, effusive as he recalled the period: "It was a wonderful time for banks. There was important deregulation in terms of our ability to offer new products and services. That brought a lot of new blood to the industry." He was part of that trend: his bank, like others, was eager to hire bright young men and women who would not feel constrained by a more traditional mind-set. "It was a wonderful time for our bank. We were growing by leaps and bounds."

During the first five years of his employment, Ben's bank increased in size by many factors. "I got to work on many wonderful things, including taking the bank public," he recalled. "We followed that with all kinds of other activities, involved with buying other banks and other types of financial institutions." What came across in our many conversations was just how emotionally attached Ben had felt, *and still felt*, to these deals. He had been empowered and excited by them, perhaps as much in his own way as did the deal makers whose names were splashed across newspaper and magazine headlines of this era.

In their embrace of risk, Ben and his colleagues were different from their white-collar counterparts during earlier postwar years. But in terms of their emotional attachment to their employer, they were all brothers under the skin. He explained to me: "You didn't have the skepticism then that you have now. The notion of loyalty existed. People were willing to work harder for the organization because they felt they would be there for the long term." Yet the fire that motivated people like Ben was sparked by more than loyalty alone. "It was thrilling. It was fun. It was great to be part of it all."

Without any qualms, Ben threw himself into the rapidly increasing demands of his job. The contrast between his own high-intensity schedule and the work lives of bankers before deregulation could not have been more dramatic. "I used to get into work by 7:30 A.M., work twelve hours a day. I always had work in my briefcase," he told me. His commute by bus and subway from an upscale New Jersey suburb added another hour to each end of the workday. Some weeks he would spend so much time at the office or on the road that he would see his children for only a few of their waking hours, coming home just long enough to grab a quick shower and snooze. It was as though he had never heard the phrase "banker's hours."

Although far from the bank's top management ranks, he felt completely devoted to—and motivated by—its fast-growth goals. "We were not making great money back then," he confided. "When I joined the bank, I was earning $50,000, maybe another $5,000 in bonuses." But that didn't matter: when it came to how hard he was working, no one at the top could put Ben to shame. "I was working enormous hours. I was in constant motion during those days."

If any single moment could encapsulate this period for him, it was the time, recalled Ben, when a messenger from a Manhattan printing firm brought him some disclosure documents. He and his wife were vacationing at a waterfront resort. In fact, they were on their honeymoon. But he was prepared to work if necessary—and, of course, it was. The delivery arrived while the newlyweds were sunbathing on the beach. Ben received documents that were single-spaced, hundreds of pages long, all tied to a financing deal with which he was involved.

"I remember reading them while my new wife and I were lying on the sand." He was silent for a moment, perhaps picturing the scene in his mind. "That kind of captures my ethic back then." But he was far from alone, Ben emphasized. "It was the $15,000 accounting clerk and all kinds of other people. It was a unique time. You weren't driven by fear, but a sense of satisfaction." Some of that golden glow undoubtedly comes from nostalgia; but the banker's reminiscences also suggest a powerful sense of identification with his employer. He characterized it this way: "The company and the employee were on the same wavelength."

During the decade of the deal, what a highly charged wavelength it was! "When I worked on a transaction, I would go until I dropped," he confided. "I remember when I completed work on the public offering for the bank, I told myself, Well, that's it. Now I can coast. But the time never happened when I could coast. We used to joke at the bank that for every one year we worked there, we got ten years of experience."

He paused, then added, "When you're truly in a deal perspective, you lose sight of everything else." His lack of caution about money was a good example. "During the eighties, when I was climbing up the ladder, I bought a house. Stretched myself, because I felt I could grow into it." When a daughter entered college, he borrowed against the value of the family's house with a home equity loan, also confident that he would be able to pay it off as his salary and the value of his home kept rising.

But although he had thrown himself into an industry that was reinventing itself at a supercharged pace, Ben—like many of his white-collar colleagues across corporate America—had retained a fairly traditional set of expectations about hard work and its inevitable rewards within the workplace. During his early years on the job, regular promotions, raises, and a rapidly growing retirement account all reinforced those expectations.

But if the savings and loan industry's soaring phase epitomized one side of the 1980s, then so did its crash-and-burn conclusion, which Ben began to see signs of even before the stock market crash of October 1987. His bank "had entered into some very high risk loans, like high-rise construction," he explained to me. "Then, bank regulators started cracking down on capital requirements for us and other institutions. That just devastated our bank. Put us into a death spiral." Meanwhile, real estate values collapsed across the United States (and most especially throughout the Northeast, where the bank's mortgage portfolio was based). Junk bonds and other investments collapsed. His bank's stock price collapsed. And his career prospects went downhill along with his company.

He paused. "Within a couple of years, the world changed dramatically for me. And the banking world changed. We went from a high-growth to a try-to-survive mode. Imagine feeling as though you've been climbing a mountain and you've almost made it to the top. And then suddenly you're on a river and about to go over a waterfall."

The postscript to Ben's 1980s experiences should be all too familiar to followers of the banking industry. Saddled with disastrously performing loans, his S&L teetered on the verge of bankruptcy, surviving only because of the intervention of a federal agency, which brought in new management, recapitalized the bank, and eventually sold it to a competitor. Ben held on to his job for a while, but he faced ever more voracious demands on his time and energy, all in the less-than-thrilling interest of shrinking the bank back down to the same small size it had been when he originally joined it.

The good days were over. At first he considered himself fortunate to have avoided the pay and benefit cuts he kept hearing about from his counterparts at other struggling banks. But his retirement savings were devastated by a total loss of his investment in the company's once-soaring stock. Although I'd known the ending in advance—after all, I had met Ben at that gathering for unemployed executives—his recollections of the downturn were painful to hear. "It was emotionally debilitating. I poured a thousand percent of my energy into the efforts to save the bank." His tone became harsh. "If I had it to do over again, I never would," he said, pausing, "because I'd probably be a million times better off now if I had directed that energy to refocusing myself and my career."

He was silent for a moment, reflecting on his comments. Then he spoke again, his tone appropriate once more for a well-balanced banker: "But that's me looking at the 1980s from a 1990s perspective."

Allegiance to the Corporate Parent

Not every white-collar staffer succumbed to the thrills of the go-go 1980s the way that Ben did during his bank's meteoric, if brief, rise. Many people experienced the decade as one anxiety-producing corporate crisis after another, whether prompted by pressures from Wall Street, deregulatory trends, or global competition. In any case, the end result was similar: As corporate perspectives became focused upon ever more short-term goals, people's job conditions became increasingly unpleasant, unrewarding, and unrealistically demanding.

Not every employee stayed on at a troubled company, of course. But large numbers of men and women did—accepting heavier and heavier workloads, often while their salaries and benefit packages were frozen or reduced. For these people, workplace conditions were far from exhilarating. But they stayed on because they were prepared to do whatever it took to help their companies survive the challenges of the 1980s. Trapped in an emotional mind-set nurtured during three decades of paternalistic management practices, many found it difficult, if not impossible, to cut ties when they still believed in the "rightness" of a business world built upon mutual loyalty.

There may be no greater example of this dynamic than the AT&T divestiture, which was mandated in the early 1980s, at a time when the company employed about 1 million people in all forty-eight of the contiguous U.S. states. No other single event in the decade's history had a more dramatic impact on more people's work lives. For all the long-term opportunities that divestiture created, in the shorter term many white-collar staffers found themselves required to work harder then ever before in order to help effect enormous transitions—while increasingly recognizing that their own prospects now included job loss, demotion, transfer, or some other unexpected and seemingly undeserved turn in once-thriving careers.

Why didn't they just leave and seek to reestablish successful careers elsewhere? (It's the same basic question again: Why did they fail to resist the new work-world order?) In my efforts to resolve this, I conducted long interviews with nearly a dozen men and women who had lived and worked through these difficult years at AT&T and its Baby Bell offspring.

These people did not feel the same sense of thrill and limitless potential that someone like Ben did as he went along with the ever-intensifying demands of his workplace: there usually were not many goodies to go around in a crisis situation. Yet they still felt a strong sense of attachment to—and identification with—their corporate parent. This motivated them to work harder, despite increasingly demoralizing job conditions. All they really wanted was to help their employer get past the current set of challenges and restore the company (as well as their work lives) to what had once been the norm.

I interviewed Fred on a number of occasions. We spoke by telephone: I in my New York City office, and he in the retirement home he shared with his wife in Arizona. At that time he was sixty-one years old. He had worked for AT&T for his entire adult working life, starting out as a part-timer while still in high school.

We discussed his whole career, which encompassed transfers to more than a dozen different cities, divorce, a rise to the ranks of upper-mid-management, and a seemingly irrevocable split with an adult child who blamed him for paying more attention to the company than to the family during his years as a corporate up-and-comer. Then we focused our talks on the divestiture and its impact upon his life.

"I've always been a hard worker," Fred told me. "Rarely did 6 A.M. come when I wasn't in the office. I'd stay till 6 P.M., 7 P.M., 8 P.M., and often work on Saturday. I had a work ethic that said that if I'm supposed to do it, I'll do it right. I'll defend her"—meaning AT&T—"to the end."

That was *then*, he emphasized. "That was how I felt. There isn't anyone I worked with who cares anymore. There isn't anyone who gives a whit about the company. Loyalty is gone, without doubt. There's distrust. There's anger. The piper will have to be paid." He paused, then added, "We used to have a saying in the old days that AT&T was almost like a religion. We defended it just like a family. No more."

At that point, he proposed sending me a copy of the handwritten diary he had kept during the prolonged period of divestiture. He thought it would help me understand the massive changes he had come to experience, not just in the conditions of his day-to-day work life but in his attitudes toward his job and his employer.[18]

After reading dozens of the pages, I agreed. No conversational summary, distorted by the conclusions of hindsight, ever could have
fully described what had happened to him and why.

Excerpts from Fred's January 9, 1982, entry do a blunt job of setting the scene for corporate crisis: "The year is off to a beginning
which looks, from my perspective, to be dim and without promise
insofar as the job is concerned. Yesterday, my boss . . . called all the
department heads together for an impromptu meeting. When we
were all seated, he held up a piece of blue line paper with three
words on it: 'Ma is dead.' He was referring of course to the news that
AT&T had settled the Justice Department antitrust suit which has
been going on for seven years . . . There are a lot of unanswered questions and I hope and pray it won't be as bad as I see it, but January
8, 1982, will be a day not soon forgotten by us telephone people."

So much was conveyed in so relatively few words. "Ma is dead"
may have been a workplace quip, but it held much more meaning
for the participants in this room. The words evoked that close,
almost familial bond that AT&T's employees—and, indeed, many
white-collar workers—still felt for their employer during this
tumultuous decade. "Ma," and the corporate way of life they had
grown to expect and believe in, *was* dead (or at least dying, in industry after industry across the United States).

Finally, Fred's conception of "a day not soon forgotten" may be
bleak, but it also had a mythic quality about it—if only that of a
small myth cherished by an anonymous corporate employee. Like
Ben, like so many other white-collar professionals during the eighties, this AT&T manager felt that he was both a witness to *and* a par-
ticipant in important and unparalleled changes that were sweeping
across corporate America. That sense of being involved in a larger-
than-life workplace experience helped motivate him and others to
go along with the new program, at least for a while.

It took about half a year for Fred to begin to admit to himself, in
the privacy of his diary, the possibility that divestiture might wreak
havoc on his own career. June 20, 1982: "I *am* deeply concerned
about the possibility of demotion and/or transfer in the new regional organization. The problem is that there are, for example, three
general managers all doing the same thing in my discipline (and

most disciplines for that matter). If I were the Chief Executive Officer for the region, I'd say, hey! We only need one of you to do——, and God only knows what would happen to the other two."

But despite those well-founded personal anxieties, he remained as committed as ever to helping the company get past its crisis. The world of work might be changing, even changing drastically, but people like Fred still retained traditional beliefs about the importance of doing one's duty to the employer, rising to whatever challenges might present themselves, and hopefully receiving their just rewards in return.

August 5, 1982: "The plan of reorganization was filed with Judge Greene . . . so the die is cast. . . . 1983 will be tough, but if we can get thru [sic] it and 1984, I think we'll begin to see the operation as it will exist in the late '80's. Let's go for it!"

Entries like these conveyed a kind of corporate fortitude, reminiscent of Fred's descriptions to me of his predivestiture work life. "It was always hard," he had told me. "Back in my travel days, I remember one night, I was in a strange bed. Once I turned out the light, I couldn't remember where I was. Then I said, 'It's okay, it's Atlanta.' I almost fell asleep, then I said, 'No, it isn't Atlanta, it's Denver.' Then, laying there, I said, 'No, it's not Denver, it's Cleveland.' Finally, I could not figure out where I was, so I turned on the light and looked at the area code on the phone. It was '415' and I said, 'Oh yeah, it's San Francisco. I'm in San Francisco.'"

But as the decade progressed, Fred began to show signs of overload. By March 6, 1983, he wrote: "Stress is high in my life right now. Principally because of the job. The problem is that I see myself standing alone. . . . It's damn near impossible to keep from going crazy. . . . Sometimes I feel that this stress is self-induced because of my conscientiousness. . . . In this era of ambiguity, uncertainty and inordinate turf battles, the manager who *really* cares may well kill himself with anxiety and worry and what those emotions generate—stress."

This basic tension—between the corporate *mythology* that was motivating Fred (the historically unparalleled business crisis during which he was "standing alone") and the corporate *reality* (he was working too hard, stressed, not fully appreciated)—recurred throughout later pages of his diary. He complained about stress and overwork repeatedly as the demands of his workplace kept ratcheting up in intensity, almost on a month-by-month basis. But for much of the first year or so after the divestiture ruling, Fred expressed in his diary a willingness to pay a personal price, in large part because he saw it as a temporary sacrifice.

Then came an undated entry in 1985 which signaled his first (at least, his first written) sign of doubt. "The job is not settling down much—leaving for Atlanta tomorrow and New Jersey next week. This divestiture has been tougher than I thought it would be. I'm also angry at the 'company' and my boss. For two years I've worked my guts out to get this region ready for divestiture—I've stretched myself *past* the limit and gone every *extra* mile. And for those two years of commitment and delivery, my salary has been increased 5% per year. . . . I am upset and discouraged."

In retrospect, that sounds a lot like burnout. Whatever *had* been driving Fred at his accelerated pace during these years (whether it was the adrenaline flow from the toughest challenge of his career, the emotional attachment to a dying "Ma," or the work ethic of a part-timer who had risen to management heights), his spirits were flagging in the face of mounting 1980s realities such as cost-cutting, salary freezes, and career glitches. Yet he continued working at that same intensified work pace, perhaps unable to believe that a payoff would not come along at some later point, when the crisis was finally behind the company and life at his workplace returned to the way it had been before divestiture.

Then came September 19, 1985. "Last Friday was the 13th and it turned out to be an appropriate Friday the 13th kind of day. Having just returned from NYC, I was told . . . that there was no job for me. . . ." He had been kept "on a yo-yo," he complained, "one day I'm a candidate for the operations job—the next day, I'm not. Anyway, now it's final, I'm *not!*"

The entry continued. "There's a lot of mental anguish this decision causes me. . . . I'm having trouble sleeping and even thinking on an even keel. . . . I can't handle the loss of face—What did all that work mean? What was the point?" From here on, demoralization seems to have set in fairly quickly. January 3, 1986: "Now to the wonderful world of work: I hate it! Ever since I lost the operations job on September 13, I've been assigned to menial projects that *any* fool could handle."

Later in the same entry he unveiled a plan to finally leave the corporate womb: "I believe my wife and I can make it on my pension *if* our 2nd mortgage was paid off plus the credit cards. The MIPP [Management Incentive Pay Program] would do that as I honestly believe that leaving that outfit will be the solution to a lot of problems I'm having—namely sleeplessness, anxiety, worry and others that perhaps are best unsaid. So we shall see—it's interesting to note that early in 1982 I wrote of worry and of being too conscientious. That's nearly four years ago. Maybe I'm at the end of the rope."

By then he was earning about $75,000 a year and had worked for AT&T for more than thirty years. When he decided, later that month, to leave the company, he received an early-retirement package that consisted of six months' worth of salary plus the cashed-out value of his unused vacation days. On January 26, 1986, he wrote, "[W]hile we'll end up having almost nothing in savings, we will be able to get by on the pension payments. Our savings plan will be wiped out paying off the 2nd mortgage and the other 'short term' debts. It will leave us with a $600 per month house pay [*sic*] plus the other current monthly expenses—we *just* make it. But the other side of the coin is that I'm not even 50 years old so it's too early for the rocking chair. . . ."

Contrary to Fred's rosy expectations, he never did succeed in finding another job, despite his many career achievements and qualifications. He likely was handicapped by what had once seemed his greatest strength: lifelong experience as a "Bell-head." (The downside was his inexperience of the business world as anything other than an AT&T employee.) Like Ben, he probably damaged his future prospects by staying on way too long in an industry that was destabilizing and a corporate world where opportunities were shrinking.

So eventually he decided to make his "retirement" official with a move to Arizona where, among other things, the cost of living was much lower than in his midwestern home state. But his diary suggests that even had he known this ultimate outcome, he would probably have made the same decision today: "There *is* a sense of peace now—knowing that I have but one more month to put up with the idiocy that abounds in that outfit that I gave nearly 32 years of my life to!"

Breaking the Ties Too Late

As the decade progressed, its economic achievements began to look shakier, especially after the stock market crash of 1987. One large company after another began hemorrhaging staffers, creating a specter of long-term unemployment that loomed even larger than it had during the dismal years of the late 1970s: 15 percent of all those people who got laid off during this period remained unemployed for six months or longer.[19]

After a certain stage, which occurred at different times during the decade in different industries, white-collar men and women accepted deteriorating workplace conditions not because of their sense of attachment to their employers but because they realized they had little other choice. As Ben's and Fred's stories illustrate, even the most motivated and committed corporate staffers came to sour on the workplace changes of the 1980s once it became clear that they were not short-term sacrifices but rather an unpleasant new way of life.

Their emotional transitions were often quite dramatic, whether they took the form of growing self-doubt, employer distrust, demoralization, or burnout. But negative feelings were scarcely limited to people whose career progress was stymied or halted during the decade. Geoffrey is a good example: he is a Wall Street research analyst who spent much of the 1980s at the investment house of Drexel Burnham, later rising into management at several other firms, including Goldman Sachs.

Recalling earlier business conditions, he told me, "Wall Street wasn't as obsessed with youth. They wanted young people, but the idea was, you were supposed to learn. You would grab your experiences and let them mold you. That's what breeds health—in a healthy environment, you have someone with experience.

"But in the 1980s, especially the mid-1980s, companies gave up on that philosophy," he told me in the course of a long breakfast interview during which we discussed his twenty-plus years on the Street. "Companies weren't going to look at things from the long term—how to build a healthy organization—but to look at the very short term. The question became, Who's going to make money for you quickest in the short term? That's the sellout mentality," he emphasized. "They're selling out the healthy organization. It's just like stock. They're looking at their own companies like stock, not like an organization."

His conclusion? "You take the focus you grew up with. That's incredibly loyal allegiance to an organization. You realize it has nothing to do with reality. They're using you as a piece of their machine to make more money. That fact that *you* worked for me ninety hours a week for all these years doesn't matter."

What *did* matter? By the end of the decade, many white-collar workers were no longer sure.

Changes took place during the 1980s that accomplished important financial goals. Large corporations either learned to cope with new, global competition or disappeared from the horizon. Many began the process of investing in new technologies that laid the groundwork for future gains. The business world shook off the doldrums and anxieties that had taken hold during the seventies, setting the stage for a truly remarkable bull market and a prolonged period of economic prosperity.

But many of these changes were purchased at an unnecessarily high cost in terms of their effect on the work and home lives of white-collar Americans. The decade was one of excess—most especially in terms of the way that growing numbers of corporations chose to degrade and discard their once-valuable human capital. Despite all the talk of building a new and better economic order, viable companies were destroyed for no reason other than their bust-up value. Enormous sums of money were wasted on Wall Street fees for deals that fizzled, greenmail payoffs, and complex stock-driven maneuvers that generated paper profits rather than real-world gains. For all the money that corporate America invested in its future, huge amounts of capital were simply drained from the system in order to pay off teetering debt loads tied to the destructive financial transactions of the time.

By the end of the 1980s, vast numbers of men and women found themselves in a situation that one might characterize, without too much exaggeration, as the worst of all career worlds. During key transitional years, when they might well have resisted the new culture of overwork and underreward, most had not done so; many, in fact, had acquiesced to declining conditions, because they were emotionally attached to their employers and swayed by the mood of the times.

By the time they, like Ben and Fred, began to experience a different set of emotions that *might* have motivated and equipped them to resist tougher working conditions, corporate America itself had evolved in ways that seemed permanent and inflexible. Regardless of whether white-collar workers now sought to avoid these conditions, by the dawn of the 1990s the "sweatshop" corporation had become an integral—and perhaps inescapable—part of the United States' business landscape.

SEVEN

"Raising the Bar": Why Work Now Worsens As Companies Prosper

Given the enormous success achieved in recent years by companies within the United States' diverse technology sector, one might have assumed that the high-tech world would have emerged, after the tumultuous 1970s and 1980s, as our contemporary equivalent of the postwar paternalistic workplace: a thriving environment in which white-collar workers could share the rewards of corporate prosperity through better working conditions, more lucrative benefits, and increased long-term security.

The opposite, in fact, has been the case. During the past decade, work life has deteriorated in innumerable ways at many of the nation's most successful technology companies—not *in spite of* their favorable results but, in a sense, because of them. Unlike their business counterparts of fifty years earlier, these large corporations and their executives believe in the bottom-line benefits of a workforce motivated by fear, insecurity, and ever-increasing job demands, and they have acted accordingly.

"Sweatshop" management techniques such as layoffs and other cutbacks, reliance upon contingent labor, and employee overwork and stress flourish within these companies, no matter how well they perform. With a stock market that has reinforced the belief in the "rightness" of these high-tech strategies—and a larger corporate universe eager to implement them at any cost—there has been no going back to better conditions for white-collar men and women.

Could there be a better place to examine this dynamic than in California's Silicon Valley? I first encountered Brian, a software engineer with expertise in the most complex reaches of the Java programming language, through the Internet. In response to a web page I had posted describing my research, he sent me an intriguing e-mail: "It's absolutely stupefying to watch the industry changes going on . . . 75% to 80% of the engineers where I work are consultants. Their average lifetime—3 months. The policy: 'Just finish the task and get out.'" He concluded, "These changes are turning the workplace into an unending survival exercise."

Over the course of the months during which Brian and I conversed by telephone and continued to swap electronic mail, I came to appreciate his perspective, colored though it was by two important factors. First, at the age of forty-three, with a nonworking spouse and a young child to support, he was struggling to stay afloat in what he and others viewed as a "young man's business": "In this industry," he told me, "there's a tremendous fascination with twenty-year-olds. There's a saying here, if you're in your thirties, you're expendable. If you're in your forties, you're unhirable."

Competing as he always was for new short-term assignments, he could not escape his own ever-increasing age liability: "The older you are, the harder this gets. There aren't that many people who know how to do what I can do. But I've lost count of the number of résumés that I've sent out where I've exactly matched the qualifications of the contract and I don't even get a call. And instead, you'll see job specs that ask for 'senior engineer—one to two years experience.' What does that say? *How* can you be at that level, with that little experience?"

Brian explained the career-defense strategy that he and his friends relied upon: "multiple levels of redundancy" was the term he used—a phrase that may give new meaning to the image of man as machine. For him, it referred to the practice of simultaneously signing up for several, or more, different consulting jobs (whose demands between them added up to much more than those of any one full-time job) in an effort to lessen the threat of work loss. "At any moment, your primary revenue stream can be gone. So you have to build up different work projects to make yourself more secure."

Yet job security can be an illusive commodity these days, especially for "mid-career" computer programmers in Silicon Valley.
According to one trade industry journal, "[D]espite a growing economy in 1998, the mean duration of unemployment among our
members has increased from 84 weeks in 1995 to 103 weeks in
1998. . . . [E]ach additional year of age of members seeking new jobs
translates into three additional weeks of unemployment."[1]

With all of Brian's short-term assignments coming from the
quicksilver, pressurized world of high-tech companies, his work
pace seemed almost superhuman. "My life for the past several years
has often literally consisted of coming home and picking up the
newspaper with the sun coming up. Six month stretches of working
six or seven days a week, with my average workday eighteen hours
long."

What was the emotional toll of that pace, I wondered. "In regimes
like this, where people are working under the conditions I am," he
commented, "I've gone through so many years of this, lived with
such extended sleep deprivation, worked through such extended
burnout. . . ." He paused, then concluded, "This is like being a sol-
dier, in a way. You have a problem that any shell can hit you. But
you can't turn around or stop. Because if you do that, you're going
to be hit. The only hope is to keep going."

Permanent Jobs Become Impermanent

Despite all the hoopla about secretaries and twenty-somethings
who have become stock-option millionaires in Silicon Valley and its
high-tech sister region surrounding Seattle, Brian's precarious work
experience is, unfortunately, far closer to reality for many of the
industry's working men and women.

Heavy workloads might seem tough but fair if white-collar workers could count on employment stability in return for the extraordinary commitments they are called upon to make. But that's
seldom the case, since the industry aggressively relies on layoffs and
other workforce-churning techniques that make a sham of the
notion of permanent employment.

There's little taint attached to layoffs within the high-tech community, where what matters is not the negative impact upon indi-

vidual workers but the positive benefits to be drawn by corporations
and shareholders from lean cost structures and pared-down, flexible
workforces. As a result, cutbacks are often timed with hair-trigger
precision to respond to changing marketplace conditions or unex-
pectedly poor short-term financial results.

By most measures, 1998 was a stellar year for both the U.S. economy and much of the technology sector. Despite all the good news,
though, the year witnessed more job cuts by corporate America than
any previous point in the decade: over 677,000 of them, which was
a good 10 percent higher than the previous record, logged in 1993.
(To get a sense of the way the economics of layoffs has changed during the past decade, consider that 1993's former-record-holding level
of cuts came on the heels of the 1991–92 recession; 1998's followed
a handful of years during which the U.S. economy, and its stock
market, had soared.)

Significantly, a good 20 percent of 1998's job cuts, or about
135,000 layoffs, were carried out by companies in just two industries: electronics and computers.[2] Since many of the high-tech
employers wielding the ax performed well before, during, and after
these cuts, their necessity seems debatable. Yet they were quicksilver responses, all the same, to a series of marketplace catalysts,
including shifts in consumer demand to new low-cost personal
computers, fears of repercussions from Asia's then-unfolding economic problems, and a downturn in the semiconductor industry.

Were the staffing cuts carried out too early or too aggressively?
Not, apparently, from the stock market's perspective, since the
technology sector remained one of the powerhouses driving the bull
market during this same period. And for most technology executives, whose personal wealth was tied to their stock holdings, that
was the only perspective that mattered.

Some of the tech industry's most prominent leaders promoted
the rise of job *insecurity* with an almost missionary zeal. "Until
very recently, if you went to work at an established company, you
could assume that your job would last the rest of your working life.
But when companies no longer have lifelong careers themselves,
how can they provide one for their employees?" asked Andrew
Grove in his book *Only the Paranoid Survive.* "The sad news is,

nobody owes you a career," he went on to emphasize. "Your career is literally your business. You own it as a sole proprietor. . . . It is your responsibility to protect this personal business of yours from harm. . . ."[3]

Grove's book sold handily, since its no-guilt, no-regret tone helped provide an intellectual framework to justify changes in the increasingly nasty new corporate workplace. From an employee's perspective, however, the impact of workforce churn-over was all too depressingly clear. "At Microsoft, you would hear, 'we don't guarantee anybody a job.' I felt a profound sense of resentment," confided Marvin, a technical writer at Microsoft.

"Here I am working one hundred hours a week," he told me, "and yet I'm going to wind up with nothing." The fact that he and his peers had bolstered their personal savings with impressive stock-option packages did little to relieve the shame and disappointment they felt at being branded disposable commodities. "On the level I was— the high professional level—people got ticked off. They were mad."

In congressional testimony before the U.S. House Judiciary Committee, Dr. Norman Matloff, of the University of California at Davis's department of computer science, argued that the software industry, for one, artificially kept its labor costs for programmers low by discriminating against older workers—instead hiring mainly from two categories: "new or recent college graduates, who are cheaper in salary than established programmers, cost less in terms of benefits because they are typically single, and whose single status facilitates working large amounts of unpaid overtime"; and "foreign nationals on work visas, who often work for lower pay."[4]

Matloff blamed age discrimination for shortening the careers of most software programmers. "Five years after finishing college, about 60 percent of computer science graduates are working as programmers; at 15 years the figure drops to 34 percent, and at 20 years—when most are still only age 42 or so—it is down to 19 percent." As a point of comparison, more than half of the nation's civil engineering majors were still working in their profession twenty years after graduation.

Matloff argued against the tech industry's intensive lobbying efforts to win increases in the United States' yearly quota for H-1B work visas for foreign-national programmers; he cited statistics showing that technology companies then hired only about 2 percent of all programmers who sent in their résumés. "The only shortage is one of cheap labor, especially in the form of foreign nationals, who make on average 15–30 percent less than comparable natives."[5]

This allegation—that high-tech employers used the high-skills visa program to help undercut white-collar salaries—was reinforced by a 1996 Labor Department study which found that although participating employers were required to pay foreign workers the prevailing wage U.S. workers would receive for the same job, three quarters of those companies audited could not provide evidence that they had complied with this rule. Nearly 20 percent of those companies audited were found to have paid foreign nationals less than the software industry wage promised on their visa application.[6]

This is symptomatic of a larger problem within the high-tech sector in general. Employers often provide few financial rewards for experience or career longevity—mainly because *too much* time on the job is viewed as a worrying sign that someone's skill set may be out of date. According to a University of California at Berkeley study, the average U.S. professional with twenty years of experience in 1995 earned 73 percent more than a comparable new hire in his or her field. The reward differential for experienced engineers or other high-tech professionals was far lower, as might be expected in a "young man's business."[7]

Conversion to Contingent Labor

Another way that the high-tech industry squeezes more work for less reward out of its white-collar workforce is through the increased use of contingent labor, typically temporary staffers or independent contractors.

Technology companies are scarcely alone in this regard. Back in 1986, about 800,000 temporaries were employed daily across the United States; by the end of 1998, nearly four times as many Americans were "temping."[8] For most companies, the decision to rely upon contingent labor is strictly a financial one: temps—although somewhat more costly than traditional staffers in terms of their salaries, thanks to agency fees—can save 25 to 33 percent of an employee's paycheck because of skipped benefits.

The trend is heavily entrenched in the technology sector: by one estimate, as many as 40 percent of all workers in Silicon Valley are contingent workers.[9] After surveying more than twenty-five hundred companies, Rosabeth Moss Kanter reported, "Greater use of contingent workers—that is, temps, part-timers, independent contractors—prevails even in companies enjoying employment growth in emerging technology fields. In fact, such companies are especially reliant on contingent employees."[10]

Within the high-tech sector, some temporary workers are relied upon for such long periods of time—spending many months or even years in the same job—that they have taken to calling themselves "permatemps." Despite their extended tenures, they remain either self-employed contractors or employees of temporary-staffing agencies. (In some, even more confused cases, the temps are employed on a contingency basis by temporary agencies that are *owned* by the technology corporations themselves; they're still not considered full-time employees, however, even though their temporary postings may last indefinitely or be confined only to this single company.)

The permatemp phenomenon is worth focusing upon because these employees within the high-tech industry and elsewhere are the second-class citizens that many white-collar workers could easily become—as layoffs, benefit cutbacks, and other workplace changes degrade and destabilize their career prospects. It has been estimated that at least 200,000 men and women now fall into this category at large corporations that include Hewlett-Packard, Intel, AT&T, and Microsoft.[11]

Long-term temps often have a pretty good sense of the corporate motivations behind the trend. "I took a permanent/temporary job almost two years ago to gain experience in the computer field," reported one visitor to an Internet work-related website with whom I carried out an extensive e-mail correspondence. "It doesn't matter how excellent your work is or how competently you handle your position—it will always be a permanent/temporary job," she added.

"This company, like all other global companies, worships at the altar of outsourcing."

This visitor, currently permatemping for IBM, added, "The frustrating thing . . . is that they rarely hire the temporary or contract workers in any other position. . . . The job postings are not accessible to non-employees. . . . There must be some unwritten policy not to hire the contingents. I would like the perks of being a permanent employee—the medical benefits, increasing vacation time, sick days, personal holidays, 401K, and the promotions."[12]

As a permanent/temporary staffer, "Beejay" explained to me that she qualifies for Christmas, Thanksgiving, and four other annual holidays, "but there are restrictions. We must work the day before and the day after a holiday to get holiday pay. In other words, we had better not get sick!" She also earned one week of paid vacation—from her agency, not from IBM—after she logged fifteen hundred hours of employment during her first year of temping. IBM did not provide her with any benefits, but she was able to purchase her own "catastrophic illness" health care policy from the temp firm at a cost to her family of over $300 per month.

As for her permatemp colleagues on the job, she reported, insurance was often a matter of catch-as-catch-can: "Several single mothers were able to . . . get their children on Medicaid. . . . The coverage is excellent . . . [but] the single mothers are living dangerously because they have no health insurance for themselves."

Such considerations scarcely matter to high-tech employers, whose management priorities focus upon bottom-line results and their stock-price impact. Microsoft, for one, has been an avid user of temporary-agency staffers and independent contractors for years. Back in 1997 it dismissed about ninety receptionists in order to replace them with temps. "We were overpaying them," Bob Herbold, the company's chief operating officer, reported to one journalist. (The receptionists' benefit package even included stock options.) "Boy, it's had a positive impact financially," he added, referring to the company's larger use of temporary workers.[13]

Not all temporary workers are so-called permatemps, of course. But at Microsoft, where some temporaries worked in positions for five years or longer, the company's practices captured the national spotlight, thanks to a high-visibility class action lawsuit over denied benefits for long-term temporary employees.[14] Citing the lawsuit, which wound its way through the legal system throughout most of the 1990s, the company now prefers not to comment on its temp workforce, other than to note that the current average employment tenure for contingent (so-called agency) employees is ten months.[15]

Yet a two-tier staffing system was well entrenched at Microsoft during the 1990s. According to one estimate, by 1998 Microsoft employed "about 5,000 temps, including 1,500 long-term ones," who had worked for the company for at least one year. "These temps work next to Microsoft's 17,000 domestic employees," the *New York Times* continued.[16] Their positions ran the gamut from writing software manuals and designing Internet websites to performing clerical support services.

In many cases, the company's temporary employees performed job functions no different from those carried out by permanent—meaning noncontingent—employees. They also frequently put in the fifty- or sixty- or seventy-hour workweeks that were common throughout the high-tech sector. Yet the disparity between these second-class citizens and the company's regular workforce made work life worse for both groups in a variety of ways.

Within any corporation, the heavy use of temporaries and independent contractors creates an underlying tension for all of its staffers; after all, permanent employees are themselves vulnerable to replacement by outsiders—a message that is clearly conveyed throughout employee ranks when whole job categories (such as those ninety receptionists) get converted to contingent status. With that kind of unspoken risk to worry about, white-collar workers usually are less likely to make big demands upon management, whether in terms of salary increases or benefits enhancements; they will also hesitate to refuse to work longer hours, nights, or weekends, or to accept heavier job loads. This tension plays itself out in the problematic relations that often exist between temporary and nontemporary workers (since the former covet the latter's jobs, and the latter fear that the former may one day replace them).

Meanwhile, temp status degrades the work lives of contingent employees. Within Microsoft's hierarchy, for example, these men and women are typically referred to as "A dashes" (because their e-mail addresses are listed, in the corporate directory, with an "A—" that labels them as agency, rather than corporate, employees). Many of the company's temps—who work there on three-month contracts that can be canceled at any time—choose to underscore their second-class status by calling themselves "alien dashes" and "dash trash."[17]

Lest they forget their second-class status, they must wear orange identification badges, in contrast to the blue badges that permanent employees carry. Those badges disqualify them for various job perks including a discount at the company store, job-training programs, and the use of the company's basketball courts. They don't even get invited to the company picnic. When you are a temp, "they treat you like pond scum," is the way one former contractor put it.[18]

All these infringements upon workplace status might not matter so much if temporary workers could count on the same lucrative financial benefits their noncontingent colleagues receive—most especially the stock-purchase plan, which permitted equity purchases at a 15 percent discount from current trading levels. Indeed, the effort to gain entry to this plan was the cornerstone of the permatemp lawsuit against the company. As one longtime temp put it, "People who started at the same time as I did are cashing in their options and paying for their houses in cash. Meanwhile, I live in an apartment. I'm still paying $200 a month for health care."[19]

The most recent court ruling favored the litigating permatemps, thanks to a decision by a three-judge panel of the Ninth Circuit Court of Appeals which concluded that federal law required that retirement benefits be uniform for all employees. (Employers were given more leeway on vacation and health care matters.) Since the U.S. Supreme Court declined to review that decision during its winter 2000 session, it appeared at the time of this writing that Microsoft might owe as much as $100 million in lost benefits from discount-stock-purchase opportunities denied to a pool of temporary workers and freelancers that conceivably could include as many as ten thousand people.[20]

Within the thriving technology sector and other industries as well, this is one workplace issue that shows no signs of quietly fading away. Other companies, including PG&E, U.S. West, and Capital Cities/ABC, have been involved in lawsuits that basically center on the question of which benefits long-term temporary workers should be entitled to receive, if any, and from whom.[21] Not surprisingly, the highest-visibility cases so far have focused on the most potentially lucrative benefits that temps and freelancers lack: stock options, discounted-stock-purchase opportunities, and participation in corporate retirement plans.

More litigation seems inevitable. But rather than halting their use of contingent labor, companies may simply try to limit their exposure to the permatemp risk. Microsoft, for example, instituted a new policy in early 2000 requiring that all temps take a one-hundred-day hiatus after working within the organization for a full year.[22] From the vantage point of white-collar Americans who are increasingly vulnerable to contingency conversions, such cosmetic changes scarcely represent an improvement.

The Equity Carrot and Stick

It's little wonder that temporary workers are preoccupied with all that company stock they can't get their hands on at Microsoft and elsewhere. Equity is an obsession within the high-tech community—for company founders, key executives, and (to an extent that is seldom the case elsewhere in corporate America) for other employees up and down the job ladder. But although the use of equity can help companies achieve key performance goals, this technique can carry with it a heavy cost, as technology corporations and others often use equity to manipulate workers to accept inhumane job demands.

From an employee's perspective, the best "carrot" is a stock grant that translates into immediate ownership of a company's shares. But because employers are always looking for ways to squeeze greater productivity over a longer period from their workforces, most prefer to dangle some form of delayed gratification before staffers. That typically involves participation in a stock-option plan—one that will permit employees to buy shares at a discounted price *if* they can hold on to their jobs long enough to gain "vested" ownership of the options. In return for the promise of that carrot—as many as five or seven years down the road—people put up with unbelievably intense job demands, often requiring them to work weekends and long into the evening hours.

The allure of stock options is so powerful within the high-tech world that in some cases, even the *promise* of one day receiving options is sufficient to motivate employees to put up with tough working conditions. "I know it's ridiculous," one software expert told me at a dinner party, "but I haven't looked for another job because my boss keeps telling me he's going to give me options sometime soon." That point of reward kept getting delayed—for vague and unspecified reasons—but this man was still waiting. "It's very hard to leave because you feel so close . . . even though stock options themselves are no guarantee that you'll make money, and the *promise* of stock options is even less certain than that."

"I pretty much walked to the altar of Intel and bowed to that god," is the way Henry, one senior manager, described his rise within the corporation, accompanied by participation in Intel's stock plan. The potential to build equity wealth came for him at a heavy personal cost: "I was working sixteen hours a day. I felt like I was drowning in the demands of the job. My wife stopped sleeping in my room. She didn't want to wake me."

Many men and women within the high-tech community are remarkably frank about the Faustian bargains that they, like Henry, have made, often sacrificing what seems like every other aspect of their lives to employers for however many years it takes them to gain ownership of their stock options. Many motivate themselves to survive brutal work schedules by fantasizing about the date on which they will become vested and can then quit their jobs and return to a normal existence elsewhere. "People have parties on the day that they're vested. They know that now you can tell them to stuff it," Marvin, the technical writer at Microsoft, told me. "But if you get higher, the bonuses get much higher," he added, "and people get sucked into staying."

Not surprisingly, the company's equity is an obsession for employees of the software giant, which is probably just fine with

Microsoft, since this preoccupation keeps them working hard, their attention firmly focused on stock market listings, if not the overall bottom line. (One newspaper account compared the company's 1997 annual meeting to a "revivalist celebration": "'Why are we at Microsoft?' bellowed billionaire Steve Ballmer, then the company's executive vice president, to a crowd of nine thousand employees packed into the Kingdome, Seattle's indoor stadium. 'For the money!' he screamed. 'Show me the money!' The crowd responded with a roar: 'Show me the money!'")[23]

With a stock price that seemed virtually invincible during the nineties, ownership of a tiny piece of this equity pie offered Microsoft's employees the potential of a payoff big enough to compensate them for all those long, hard, high-pressure hours at the office. But the equity obsession could work like a stick as well as a carrot. "It's not good when the price goes down. People get worried. You can tell. It gets really quiet in the cafeteria," Marvin explained.

It would be naive to dismiss the technology industry's use of equity as, in itself, a workplace evil. It has proven to be a powerful motivation, offering many employees the prospect of lucrative rewards, especially during the stock market boom of the 1990s. Indeed, in a world in which corporate executives and shareholders seem preoccupied with one single indicator of business success—a rising stock price—stock options and stock-purchase plans serve to unite workers' interests with those of other owners, key executives, and outside investors.

Whether or not this alliance proves to be shortsighted in its fixation on near-term stock prices is another question. But during the brave new corporate world that flourished in 1990s America, equity seemed to compensate—or at least to substitute—for long-lost motivations such as employer and employee loyalty. The allure of one day becoming a "Microsoft millionaire" or its equivalent is apparent in the persistence with which many, many people pursue jobs at any of the United States' high-tech giants, despite these companies' reputations as hard-driving employers (who occasionally throw some beer bashes to help overwrought workers unwind).

Equity also played a role in motivating the high-tech industry's huge contingent workforce to perform—and *keep* performing—

under intensely demanding job conditions. "Contract employees are always reminded: Keep busting your ass. Because the carrot was always there: getting hired full-time," recalled Patrick, who spent most of his mid-twenties working in Intel's back-office operations.

That was the pot of gold at the end of Patrick's career rainbow: a permanent job on Intel's staff, which would bring with it immediate employee benefits, the potential to rise within the company, and hopefully, one day, a small equity stake. "I temped for a year and a half," he recalled. "Had no medical benefits. I earned less than $8 an hour. I worked from seven in the morning until four-thirty in the afternoon. Things like overtime would look good, so I did it."

His original "temporary" assignment was scheduled to last for twelve months. "After that, they said they would extend me for six more months. I was elated because I was still there. Some of the managers made me feel I was the luckiest guy in the world. I was always the aggressor—I really wanted to be hired."

But the work pace, combined with all the uncertainties of his position, exacted a grueling toll. "I hated being contingent because of the feeling of insecurity. It didn't feel like I was a solid provider. Maybe that's an old-fashioned feeling about manhood," he commented, then added, "I felt like I never had a future. I'd see those temps come in and just wanted to say to them, 'Just leave, man.'"

After eighteen months as a permatemp, Patrick's dream came true—sort of. "Finally I got hired. I was known as an Intel temp: 'ICE,' Intel contract employee." To anyone less preoccupied than Patrick was with the company's hierarchical structure, it might have been difficult to determine *how* or why his working conditions had improved, since he was doing the same job he had done before and was still considered a contingent staffer, who could be dismissed at any time. He still had no benefits. But he felt that he had made real progress, since he was no longer an agency temp; he was an Intel temp. Surely, he told himself, that brought him a little closer to the company's stock.

"I was under six months' review. 'We'll decide if we like you,'" was the message that came across to him. That's when the pressure "really increased," he recalled. "It was like I was halfway there." Ironically enough, Patrick was eventually hired for a full-time permanent position within the company—complete with stock options—but left it before he could ever cash in, because he burned out on the workload.

Stress and Overwork

"Joeoverwork" described his pace of work in an e-mail message that he sent to one of my Internet chat rooms: "One particularly vile form of employer theft is the popular practice of putting people on a salary basis and then proceeding to work the living daylights out of them. As an engineer . . . I was on salary and told I was REQUIRED to work a MINIMUM of 60 hours a week for the next 6–8 months!"[24]

Other tech-industry insiders suggested that "joeoverwork" should have been grateful, if nothing else, that the end to his employer's overtime demand was within distant sight. One former Microsoft employee advised me to pay attention to technology companies' parking lots, which are typically jammed with cars on weekends and well into the evening hours. "You're never sleeping," he noted. "One time, I drove home after working a really long stretch—couldn't find my way home. I forgot where I lived."

In the high-tech industry, tales of employee overwork, job stress, and burnout are rampant, yet employment is still avidly pursued, especially by recent college graduates and other younger workers. So, one might ask, how bad could things be?

Some business experts might argue that workplace conditions have not deteriorated for white-collar men and women within the technology sector: work patterns are just different from earlier postwar norms. Other business observers, many of them, might claim that declining conditions are a price well worth paying in return for bottom-line results as strong as those reported in recent years by many tech companies, whose stock prices drove the market boom of the late 1990s.

Few of us realize, however, just how difficult conditions have become—and how severe the personal toll can be—in leading-edge industries like technology that have aggressively embraced harsh workplace changes. Even the most ardent of bull-market investors might balk at some of the truly ugly employee-management practices that have helped fuel recent growth and profits at some of the United States' best-respected corporations.

By any measure, Intel is one of the great success stories of the modern business era. The computer chip manufacturer's revenues grew within the space of a decade from less than $2 billion to over $25 billion. Meanwhile, its stock price, in the ten years following 1987, multiplied to a value fifty times higher.[25]

Given that level of performance, as well as the general American preoccupation with the stock market during the late 1990s, it was scarcely surprising when *Time* magazine anointed Intel's then chief executive officer, Andrew Grove, with its coveted "man of the year" award. Such praise notwithstanding, Intel provides a fascinating case study for those interested in exploring the intricate relationship between *increased* corporate performance and *deteriorating* white-collar conditions within the new U.S. economy.

I first became aware of employee discontent at this high-tech giant when I came across a website maintained by a group of the company's "former and current employees" (who called themselves "FACEIntel").[26] In its early stages, this site, which was launched on the Internet in 1997, consisted of a graphic design and format that were about as simple as they could be. With one main illustration, a scanned photo of a *staged* demonstration that was meant to invoke the specter of a union picket, the early web pages outlined the group's grievances, which included allegations that Intel practiced a policy of discriminating against employees on the basis of age and medical disability.

Within a couple of years, the website had become much more complex and elaborate, although its slogan—an Arnold Bennett quote, "The price of justice is eternal publicity"—remained the same. In its cyber-statement about the group's "campaign focus/goals for 1998," FACEIntel made this pledge, among others: "Group members and our supporters at all major Intel sites will campaign in the community churches. We will inform and educate clergymen in the communities about the ugly side of Intel's face and Intel's predatory and inhumane human resources policies and practices." The website, now quite large (as well as hyperlinked to numerous other work-related sites throughout the Internet), also included multipage electronic sections on such startling subjects as "Suicide and Heart Attacks, Stress Kills." These were FACEIntel's attempt to document, on an anecdotal basis, what the group alleged to be dire health-related consequences of the company's demanding pace of work.[27]

In an effort to get beyond the various layers of rhetoric (both for and against the company) that surround Intel, I conducted a long series of interviews with current and former staffers, some of whom were members of FACEIntel and many others of whom were not. I also began extensively tracking the company's present and past history through the media, as well as in published books, which included Andrew Grove's *Only the Paranoid Survive* and Tim Jackson's unauthorized corporate history, *Inside Intel*. I contacted Intel on a number of occasions with requests for information and comment, but the company did not respond to my requests. My goal was to understand what working conditions were truly like within this high-tech giant and to assess—if indeed those conditions had deteriorated during the 1990s—whether negative employee-management strategies had helped contribute to Intel's extraordinary success during the decade.

First, some background. Intel's basic upward swing in recent years was undeniable, but the company had been forced to negotiate some troubled and challenging turns. These included a massive restructuring of its business line during the mid-1980s (when it switched its whole business operation from manufacturing computer memory chips to producing microprocessors), as well as a disastrous launch and eventual recall of a flawed Pentium chip in 1994. Surviving those challenges—and in fact growing more successful despite them—had required an enormous amount of focused, intensive energy on the part of the company's employees and its management team.

During this period, the company also experienced a major change in management, when cofounder Robert Noyce, a paternalistic if demanding leader, was replaced by Grove, who prided himself on a take-no-prisoners management style with a single-minded focus on building the business. During the eleven years that Grove ran Intel, his temper became legendary, as did his aggressive use of corporate lawsuits to pursue ex-employees or competitors that might be encroaching on the company's turf. Grove vacated the CEO's seat in 1998 (while remaining the company's chairman of the board).[28] Intel launched a lawsuit against FACEIntel that same year to prevent the group from sending its mass e-mailings to company employees.[29]

Grove's people-management skills set a style for Intel that was anything but warm and fuzzy. According to one report, when a high-level staffer appeared at a meeting several minutes late, "Andy Grove was sitting there, holding a stave of wood the size of a baseball bat. At the end of the stave was a hand shape, encased in a protective glove of the kind used inside Intel's fabs, with the middle finger extended in an obscene gesture. Grove had just slammed the wood onto the surface of the meeting-room table—and was now shouting at the top of his lungs: 'I don't ever, *ever,* want to be in a meeting with this group that doesn't start and end when it's scheduled.'"[30]

That may have been just background noise. But according to many of the sources I interviewed, work life at Intel did begin to change in the early 1990s, not because of the chief executive's temper tantrums but because of some key employee-management decisions, which coincided with changes taking place elsewhere in the technology industry.

One was Grove's mandate that the company needed to place its hiring emphasis on NCGs (in company jargon, that meant "new college graduates"). The business rationale behind the decision was obvious: recent grads would possess up-to-date technical skills, demand lower salaries than experienced professionals, and probably be willing to work the same long, intense hours they had become used to in college.[31] Recent graduates likely would also impose a lighter burden on the company's benefit system, since younger staffers (especially those without families) probably would have lower medical costs than older workers.

One senior manager recalled the change this way: "Andy Grove took over. He came up with the push about new college graduates. One board director gave this speech about 'we have to create turnover. Employees have been around fifteen, sixteen years. They're at high grade levels. We have to turn that around.' I looked around the room. I was about forty at the time. I looked at the other senior managers and said to myself, 'Don't these people realize that we're the ones that are being talking about?' "

During this same period, Intel changed the terms of its employment contract with staffers. One former engineer explained to me, "It changed around 1991. Before this, everybody had a 'for cause' employment contract: In order to terminate you, they needed to have a cause. They came and changed it, disguising the change under 'we want to protect our intellectual property.' But in the new contracts was a clause saying, this contract is being changed to 'at will.'" Most large corporations have made similar changes during the past decade. "If you did it to me now, I'd understand," this staffer commented. "But then, I was naive."

Then came the R&Rs. In Intel-speak, that meant "rankings and ratings," another Grove initiative, which was a standardized system for evaluating all employees. Tim Jackson explained the system in *Inside Intel:* "Rating meant that most Intel people were put in one of four performance categories: 'superior,' 'exceeds expectations,' 'meets expectations,' or 'does not meet expectations.' These soon became so ingrained in the company consciousness that Intel people in casual conversation would describe an underperformer as simply a 'does not meet.' Ranking meant that every employee was also told how the company believed he or she matched up against others doing similar jobs. Pay raises—and, more important, awards of stock options—were based on this system."[32]

But what started out as a simple staff-evaluation system soon became something much more complicated when coupled with Intel's new hiring emphasis on recent college graduates and the company-wide transition to "at will" employment contracts. "For most of my years at Intel, I was a manager myself. I knew all about how ranking and rating worked. Back in the late eighties, there wasn't much of a process. They had a scale of categories, nearly everybody was satisfactory or above. It was fairly mild," commented one electrical engineer.

"Then in the early nineties," this engineer added, "I'd equate it with the whole stock market boom—they came in much more aggressive. You're either above, cutting it, or not. As a manager, you would get this number and the number would be high. Somewhere between 5 percent and 10 percent. You were told you had to have that many below the average and had to have that many above the average. They want to have a nice bell curve."

The engineer went along with the process at first, without complaint: "The first year it was tolerable. I would agree that there were definitely some people who were not so qualified. But after a few years of it, it became harder to do. I didn't want to face this thing of having to tell my people." Little wonder. The consequences of being on the wrong side of Intel's bell curve meant that employees could get CAP'ed. (Another ominous company term, this was shorthand for being placed on a "corrective action plan," which for many ended up being a ninety-day or so trip to unemployment.)

Here was another manager's assessment of the R&R process: "You are dumped in a hat and have to be compared to everyone else. They put it on a bell and X percent have to fail. Granted, I can see them doing it once or twice. There was some fat originally. There was. But it is very abusive. It's demoralizing. Using the bell curve, in the end everybody must fail."

This manager eventually found himself on the wrong side of the review process, in part because he objected to quotas that seemed arbitrary and unfair. "I wasn't on a CAP," Drake told me. "I was 'trended' as a 'slower than' my peers. That means you're not keeping up with the pack. The next step would have been a CAP and everybody knows that with the CAP, even if you meet every part of your plan, your manager has the authority to say you could have done it better."

It's not hard to imagine how stressful life at Intel became during these years, especially for more experienced workers who feared that their ages and salary levels were working against them. What had once been, by many accounts, a collegial and collaborative environment became increasingly competitive. "Intel used to be a great place for teamwork. But it got so bad you were afraid to help other people," explained one software writer. "That's because, if they were ranked and rated higher than you, you'd be screwed. They could make it and you'd be out."

Another employee told me, "One trick my boss used with us: R&R is supposed to be confidential, but he would say, 'I'm not supposed to tell you, but so-and-so is ranked ahead of you.'" He took a deep breath, then added, "I was gaining weight, stopped doing exercise. One of my trademarks is to never lose my temper. But I was changing my personality. You didn't have time for patience. If you were training someone and he didn't get it, you didn't have an hour to waste."

Why did people continue to work under these conditions? "You get trapped by big houses, big cars, the lifestyle, the nice vacation," one senior manager told me. "You look around and say, 'Where could I get this salary?' You keep hearing downsizing, rightsizing, 'reorgs,' reengineering. You don't need to hear the layoff term to know what they're talking about. In today's world, you know if you leave a job, you're going to earn less. People feel trapped."

Grove, who during the 1990s gained his own gurulike stature as a management theorist, wrote in *Only the Paranoid Survive:* "The quality guru W. Edwards Deming advocated stamping out fear in corporations. I have trouble with the simple-mindedness of this dictum. The most important role of managers is to create an environment in which people are passionately dedicated to winning in the marketplace. Fear plays a major role in creating and maintaining such passion. Fear of competition, fear of bankruptcy, fear of being wrong, and fear of losing can all be powerful motivators. How do we cultivate fear of losing in our employees? We can only do that if we feel it ourselves."[33]

By 1993 it was clear that fear, or *something,* was producing the kind of corporate results Grove wanted. No matter how unpleasant the workplace had become—at least for some staffers—the company's revenues had risen from $3.1 billion in 1989 to nearly $8.8 billion just four years later. Perhaps more significantly, the emphasis on controlling operating expenses (which included salary and benefit costs, kept low by all those new college graduates) helped the company increase its net profit margins from 14.2 percent in 1989 to 25.9 percent in 1993. The stock was on the uptick.[34]

A phrase that began to be used within the organization was "raising the bar." Emblematic of an ethos that increasingly spread across corporate America during the nineties, the phrase conveyed the idea that great companies didn't just stay the way they were; they kept raising their standards and goals, and reinventing themselves, while constantly pushing themselves to be better and better. As a theory, it had great appeal. But in reality, at corporations like Intel, raising the bar often resulted in workloads that kept mounting as well, with a set of constantly rising standards that became more and more difficult to meet.

One measure of how well, or poorly, an Intel employee was coping with the "bar" was how he or she was "trended": Intel-speak for how well the staffer was learning new skills compared with colleagues. (Remember Grove's message about owning your own career? He also wrote, "Who knows what your job will look like after cataclysmic change . . . ? Who knows if your job will even exist and, frankly, who will care besides you?"[35] Messages like that undoubtedly added a desired element of fear to the "trending" experience.) At Intel, employees might be experienced, productive, and motivated, but if they were "trended" as "slower thans," they were probably goners.

One manager ultimately decided to bring his objections to his own boss. "One day I said to my manager, 'Statistics tell you that the probability is such that sooner or later I—and even you—are going to hit a break-even point when the expectations are more than we are humanly capable of. We're going to reach our limit.' He said, 'Well, have you thought about what you're going to do for the rest of your life?' and that was a pretty good indicator," he told me, "that my number was up."

There was another employee-management tool that kept fear in the workplace, as desired. "Your job just disappears," explained one staffer. "You go into what they call 'redeployment.' You are put into a room where you sit at a computer and apply on-line for jobs that are listed within the company. If you don't find a job within ninety days"—or whatever period is assigned—"you are terminated. Or you can take the pay and consider that ninety days a voluntary buyout." He waited a moment, then described to me, "That's besides the trending, the rankings. It leaves people so driven down emotionally. You can't fight back. And you don't even understand what's happening to you or why it's happening."

For many people, as the decade progressed, the workload at Intel began to seem overwhelming, even by the high-tech industry's pressurized standards. "The beauty of it is, they don't say, you are going to have to work X amount of hours—even though, once in a while, they'd come to the office and write down your hours. But you are not going to survive, not going to be able to stay afloat, if you just work nine to five. R&R is the whip—everyone is competing against everyone else. But the other thing is, the amount of projects you are given. Nobody is going to ask you to work nights or weekends, but you are liable to complete *so* much. Meanwhile, all things are driven through meetings after meetings after meetings," reported a staffer from the company's Folsom, California, office.

There are plenty of people at Intel—as elsewhere throughout the hard-driving technology sector—who *do* buy into the work-until-you-drop mentality, which seems to have a certain machismo appeal. One visitor to FACEIntel's website sent this e-mail message: "The straw that broke the camel's back for me was when my supervisor said with glazed over Intel blue eyes: 'We need people that love this place. Like me. My wife has to call me every night to come home, or I'd just stay here all night and work. I love this place and you don't. That's your problem.'"[36]

Since stories of overwork, insecurity, and emotional stress *were* so commonly reported during the course of my interviews, I started asking Intel's current and former employees how they coped. "Everyone in my division is a coffee freak. A lot of people are sugar freaks too. Candy bars, doughnuts, I was in the boat," one man told me.

Another explained, "Sometimes I would crash. A crash would mean I'd sit there and stare at my computer—couldn't move, couldn't hear anything. One time, I got a warning from my supervisor. He told me I was going to get a CAP." He paused. "I was able to avoid it by going to a psychiatrist. He put me on Prozac."

Not surprisingly, even that age-old psychological defense, racism, surfaced as Intel's employees attempted to make sense of their working environment. One technical staffer confessed to me that he had been "surprised by the level of work demands—the culture is overwhelming—I don't know how to deal with it," and then theorized that the reason for the "hardship" was that "Andy Grove is a Jew. They don't believe in cooperation."

The more I talked with people from Intel, the less I was able to think of them as Grove's paradigmatic owners of their own careers, sole proprietors responsible for their own successes and failures. Nor could I even view them as part of a well-functioning corporate team.

On the contrary. Many of the people I spoke with seemed emotionally or physically crippled, as though they had been wounded by the very act of giving too much to their jobs, under such intense conditions, for way too long. "As far as stress, it's rampant. I saw it on everything," one former manager told me, "from the very young heart attack victims, to suicide, divorce, people having nervous breakdowns. People were mean and angry. Stress-related injuries— everything from wrist problems on up."

Added another, "If you make the choice to have a home life, you will be ranked and rated at the bottom. I was willing to work the endless hours, come in on weekends, travel to the ends of the earth. I had no hobbies, no outside interests. If I wasn't involved with the company, I wasn't anything."

Yet, as in the earlier years of Andrew Grove's leadership, this demanding pace produced its desired corporate results. Revenues continued to grow during 1994 and 1995, despite a temporary downturn in net profits, mainly due to the cost of the Pentium chip recall and its fallout. By 1997, with revenues up to $25 billion, net profit margins were at their highest level in the company's history, 27.7 percent.[37]

When this key profit ratio dropped somewhat, amid industry problems in 1998, to 23.5 percent (which was still much higher than the company's profit level in 1989), Grove and Intel's new chief executive, Craig Barrett, responded quickly. The corporation planned to cut three thousand jobs, among other operating costs.[38] Few insiders were surprised. Barrett had formerly served as Grove's second-in-command and earned some degree of notoriety within the high-tech community for this comment of his at a shareholders' meeting: "The half-life of an engineer, software, hardware engineer, is only a few years."[39]

In the case of these cuts, the investment community provided prompt support for Intel, projecting sizable shareholder returns for the foreseeable future. "The bottom line is apt to benefit from cost reductions, primarily stemming from a lower employee count and greater manufacturing efficiencies," predicted one market analyst, who endorsed the company's stock with his highest level of timeliness as a "buy."[40]

With encouragement like that from the stock market, it was no surprise that Intel (and other thriving firms within the technology sector and elsewhere) persisted with harsh management styles, regardless of the toll exacted upon workers. Although conditions were prosperous, these companies saw only risks—never the potential for benefits—in the more balanced demand-and-reward structure that had flourished during an earlier era of business prosperity. But "sweatshop" management strategies are no more a guarantee of long-term corporate success than earlier, paternalistic practices proved to be, as an examination of contemporary industries in trouble will show.

EIGHT

"Like a Boulder Rolling Downhill":
Declining Job Conditions,
with Little Payoff

The United States' struggling industries—and there are still many of them, despite the economic boom of the 1990s—are worth examining closely in an effort to understand the dynamics of recent workplace changes. Their troubled paths offer clues to future challenges and problems that white-collar workers likely will face in the years to come.

Even more important, perhaps, these industries offer a real test of whether harsh management styles—which often include frequent layoffs, increased use of contingent labor, benefit cutbacks, and a variety of overwork techniques—can promote business growth and prosperity in the face of serious marketplace challenges. I would argue that they do not, and may in fact handicap struggling companies by destabilizing and demoralizing their workforces.

A Closer Look at Banks

The banking industry offers a virtual test tube in which to observe the impact of negative workplace trends upon financially challenged corporations and their employees.

Most U.S. banks have struggled throughout the 1990s to reinvent themselves—mostly as financial giants capable, at least in theory, of squeezing profits from business lines with razor-thin margins while at the same time withstanding fierce competition from the domestic mutual fund industry, global banking entities, electronic-commerce ventures, and more.

Banks were hardly the only corporations forced to grappled with the tough marketplace conditions that thrived in many pockets of the United States' boom economy during the 1990s. But there were not many industries that faced as many financial trends turning against them as this one did during the years approaching the new millennium. (Even the millennium itself proved a source of financial turmoil, as "Y2K" expenditures associated with computer-system adjustments for the year 2000 neared $3.5 billion simply for the nation's fifteen largest banks.)[1]

An even bigger problem for the industry was the erosion of its various customer bases. Back in 1980, banks controlled 90 percent of American households' financial assets; by 1997, that dropped to about 55 percent. (The mutual fund industry picked up most of the slack, with its share of household assets rising from 10 percent to about 45 percent.) During this period, banks lost significant market share even when it came to the commercial credit products and services that were a crucial source of industry revenues: In 1980 they handled about 50 percent of the nation's commercial credit business; by 1997, that dropped to 35 percent. William McDonough, the president of the Federal Reserve Bank of New York, put it bluntly: "Something called a bank does not have a monopoly on much of anything."[2]

While some banks responded to new competitive pressures by making forays onto the Internet or into new customer markets, two strategies were far more typical: merge with other institutions to become ever-larger financial powerhouses (mainly by coupling with other commercial banks or investment houses); and cut operational expenditures, primarily by laying off staffers and otherwise reducing workforce costs.

During what has been described as the "largest merger-and-acquisition binge of modern times," the banking industry completely reconfigured itself: More than 30 percent of the fifteen thousand financial institutions that existed on December 31, 1990, had disappeared as independent entities less than nine years later.[3] Along the way, some institutions proved nothing short of rapacious as they merged and acquired their way into the financial galaxy. BankAmerica, for example, coupled with Security Pacific, and then with Continental, and then with Robertson Stephens, and finally with NationsBank, which had itself merged with Boatmen's Banc-shares, and then with Montgomery Securities, and then with Bar-nett Banks before the BankAmerica deal.[4]

With each merger, at these banks as throughout the entire indus-try, layoffs inevitably followed, as institutions looked for ways to cut costs by eliminating so-called organizational redundancies and realizing economies of scale. After Wells Fargo & Company merged with Norwest Corporation in 1998, the combined company soon announced plans to eliminate 5 percent of its total workforce, or about 4,600 positions.[5] In all, during the six-and-a-half-year period that lasted from January 1993 through May 1999, more than 104,000 jobs disappeared because of mergers among financial cor-porations. That added up to more than four times the size of merger-related cuts in the next largest industrial category, aerospace and defense.[6]

Other cost-cutting initiatives flourished, too, often to the detri-ment of the banking industry's beleaguered workforce. Manage-ment consultant Alan Downs cited an example in his book *Corporate Executions:* "In February 1993, the Bank of America, after laying off 28,930 workers, proudly announced what was believed to be the highest profit for any banking institution *in his-tory,* $1.5 billion. Its CEO, Richard Rosenberg... followed that stun-ning report with an even more surprising announcement: 8,000 of the bank's white-collar employees would be reduced to part-time status of just nineteen hours per week—a move that made those employees just one hour shy of eligibility for benefits and saved the bank an additional $760 million while leaving thousands with a severely reduced paycheck, no health care, no paid vacation time, and no retirement."[7]

White-collar cutbacks proliferated throughout the industry. Soon after Citicorp's $50 billion merger with Travelers Group in the fall of 1998, the megabank publicized its intention to cut at least 5 per-cent of its 160,000-person workforce.[8] By the spring of the follow-ing year, the newly combined entity also unveiled its decision to join the ranks of penny-pinching corporations that were downgrad-ing their employees to new and controversial "cash balance" pension plans.[9] Travelers already had a cash-balance plan in place. Citicorp's new partner had also already built up a reputation—long before *this* merger—for its willingness to follow up on acquisitions with aggressive human resources cuts.

Chaos and Cutbacks Degrade Work Life

What is the personal cost of working within an industry like this one that is increasingly so full of personal risk, I wondered. What happens when someone's daily work life includes the real yet utterly unpredictable prospect of a layoff, loss of full-time employment status, or reduction in benefits or retirement savings—or the likelihood that one's employer will someday soon either acquire or be acquired by a competitor (thus destabilizing the workplace entirely)?

Richard Sennett explored a related issue in his book *The Corrosion of Character.* He noted, "[I]n everyday life people are more concerned about losses than gains when they take risks in their careers or marriages as well as at the gaming table. . . . It's for these reasons that risk-taking is something other than a sunny reckoning of the possibilities contained in the present. The mathematics of risk offer no assurances, and the psychology of risk-taking focuses quite reasonably on what might be lost." In words that might well describe the daily regimen for many of the banking industry's white-collar workers, he concluded, "Being continually exposed to risk can thus eat away at your sense of character. There is no narrative which can overcome . . . 'always starting over.'"[10]

In an effort to more fully understand what it felt like to work under erratic conditions like these, I interviewed a number of men and women who were employed (or had been employed) within the banking industry in recent years. Evelyn's story was particularly evocative, because if the corporate world were a more logical, let alone fairer, place, her career would certainly have added up to a "success."

Instead, she had been forced to struggle simply to hold on to her position during one banking merger after another (after quite a few of them, in fact). By the time I spoke with her, she was in the process of attempting to reinvent herself, at the age of fifty, as the owner of a small dry-cleaning operation whose franchise she had bought after cashing in her retirement savings.

Evelyn had risen from an administrative assistant's post to a vice president's spot within her bank's hierarchy, thanks to financial skills that proved so acute that she and her team eventually started consulting on management issues for other corporations as well. For more than a dozen years, she spent about two weeks out of every month on the road, juggling her responsibilities as a parent with the ever-increasing demands of her job.

"I was a person who loved my job. I loved it. No one ever heard me complain," she told me. "I've spent the night on a bench in O'Hare Airport. I got hung up in Oklahoma City when the air traffic controller strike happened. For three days, I couldn't get home. Not once did I ever dislike my job."

But all that changed when merger fever hit her industry. "When the first merger at my bank came along, I heard about it on the radio on my way to work," she recalled. "My first reaction was, there was no way that we'd be affected, because we were so good at what we did." She paused, then explained to me, "I'd seen mergers at other banks. When we went through the first one, I thought, We helped save our bank millions of dollars. We were out there consulting to other companies. How could anyone eliminate us?"

She soon learned differently. "We were going to be let go. But there were people who came to bat for me. They let us evaluate how the other bank performed our function." With a strong reputation and track record both within her corporation and the industry, she managed to hold on to her job. If only that battle for survival had been her last! After the merger, Evelyn found herself working harder than ever—but she was motivated to do so because she still felt emotionally invested in the success of her employer. She even cherished some illusions, in these early days, about her ability to prove her value and rise yet again within the bigger (and allegedly better) corporate structure.

But not for long. A second merger followed fairly closely on the heels of the first one, and although she again managed to hold on to her position, she began to recognize that "it was always chaos during the mergers. Every time we had a merger, the morale of everyone went down completely." There was one reason why, at least from her vantage point: "I learned eventually, it's all a political system. If one side"—that is, one of the two merging corporations—"gets a department, then they get it. No one determines who's doing it best."

That kind of attitude can fuel feelings of cynicism and futility, polar opposites of the emotions Evelyn had always prided herself on bringing to her job. So it was not too surprising that she and her colleagues found themselves searching for some type of meaning amid all this mayhem. "I talked with all kinds of people who had very high positions in the bank. I never found anyone who understood why it was all happening. Or who believed that we were going to do anything for the customer that we couldn't do before. Or, who knew," she added, "what we would pay off to the shareholder that we hadn't been able to do before. I never understood why any of the mergers took place."

But they did keep happening. "The last merger was the worst. That was about two years before I was let go," she recalled. "It was clear that the pay scale would be changed. Benefits would be changed. When the new bank came along, it was clear that they didn't have the kind of philosophy we'd had. We knew we'd lose our jobs."

Two factors combined to create personal difficulties for Evelyn. First, there seemed to be no end in sight, at least when it came to all that merger-induced turmoil. There also seemed no justification for it, which made it hard to find any meaning in the downturn. Confronted by a workplace situation in which there seemed neither logic nor predictability, she felt helpless to control her day-to-day reality as well as the long-term trajectory of her career. Worst of all, she didn't know how to protect herself—or her family's well-being—from all the negative consequences that she feared.

The emotional and physical stresses that this generated were unparalleled in Evelyn's life. As she liked to point out, she had always thrived on work-related stress in the past, priding herself on meeting even the most difficult of challenges, keeping up with the heavy pressures of her job and travel schedule, and constantly adjusting to the changing workplace norms and intense demands of her various consulting posts. But the stress from her new work life was as deadening as it was different, since there was virtually no relief in sight and still less hope of personal reward or recognition.

"The final two years, I hated my job. I couldn't stand to be in the office," she told me. "I saw the change take place in people all around me—coming in late, taking off for lunch, leaving early. Everybody knew." Unspoken, but implicit, were two more words: "Nobody cared."

"For the last year I worked at the bank, I literally had nothing to do." Evelyn's story finally wound its way to a conclusion. "I basically spent my days doing personal things. The new merger had eliminated my department. After all those years, I wasn't going to quit. I wanted the severance package." After a waiting game that lasted nearly a year, the megabank sent her department "a letter saying that through no fault of our own we would be let go. I was given six months with pay."

In today's lean-and-mean corporate universe, that can be considered a pretty fair handshake. (One woman whom I interviewed, a veteran of the publishing industry, confided that she had received a severance check that added up to less than a month's salary, despite the fact that she had spent eighteen years with the same employer. The company that acquired her firm took the position that she and her colleagues were *its* new employees, and thus didn't deserve anything more when their jobs were eliminated.)

As for Evelyn, although she had risen higher on her bank's career ladder than she once might have imagined possible, she was *not* a top-level executive. On the one hand, that meant she never had any illusions that job loss might be cushioned by stock options, a departure bonus, or a golden-parachute payoff. But although she had no hopes to be dashed, the actual terms of her severance deal left her filled with bitterness and disappointment.

"A year ago," she told me as our conversation drew to an end, "I found out I had a serious disease. For some months now, I've had a very difficult time working. When I think about all those years when I worked for the bank—how now I don't have any of the disability benefits I used to have . . ." Her voice faded away for a moment. Then she said, "All my life, I worked really hard. And it was always for somebody else. I don't know of anyone who doesn't dislike their job now. Most of my friends do. That's the way it is now."

Emotional Detachment as a Survival Strategy

Evelyn's experiences within this tumultuous industry are all too common.

When CoreStates merged with Meridian Bancorp, 10 percent of the premerger workforce, or nearly two thousand jobs, were eliminated. When Bank of Boston merged with Baybanks, the layoff toll was nearly 8 percent, or another two thousand people. And when Chase Manhattan and Chemical banks merged in the mid-1990s, the combined entity axed about twelve thousand jobs, or more than 16 percent of its premerger workforce. "It all seems like a quiz show," one Chase staffer told a reporter. "Who will win? Who will lose? Do you know the missing letters of the puzzle so you can come back to play again next week?"[11]

One can scarcely blame people for resorting to black humor or for trying to psychologically detach themselves from a bleak workplace situation over which they have no control. It's an emotional-survival tactic that makes sense in a corporate world that increasingly does not: a form of self-protection against employers who keep increasing their demands even as they reduce and eliminate their commitments to overburdened staffers.

Corporations often reinforce such detachment mechanisms through measures that encourage executives and surviving employees not to dwell too much on any of the human costs involved in cutbacks. That strategy makes sense from the corporate perspective: if staffers *did* spend too much time thinking about the sufferings of their former colleagues (or became overly anxious that the ax would soon fall upon their own necks), job-stress levels might rise so high as to prevent people from meeting the ever-increasing productivity goals that usually accompany workforce reductions.

Thus, after the Chase-Chemical merger, laid-off employees were simply referred to as "saves" (a term that actually suggests that the job-loss experience was positively benign, at least from someone's perspective). Meanwhile, the megabank distributed a twenty-six-page booklet to help its managers cope with "nonselected employ-ees" (another interesting euphemism, since it conveys not a nega-tive action—like firing someone—but the *absence* of an action, which is much harder for any particular person to feel guilty about).

The booklet suggested that managers rely upon fill-in-the-blank scripts like this one: "Today is your last day with the company. Please turn over your files on the ABC project to (name of employ-ee) and spend a few minutes bringing him up to speed." It also urged people to spend no more than five or ten minutes on these conver-sations with their "nonselects" (another detachment measure). Workplace survivors were instructed to take adequate precautions against possible acts of retribution, which might include physical violence or computer sabotage. Other tips included trying not to fire people on their birthdays.[12]

Elsewhere in the banking industry, employer efforts like these ranged from the ridiculous to (what one can only hope were uncon-scious) acts of corporate sadism. Consider the "tribute packages" CoreStates Financial Corporation provided to its nineteen-thousand-plus employees after merging with First Union Corporation, at a time when about seven thousand of them were expected to lose their jobs. The packages included disposable cameras (to be used and discarded, the same fate many recipients faced) and pop-psychology messages such as "Good luck, be reflective and choiceful, and have fun!" and "Don't compromise yourself, honey. You're all you've got."[13]

During the course of my interviews with banking industry vet-erans, I repeatedly heard them describe states of physical exhaustion (from overwork) combined with emotional havoc (from various degrees of uncertainty about their future). These conversations left me wondering how it was possible for stressed-out people like these to keep dragging themselves to the office each day.

Most relied upon some form of detachment strategy. Margheri-ta's was a good example. A mid-level staffer who had spent more than a decade rising through the ranks at National Westminster, she first heard that her bank was for sale, during the summer of 1995, when she was on vacation with her husband and children.

"I read it in a newspaper," she told me, her anger still apparent. The news threw her workplace into a protracted state of crisis. "We went from September until around Christmas, till they found a buyer. It was horrible. Rumors were flying. You started hearing, they have to give us away. No one wanted us. The frustrating thing," she recalled, "was that all through that period from September through Christmas, we kept getting letters from management that would tell us things that were in the paper two weeks earlier. When the deal finally happened"—meaning NatWest's sale to Fleet Financial—"we heard about it on the radio." Press coverage announced that 1,800 jobs would be cut.[14]

As with Evelyn, all this uncertainty about her bank's future—as well as her own career—left Margherita increasingly paralyzed by her sense of personal risk and helplessness. "There was a total spirit of mistrust throughout the organization. We were waiting and waiting and waiting for information. It wasn't until February of that year that they started setting up meetings for the Fleet people to meet their counterparts." She noted bitterly, "You knew who was going to dominate."

She stopped wanting to go into the office each day, but with two children, a house in the suburbs, and a husband whose own corporate employer was rumored to be up for sale, Margherita had little choice. Although she knew she should start job-hunting, it was tough for this lifelong banking professional to figure out where to start. Applying to another bank seemed hopeless—even self-destructive—but switching industries would have left her feeling as though her entire worklife had been worthless. So she did nothing, except continue to show up at the office.

Then the newly merged bank's cuts began. "From February to April, they did it in pieces. One by one. By April, our department had pretty well figured out that we were not going to last. We got the sense that they were going to do it in a staggered way. One area would go, then another." She tried to emotionally distance herself from the workplace anxieties that kept building: "It was funny. Some people were crying. Some people were job-hunting. I just wanted the ax to fall. I couldn't take the waiting any longer."

The memory that stays with Margherita most strongly is not of her own dismissal, whch came later that year, but that of her division head. "He'd been with the bank for thirty years. He just saw his name on the list of cuts. He didn't know he'd be there. He thought he'd be one of the people who would be kept on at the merged bank, at least for another year."

Several years later, Margherita is still in touch with people who have managed to hold on to their jobs at the merged bank; but according to what they have told her, they scarcely feel secure even now. "The people I know who are left at the bank, they figure it's only a matter of time till they're let go too." Her description of their emotional condition was brutal: "They feel like chickens with their heads cut off. Rumors are flying. It was actually a relief to me to leave all the uncertainty, the mistrust. There were days when we literally did half an hour of work all day. All we did was talk about it all."

That's not to say that all this talk led anywhere fruitful. Despite her efforts to stop caring, Margherita still felt tormented by her failure to make sense of the whole experience. "It's like everybody's bought into this idea of bigness—it's got its own momentum, like a boulder rolling downhill and nobody can stop it. It's like they all think," she added, "everybody is becoming big, so I have to become big too. They really don't have much of a plan—just sort of mush people together." Her final assessment: "They did some quick calculations with stock prices, and then let that determine what they would do. For someone like me, all you can do is sit back and say, 'Whatever is going to happen is going to happen.'"

Margherita eventually found employment elsewhere, as have many of the people who lost their jobs within the banking industry during this past decade. They were fortunate in one important way: because their layoffs took place during a period of low unemployment and significant job creation, most were able to find work again relatively quickly.

But that's not to say that she and her peers are now better off—or even as well off—as they once were. With mergers and layoffs still flourishing throughout the banking industry, many people were forced to look for work elsewhere, in fields for which they were less qualified (and thus less effectively able to compete for posts comparable to those they once held). Many needed to accept part-time, contingent, consulting, or lower-paid positions, whether because of age handicaps or lack of relevant experience in different fields. When economic downturns or industry problems arise, they will likely find themselves vulnerable to future job loss, in large part because of their lack of tenure within the new corporate hierarchies.

For those who have managed to get rehired elsewhere within the financial services sector, there's another dismal reality: much of the new job growth that has occurred within this industry has taken place at smaller companies and business start-ups: the kind of employers that seldom offer medical benefits, retirement packages, or salaries comparable to those traditionally provided by big banks. For all but the lucky handful of working men and women who wind up with lucrative stock-option deals instead, the financial rewards of their new jobs probably will never compare to those of their last ones.

What all this means is something very basic: many of the men and women who once gravitated to work for "Mother Chase " (as its employees used to call the corporation) or Chase's large, equally paternalistic counterparts throughout the U.S. banking industry have simply run out of luck. The working conditions they once knew, understood, and counted upon no longer exist. And in an industry that is still struggling to come up with a formula for survival, let alone global success, nothing stable or predictable has surfaced to replace those conditions within the workplace.

Are the Strategies Worth the Cost?

It's hard to dispute the personal impact of the long (and seemingly endless) string of mergers, layoffs, and other human resources cutbacks that has occured among the nation's banks. But in a bottom-line-oriented business universe, this "human" cost would be deemed entirely justified if U.S. banks had succeeded in solving the industry's problems, vastly improving their products and services, and solidly positioning themselves to thrive within the rough-and-tumble global marketplace. Such changes might have helped to generate more jobs elsewhere and greater wealth opportunities distributed across industry lines—benefits outweighing whatever short-term pain the industry's white-collar workforce was experiencing.

But although most of the nation's large banks have been struggling to reinvent themselves for nearly a decade now, there's still no end in sight to the turmoil—nor any likely prospect of long-term stability that could comfort the industry's remaining, beleaguered employees. Most banks are bigger than they once were, some a good deal bigger. But it's far from evident whether increased size alone (or the cash-flow savings that can come from firing some employees and increasing the workloads of others) will lead to some kind of magic cure-all or recipe for global market domination.

For every example of a bank merger and workforce cost-cutting campaign that seems to have flourished over time, there are other signs of huge missteps. After Wells Fargo & Company acquired First Interstate Bancorp in 1996, the new entity *lost* at least $5 billion in deposits[15]—surely a sign that, at least from customers' vantage point, the combined bank was inferior to either of its two, separate components. During 1999, after First Union spent $19.8 billion to acquire CoreStates Financial (in what was then the nation's largest bank deal), the *Wall Street Journal* reported that the merger was "crumbling under its own weight. The essential problem: First Union's promise to increase sales while chopping expenses almost in half at CoreStates, of Philadelphia, just isn't coming true."[16]

These are scarcely isolated examples. According to a study of the period 1995 through 1998 conducted by Mitchell Madison, a consulting firm, the stocks of banks that had carried out mergers underperformed the rest of the banking industry 82 percent of the time.[17] Problems abounded. KeyCorp (which billed itself as the United States' first coast-to-coast bank after a 1994 merger of two regionals) laid off five thousand employees and closed three hundred bank branches as it promised to concentrate on only the most profitable growth opportunities. But something apparently went wrong. During the next four years, the value of its stock shares rose by less than 90 percent, compared with 162 percent for the regional banks it once competed against.[18]

Lagging stock prices were only one measure worth considering. A closer look at one single season, the summer of 1999, provided further evidence of continuing bank industry turmoil. Bank One stumbled with its credit card unit; Bank of New York was roiled by reports of a global money-laundering scandal; and Chase cut its earnings projections because of underperformance by its investment banking, trading, and private-equity units.[19] By the end of the season, the nation's twenty-five largest banks reported that their nonperforming commercial loans had reached a staggering level of more than $6.5 billion, up by 30 percent from a year earlier.[20] A few months later, the *American Banker*'s index of 225 bank stocks was down by 16 percent, compared with a 10 percent drop for the market-wide S&P 500 stock index.[21]

For the banking industry as a whole, one conclusion seemed justifiable: despite nearly a decade's worth of turmoil-producing changes, many of them to the detriment of the industry's working men and women, banks were still facing as many problems as ever. Meanwhile, the strategic vision driving the leaders of most of the nation's major banks—that bigger is better—seemed debatable, despite its momentum (even inevitability) in the wake of regulatory changes that eliminated longtime government-imposed barriers between banking, insurance, and brokerage industry consolidation.[22]

Writing about the Citicorp/Travelers union in the *Wall Street Journal*, business historian Ron Chernow warned that "the scale of the new enterprise gives rise to grave misgivings. The segmentation dictated by the New Deal had the unintended benefit of keeping firms relatively small and flexible. If one looks at a list of the world's 10 largest banks—the majority of them foreign—they are mostly bureaucratic mastodons."[23]

If the annals of international business history offer any lessons for the United States' continually coupling banks, it is that size alone is no guarantee of success. A *Wall Street Journal* team of banking experts concluded that "bank size mattered little in Japan, whose banks used to be No. 1. Japan's banking titans were once feared because of the sheer size of their capital base and their ability to lend more cheaply than competitors. . . . Today, as a result of overemphasizing scale, Japan's banks are feared only for their huge problems."[24]

Another, even more pressing matter is whether megabanks may wind up actually harming the U.S. economy, because of the added financial risks they impose upon taxpayers and others. Jeffrey Garten, a former investment banker who served as undersecretary of commerce for international trade in the Clinton administration and now heads Yale's School of Management, feared the problems that might accompany huge size: "For all the talk about free markets, companies such as Citigroup may simply be too big to fail. Recall how Washington bailed out Lockheed and Chrysler. Megacompanies are almost beyond the law, too, because their deep pockets allow them to stymie prosecutors in ways smaller defendants cannot. Or, if they lose in court, they can pay large fines without much damage to their operations."[25]

Other observers warn that the ultimate safety net behind "too big to fail" megabanks is the American taxpayer, still blissfully unaware of the financial risk he or she could face if any of these financial institutions run into problems down the road. "[G]iven the sheer vastness of the new megabanks—Citigroup will have nearly $700 billion in assets—a single mega-failure could bankrupt the taxpayer-backed deposit insurance fund. At a mere $30 billion, it suddenly looks inadequate," emphasized Dean Foust, who covered banking regulations for *BusinessWeek*. Foust went on to quote Arthur J. Rolnick, the research director at the Federal Reserve Bank of Minneapolis: "With the safety net starting to extend beyond banking, the potential taxpayer exposure has grown."[26]

Harsh Techniques Fail Elsewhere

Lessons to be learned from the experiences of the banking industry are relevant to other struggling sectors of the U.S. economy as well. At one corporation after another, it is difficult to detect a comprehensive and long-term payoff from turnaround strategies that have degraded the conditions and rewards of work. And yet, these strategies continue to be relied upon, if for no other reason than the illusory benefits they may offer in terms of a quick boost in stock prices and a short-term cash-flow fix.

Consider the troubled results of merger-related layoffs and cutbacks at companies elsewhere across corporate America. This process has played itself out in one challenged industry after another, along the way costing more than 250,000 men and women their jobs *just* during the period from 1995 through the spring of 1999.[27] And many more people than this have suffered from the destructive stress and work loads that typically accompany career survival within unpredictable, merger-roiled workplace environments.

Within the United States' book publishing industry, a series of high-profile corporate mergers has been followed by layoffs and other cutbacks, all in an effort to improve profit margins and create global powerhouses. The pattern among publishers is one that has been repeated across the nation's economy throughout the past two decades: an industry confronted by seemingly intractable problems (in this case, skyrocketing author advances, costly returns from bookstores, Internet-driven changes in competition, and other financial pressures) opted for the business world's favorite solution these days: workplace cuts.

Predictably, the quality and rewards of work have deteriorated for publishing staffers. "We're producing 50 percent more books with 50 percent less staff," was the complaint of Michael, an editor who has worked at major publishing houses for more than twenty years. "That means you compromise quality, diligence, and, above all else, your own time." Others made similar compromises. During the period from 1991 through 1996, American publishers raised the number of books they published by 42 percent, to nearly seventy thousand each year; at the same time, they reduced their payrolls in a number of key ways, including cutting the number of editors employed nationally by 11 percent.[28]

More work. Fewer people to do it. "This may seem crazy, but I feel betrayed by technology," Michael told me, explaining, "It's now possible to produce a book in six months or less, instead of ten months. So we do it. We accelerate the publishing schedule. But that means we also have to accelerate all the human steps that are involved in bringing out a book, which means doing them faster and less carefully and with fewer people to help. We don't even have a receptionist anymore, which means we don't have anyone to open the mail and sort out the junk. There's no time to actually edit books, except on the weekends."

Michael managed to hold on to his job, despite the sale of his most recent employer to another publishing house. But his current working conditions, as he described them to me, sounded miserable. "I'm so burned out. I'm overwhelmed." He paused. "It's not that I'm anxious about being fired, because in a way, I would welcome it. I'm just anxious about not getting the work done because it bombards me—and everyone else—every single minute of the workday."

Can these kinds of workplace changes actually be viewed as productive? Despite the virtual inevitability that many workers will lose their jobs or otherwise suffer whenever their employers dance to the merger/cost-cut two-step, it's not at all clear that this combined corporate strategy brings any *long-term* benefit for customers, shareholders, or the economy at large—certainly not one large enough to outweigh the vast human cost attached to it.

According to one study, somewhere between 65 and 75 percent of the corporate mergers that took place during the 1980s through the mid-1990s were financial failures. By one key measure alone—shareholder value—this group lost an astonishing $90 billion. With an estimated $20 billion to $25 billion paid to investment bankers for their assistance with M&A activities during this same period, it's fair to say that the ultimate cost of failed corporate mergers during this time period topped $100 billion.[29]

Examples of costly merger failures abound. Quaker Oats purchased Snapple for $1.7 billion in 1994, only to sell it three years later for $300 million. Novell purchased Wordperfect in '94 as well, for $1.4 billion and unloaded it for $200 million two years later.[30] With one trillion dollars' worth of merger-and-acquisition activity having taken place within each of two years, 1998 and 1999, one can only speculate about how many of these more recent deals will likewise fail to pay off. The only certainty is one that employees of merged companies have rightly learned to expect: as a recent newspaper headline quipped, "For Oil Workers, Merger Is Just Another Word for More Layoffs."[31]

But mergers are far from the only management strategy to fuel our contemporary workplace problems while producing only questionable results. Large-scale layoffs and benefit cutbacks have taken place at struggling companies throughout the 1980s and 1990s, many with little or no prompting from the merger-and-acquisition marketplace. In such cases, the spark was usually some type of corporate bad news, resulting in a crisis of confidence among a company's large investors or board of directors. Large-scale restructuring typically followed, involving lots of workforce reductions (often the only, or the easiest, way to restore confidence in management and prop up a flagging stock price).

In today's business world, the decision to respond to any and all corporate problems with employee-related cutbacks has practically become a reflex reaction. Thus, for example, Procter & Gamble combated tough global competition in 1999 by announcing plans to eliminate fifteen thousand jobs worldwide. This decision was made despite the fact that the company's *last* restructuring effort—which axed thirteen thousand men and women in 1993—was largely considered a failure in terms of its own stated growth and bottom-line objectives.[32] Also recently, Packard Bell responded to a loss of market share by ordering employees to cut the annual costs of every single department by 50 percent, a goal that was accomplished primarily by firing 40 percent of the company's workforce.[33]

Reductions like these create havoc among a corporation's employees, leaving those who manage to hold on to their jobs stressed, overworked, and sometimes even envious of those who were "put out of their misery" by being fired quickly. But while reducing short-term operating expenses, they are also no guarantee of a company's future success. Who says that Packard Bell will do any better a job of attracting and retaining customers just because it has fired four out of every ten employees and halved each department's expenses?

Yet, as Richard Sennett noted, layoffs like these have a logic all their own: "In the operation of modern markets, disruption of organizations has become profitable. While disruption may not be justifiable in terms of productivity, the short-term returns to stockholders provide a strong incentive to the powers of chaos disguised by that seemingly assured word 'reengineering.' Perfectly viable businesses are gutted or abandoned, capable employees are set adrift rather than rewarded, simply because the organization must prove to the market that it is capable of change."[34]

To hear what it feels like to live through this type of reengineering experience can be chilling. As one man put it, "I look into people's eyes and see a whole lot of people walking around with a thousand-yard stare. I know how they were before, and I know how they are now. We saw people in positions of influence whacked, or told, 'We've got a position for you ten levels beneath what you are doing now—the same thing you were doing ten years ago. Do you want to do it?' You witness the death of people's aspirations, and once that happens, you aren't part of a group anymore. There is no group. You are casual labor."[35]

Bobby spent nearly a decade at the investment banking house of Lehman Brothers—surviving four rounds of layoffs—before finally losing his job as a vice president in the early 1990s. "It moved to mass mayhem," was the way he recalled the prolonged chaos. "Divisions were feuding with each other. They were trying to kill each other off. By then, it had become so awful that I almost didn't care as much, even though there was a higher probability of my being a victim. You get worn down."

Although those corporate staffers who are forced to function as the foot soldiers in a layoff campaign seldom earn much sympathy, they pay a painful price in stress and guilt. "I felt lousy every day," Martin told me, recalling his participation in Revlon's layoffs during the 1980s.

"Theoretically, from the company's point of view," he explained, "they were reengineering the tasks and changing the jobs. They weren't just reducing the head count. The idea was, every department would volunteer this is what they did that was redundant. Then they noticed that cutting the redundancies didn't accomplish that much. So then they did it by setting compensation dollar goals. It seemed to me that although they cut the head count, they never cut the work."

Everyone wanted to push the actual laying-off experience onto someone else, Martin noted. "The managers had to do their own firing. They didn't want to do it. They wanted human resources to do it. But human resources absolutely insisted that they do it. Afterwards, they'd literally pick people up and help them out of the office." Ten years later, after working in a series of other jobs elsewhere, he remains bitter about the experience. "I ask myself, why did I spend all those years at Revlon building the company up only to spend the next few years breaking it up."

To management consultant Alan Downs, who himself helped carry out a number of layoffs, such a response is predictable. "Being a part of the layoff—standing by and witnessing it unfold—had a traumatic side effect that went far beyond the actual pain of terminating employees. The secrecy that borderlined on deceit and the surviving employees' loss of control over their own destiny attacked the very essence of their human dignity. It severely traumatized the very employees the company was depending upon to pick up the pieces."[36]

Was there a quantifiable payoff that could compensate for personal devastation like this? As with the banking industry, stock market benefits seem short-lived and illusory. The consulting firm of Mitchell & Company examined sixteen major firms that cut more than 10 percent of their workforce between 1982 and 1988: "[A]lthough Wall Street initially applauded the cuts with higher stock prices, two years later ten of the sixteen stocks were trading below the stock market by 17 to 48 percent. Worse, twelve of these companies were trading below comparable firms in their industries."[37]

Downs warned about the costs of an all too predictable cycle that can take hold of struggling companies: one that he termed "binge and purge." "With a watchful eye to quarterly results, company management opens and closes the hiring gate according to short-term financials, not long-term business needs. . . . This addictive cycle," he complained, "has ravaged what once was one of America's most revered companies, Eastman Kodak. The photography giant began its foray into restructures and layoffs back in 1985 and since then has restructured *five* times. The total bill? More than $2.1 billion and 12,000 jobs."

His conclusion? "[H]ere's what it got for all that effort: halved profit margins, a less than desirable stock price, and total revenues that aren't much larger than before they fell into the restructuring black hole."[38] What's compelling about Downs' argument is the fact that although the management consultant published his critique in 1995, Eastman Kodak continued to flounder for years afterward, all the while losing ground in the global marketplace. Yet despite the failure of its repeated restructuring efforts, Kodak kept making workforce cuts as the 1990s drew to a close, perhaps in the hope that one day, somehow, the strategy might actually succeed. In November 1997, for example, the corporation announced plans to lay off 10,000 people. Just a single month later it decided to raise the ax even higher still, announcing revised plans to cut a total of 19,900 people from the payroll.[39]

One can only speculate about the emotional toll of this tortuous process upon the company's survivors (who once, ironically enough, could pride themselves on working for one of the most paternalistic companies in the United States). After nearly fifteen years of cost-cutting havoc, there was little indication by June 1999 that the company had found its way to the right path. At that point, Kodak replaced its chief executive officer,[40] yet workforce problems continued.

Critics of business actions like these are growing in number. In their book *The Judas Economy*, economist William Wolman and his coauthor, financial journalist Anne Colamosca, cited a series of prominent recent studies disputing the benefits of such practices: "An American Management Association study of corporate downsizing efforts undertaken between 1989 and 1995 found that only about one third of the companies experienced increased productivity. These results are confirmed by earlier studies," they wrote. "A $2 million study of 584 companies conducted jointly by Ernst and Young and the American Quality Foundation in 1991 found that most reengineering programs achieve 'shoddy results.' In 1992, studies by management consulting firms, McKinsey and Company (of 30 quality programs) and Arthur D. Little (of 5,000 manufacturing and service companies)—both found that only about one-third of such programs had a significant impact on their companies' market success."[41]

Despite its dubious results and indisputable toll, the culture of overwork, job stress, and underreward spread through the United States' struggling industries as surely as through its thriving ones. One might have expected more of a challenge from white-collar workers or the investment community. But business executives relied upon a variety of strategies to convince Americans that this harsh new world of work was well worth its costs.

NINE

"Career-Change Opportunities": The Corporate "Spin" on the New World of Work

C orporate America's campaign to replace postwar employment practices with ever more demanding, stressful, and unrewarding workplace conditions has been fought, in large part, on the public relations front. It's been a two-pronged effort: to minimize the fallout from negative changes among a company's current employees, retirees, and laid-off personnel; and to offer a long-term rationale for change, despite its costs, to the larger community of institutional investors, government lawmakers and regulators, and potential employees and business partners.

It has been an effort to incubate a cultural revolution, as one corporation after another has attempted to reeducate Americans about the world of work and the rationale behind—indeed, inevitability of—harsh new changes. So long as the stock market soared and the U.S. economy looked unstoppable during the 1990s, contemporary business leaders were as successful in winning converts as their paternalistic counterparts were half a century ago.

But nothing lasts forever in the business world. As financial conditions became more volatile near the turn of the millennium, the limits to corporate America's spin campaign became clearer. After nearly two decades of deteriorating work conditions, many white-collar men and women no longer trusted their employers—no matter what strategies public relations and management consultants concocted—nor did they care about much of anything besides their prospects for "jumping ship" to a better corporate position or retiring as quickly as possible. With the value of most large-corporate stocks in a slump, the sales pitch for "sweatshop" management practices had apparently lost its effectiveness among investors as well.

"Selling" the White-Collar Sweatshop

When it has come to proselytizing for the new work-world order, few have been as aggressive or outspoken as Albert J. Dunlap, the once-revered, recently reviled chief executive and corporate turn-around artist whose best-selling 1996 memoir was entitled, with perfect accuracy, *Mean Business*. Dunlap ranks as one of the most fascinating of contemporary business figures, in large part because his spectacular rise and fall as a business icon reveals so much about the allure, as well as limitations, of current harsh management techniques.

Some personal background is important in understanding his success as a business "evangelist." After early stints elsewhere, Dunlap assumed the chairmanship of Scott Paper Company in 1994, at a time when that firm was losing nearly $300 million a year. His nineteen-month tenure there quickly became the stuff of 1990s business legend: he fired 11,200 people, one third of the company's workforce, drove its stock price up by 225 percent, and sold off Scott to a competitor, netting himself a $100 million paycheck in the process.

"The term 'to Dunlap' has become a verb in the business lexicon," he gloated after that sale, explaining that his very name had become a synonym for "eliminating everything that is not the best."[1] Many agreed: within the large-corporate and investment communities, Dunlap's knack for tying the leanest and meanest of management strategies to exceptional stock market results—without any apologies along the way—amounted to proof incontrovertible that his was the formula for success in the harsh and competitive global economy.

As "Chainsaw Al"'s career progressed, he went on to terminate about 50 percent of the staffers at Sunbeam, where he next signed on as CEO. There he managed to drive up the company's stock price by nearly 60 percent in one single day, just by *announcing* his agreement to take the helm. But the chief executive's aura of infallibility faded after he wound up getting "dunlapped" himself in 1998, amid signs that his cuts had decimated Sunbeam's infrastructure and product lines while failing to achieve significant financial improvements or to position the company for future profitability and growth.[2]

Regardless of its author's tarnished stature, *Mean Business* remains one of the classics of the current, hugely popular genre of books by CEOs: a not-too-surprising offshoot of the United States' equity-obsessed culture, in which the ability to keep a company's stock shares rising is viewed by some as little short of genius. One could speculate endlessly about the psychological subtext behind America's chief executives' compulsion to reinvent themselves as the contemporary business world's version of philosopher-kings.

It would seem as though business executives had more than enough to preoccupy themselves with, simply from the day-to-day demands of running their large corporations and trying to stay ahead of all that competition they keep talking (and writing) about. Jeff Papows, the former chief executive of Lotus Development Corporation, acknowledged that "[l]ife in the software industry is so intense that committing the time and effort to write a book . . . was not the most intuitive extra project to take on. Staying ahead of an industry that moves as quickly as ours is already more than a full-time job." Yet he succumbed to the trend while still in the CEO's seat with his 1998 *Enterprise.com*; after all, he explained, "it is my conviction that we are in the early years of a fundamental change in the way that our civilization works."[3]

The compulsion to reinterpret the world for the rest of us has motivated quite a few business executives in a similar direction. Often, their philosophies rest upon a "sweatshop" vision of the workplace: a corporate environment in which there is little security, predictability, or even human kindness. Instead of these old creature comforts, readers are offered a scenario for corporate success which typically runs along these lines: If they (our visionary corporate leaders) and we (their fortunate employees) all work as hard as we can, to the utmost of our capabilities, *every single moment of every single day*, we all may thrive—at least for a while—in a new economy that is difficult and demanding, but potentially rewarding.

Dunlap, who liked to compare himself to Rambo, explained in *Mean Business* that "the harsh reality of business life is that what works today won't even be satisfactory tomorrow. The predators are out there, circling, trying to stare you down, waiting for any sign of weakness, ready to pounce and make you their next meal."[4]

In his universe, there is one basic message: Business is battle and any employee who cannot cope is, or should be, cannon fodder. When it comes to younger workers (who have yet to be tested under this kind of fire), successful executives (who may share similar aggressive tendencies), and well-heeled investors (who tend to assess the corporate world primarily in terms of its stock-price swings), such management machismo has won plenty of adherents during the past decade or so. Thus, Dunlap's philosophical treatise has continued to draw rave reviews, even after his success at Scott Paper was eclipsed by his later failure at Sunbeam.

"He should run his own business school!" one reader recently e-mailed to the bookseller Amazon.com, confiding that his hours spent with *Mean Business* had taught him much more about the corporate world than years of business school. Another lauded the book as "an excellent text for anyone running, buying or attempting to turn around a business. Sure he's fired many an employee . . . [but] if shareholder value can't be increased, then WHAT if any thing is to be the endpoint of our toil? Long live the efficiency-minded Al Dunlaps of our day! May they continue to offer example and inspiration to other corporate managers."[5]

Corporate leaders are far from the only people who have taken pen to paper during the past decade or so in an effort to convince the American public of the benefits of tight fiscal controls, tough management styles, and ever-higher performance standards. But these days few books by consultants or other business experts carry the weight of those by successful CEOs, who in the current economic climate come close to attaining the celebrity stature of star athletes.

"I believe in the value of paranoia," wrote another corporate superstar, Intel's then chief executive Andrew S. Grove, in his *Only the Paranoid Survive.* "Business success contains the seeds of its own destruction. The more successful you are, the more people want a chunk of your business and then another chunk and then another until there is nothing left. I believe that the prime responsibility of a manager is to guard constantly against other people's attacks and to inculcate this guardian attitude in the people under his or her management."[6]

Elsewhere, Grove invoked a Darwinian vision of the workplace in which an individual's career success and failure were determined by the corporation's instinctive quest for survival (which, like that of any species, is viewed as utterly natural and beyond morality). "Do people seem to be 'losing it' around you?" he asked. "Think about it. You and your management have both been selected by the evolutionary forces of your business to be at the top of your organization. Your genes were right for the original business. But if key aspects of the business shift around you, the very process of genetic selection that got you and your associates where you are might retard your ability to recognize the new trends."[7]

In the business world sketched out by CEO-writers like these, the workplace changes that have taken place during the 1980s and 1990s were unequivocally good and inevitably necessary, and, above all else, produced results. Irrelevant was the impact of these changes upon corporate men and women who were forced to accommodate heavier workloads, constantly increasing productivity demands, greater intrusions of work upon home life, diminished job security, and reduced financial rewards.

Within this publishing genre, the justification for all lies squarely in one place: the U.S. stock market. That was a message plenty of people were willing to accept at face value, at least while the bull market soared.

The Tougher Sell: Executive Compensation

Corporate America's spin-masters have had far less success in persuading people to accept another key element of the new businessworld order: skyrocketing executive compensation levels.

During the 1980s and most especially the 1990s, chief-executive pay reached levels so astronomically high as to raise questions among employees and investors alike about the degree to which the nation's corporate leaders were willing to live by their own lean-and-mean creed. According to one study, the annual compensation of chief executives of large corporations (which typically included salary, bonuses, and stock grants and options) rose from an average of $1.8 million back in 1990 to $10.6 million in 1998, an increase of about 490 percent in less than a decade. This occurred during a period in which many people's paychecks barely kept up with inflation; countless others, with careers disrupted by corporate downsizings or mergers, actually lost financial ground as they spent retirement savings, sold homes, or accepted lower-paying jobs in order to meet their household obligations.[8]

By the turn of the century, magazine and newspaper articles were full of accounts of Internet entrepreneurs who became paper billionaires after taking their fledgling companies public. Or Wall Street executives, venture capitalists, and merger-and-acquisition attorneys whose paychecks and bonuses soared to unparalleled heights, along with the stock market boom. But it wasn't *their* good fortune that drove so many white-collar men and women to distraction during the period: it was the outsized rewards earned by their own, otherwise penny-pinching executive bosses.

Al Dunlap, never one to shy away from a public relations battle, engaged the issue head-on in *Mean Business,* in a chapter he called "The Best Bargain Is an Expensive CEO." He supported the notion of linking pay to performance—by awarding chief executives equity or options that would gain in value only if their company's stock price rose. But although management accountability gained widespread appeal after the corporate confusion of the late 1970s and early 1980s, few business theorists could amass popular support with lines like Dunlap's: "Even though I walked away from Scott more than $100 million richer than when I arrived, I was still the biggest bargain in Corporate America."[9]

It's hard to imagine how anyone could justify these outrageous paychecks, and few have tried. GE's Jack Welch, who earned $150 million in the three years between 1996 and 1998, responded to a question from a shareholder at the company's annual meeting by simply quipping, "Sure, I'm one of the fat cats. In fact, I'm the fat-test cat because I'm lucky enough to have this job."[10]

The disparity that developed during these past two decades between executive reward and employee cutbacks was little short of breathtaking. Back in 1978, the leaders of America's major cor-porations earned just under 30 times the pay of their average work-ers. Just seventeen years later, they earned more than 115 times as much. Indeed, by 1997 the Economic Policy Institute calculated that the average business leader worked just half a week in order to bring home as much as his or her typical employee managed to earn over the entire year.[11] According to one *BusinessWeek* report, sub-titled "Even Executives Are Wincing at Executive Pay," three of every four people surveyed believe that the top staffers of large cor-porations simply were paid too much.[12]

For most men and women, the conclusion seemed unavoidable: during the United States' recent boom, the CEOs of large corporations received a disproportionate share of the goodies while imposing the bulk of the economic recovery's cost upon their employees. No won-der that was a tough message for even the most public-relations-oriented of business leaders to sell to the American public.

For many of today's white-collar workers, plagued by overwork, deteriorating benefits, and much too much stress, the boss's salary has become an irritant they just cannot overlook. "You hear com-ments about Sandy Weill *all the time*," one Citigroup staffer told me in disgust, referring to the company's chairman. "He becomes the voodoo doll here." In 1998 Weill earned $167 million at a time when the bank planned to cut 5 percent of its workforce while reducing 401K, pension, and other benefits.[13]

Richly compensated Louis Gerstner, the head of IBM, has turned into another lightning rod for employee discontent. During a trip to Texas, he was greeted by a rather unusual form of protest from "Big Blue" employees: an airplane flying a banner behind it that read "Hey Lou. Thou shalt not steal." The staffers were irate over the company's planned conversion from a traditional pension plan to a cost-saving cash-benefit model. That same year, Gerstner earned a base salary of $2 million, a bonus of $7.2 million, and $87.7 million from some stock options that he exercised.[14]

Given these levels of inequity, it's not surprising that executive compensation has surfaced as a symbol—among a growing, if loose, coalition of white-collar workers, union activists, investors, muckraking journalists, and legislators—of something rotten in today's business universe.

Even a public relations genius could not justify some outlandish compensation packages. At AT&T, where CEO Robert E. Allen made corporate history in 1996 with his plans to terminate forty thousand employees, his pay and bonus for 1997 topped $3 million. During three short years, 1995–97, when his company's return on equity *dropped* by nearly 25 percent, Allen took home nearly $21 million in all. And when he finally gave AT&T a break and opted for early retirement, he left with a $1.5 million annual pension. Continuing the tradition, Allen's successor, C. Michael Armstrong, earned $3.8 million in 1998 at a time when he announced plans to cut another 15% of the company's workforce.[15]

An analysis of executive compensation trends reveals a clear pattern: those business leaders willing to make harsh human-resources-related cuts in the interest of boosting the bottom line (and presumably the stock price) are often well rewarded for their efforts. Xerox gave its chairman and chief executive officer, Paul Allaire, a 51 percent raise in bonus and salary (to about $7.5 million) during 1997 and then announced plans early in 1998 to eliminate nine thousand jobs, or about 10 percent of its workforce.[16]

For all those corporate staffers whose work lives have worsened thanks to such management dictates as "Keep raising the bar" and "There's no free ride," another trend has been galling: the United States' top executives simply do not seem to be held to the same inflexibly high standards as they are. At Warnaco—which lost $32 million after taxes during 1998—its chairman, Linda J. Wachner, earned a total compensation package (including options) estimated at $73.4 million.[17] Apple Computer lost nearly $2 billion under the seventeen-month leadership of Gilbert F. Amelio; the CEO still received $2 million in salary and bonus, as well as a severance payment of $6.7 million.[18]

Most disturbing of all, perhaps, was a corporate practice that first began to surface during the late 1990s, when volatility in the stock market seemed to threaten the profitability of executive compensation packages whose payoffs were tied to rising shareholder value. If one really believed in the righteousness of the universe sketched out by Al Dunlap and others, CEOs should share the pain of a financial downturn; then, theoretically, the depressed value of their compensation packages would motivate them to work harder.

But instead of following that precarious path, a fair number of companies simply repriced their stock options at lower levels so that executives could still earn equity-related profits even though shareholder values had declined. Among the corporations that went this route are Kmart, Netscape Communications, Seagate Technology, and Phillips-Van Heusen.[19]

CEOs are losing the public relations battle, at least on the executive compensation front, because the gap between management theory and reality looms large. Although there is plenty of white-collar accountability throughout the workforce, many large corporations lavishly reward their top executives regardless of whether they manage to achieve significant short- or long-term results.

Some top executives may not care whether this practice has earned them the distrust or even disgust of their current employees, retirees, or Main Street Americans. But their failure to stifle mounting criticism on this issue may end up costing them dearly. Federal Reserve chief Alan Greenspan and others have suggested regulatory changes that would reduce executive pay-related tax deductions or force companies to fully account for expenses tied to stock-option awards.[20]

Now that would be ironic. Instead of compensation levels *rising* along with stock prices, huge CEO packages could wind up lowering a company's bottom line and thus reducing its stock price as well. Chief executives might actually find themselves in a universe in which investors rewarded them for *cutting* their own pay, in much the same way that they currently reward large-scale layoffs, benefit reductions, or other workforce cutbacks. Would they respond accordingly?

The long-term resolution of this controversial issue is far from clear. But America's CEOs have already lost moral ground and management credibility over their failure to control public attitudes about executive compensation. In a business-world order that rests upon keeping regulators and legislators at bay—while motivating employees to work harder and faster within an ever-shrinking reward structure—losses like these could jeopardize the precariously balanced status quo.

The Inside Spin

There's another side to the corporate campaign to win Americans' allegiance to the demanding new world of work: internal public relations.

During the 1980s and 1990s, many large corporations launched workplace seminars, support groups, and a host of other programs that, whether explicitly or not, aimed to reeducate their current or soon-to-be-former employees about the necessities and virtues of harsh corporate changes. Typically combining New Age techniques with an evangelical thrust, these initiatives seldom focused simply upon helping staffers adjust. They aimed to win pumped-up, motivated converts who would be ready to perform and thrive under the most grueling and even hostile of business conditions.

The theory behind them might have made sense, but internal public relations initiatives have frequently backfired, adding fuel to feelings of cynicism or anger among overworked, insecure, stressed-out employees. NYNEX's "Winning Ways" program, a company-wide initiative that was conducted during the mid-1990s, is illustrative. Its objective was to nurture a new mentality among the struggling company's employees—the mentality of a winner. William C. Ferguson, the retired chief executive of NYNEX, described Winning Ways as promoting "the key behaviors and attitudes that help us exceed customer expectations and win in the marketplace. These behaviors start with integrity and leadership."[21]

Although NYNEX had thrived in the early years after the AT&T divestiture, by the 1990s the company seemed to be on an unstoppable downhill roll, thanks to a costly and divisive union strike, the expenditure of hundreds of millions of dollars on a series of failed acquisitions, and the gradual layoff of more than 20 percent of the workforce. In retrospect, this employee program seems to have been part of a "holding pattern" by the company's top executives, who spent these years floundering between one ineffective management initiative after another, only to finally resolve their problems through what was billed as a "merger of equals" (but basically boiled down to a takeover of NYNEX by the thriving Bell Atlantic).

I learned about Winning Ways from a group of mid-level employees I interviewed during my research for this book. They and their peers made no bones about their contempt for it, using a company-wide nickname to dismiss it: "Whining Ways." They viewed the seminar as yet another consultant-designed time-waster—part of a pattern which suggested to them that top management was clueless about the company's future direction as well as out of touch with everyone below the executive suite.

"First it was 'Quality,'" sneered Bobby, an M.B.A. by training, who had joined the telecommunications company during the early 1980s as part of its large administrative staff. "There were *billions* of consultants. Lots of training. A lot of it was commonsense. Then after 'quality' started costing so much, they phased it down. Then it went to 'Winning Ways.' That was the new world—where they would make you feel good about yourself while they were feeling good about letting you go."

To the NYNEX staffers I interviewed, Winning Ways was little more than an inept attempt to pull the wool over their eyes: to boost their self-esteem with some "touchy-feely" exercises, as Bobby termed them, during a troubled corporate era in which intelligent men and women could not help recognizing that there were plenty of reasons to lose confidence in the company's future, as well as their own.

Attendance was mandatory. "It was required of us. It was absolutely required. You had to sign that you had gone," complained Joan, a computer technician. "There were things like pictures that could either be an old woman or a young woman. The point was, things are different depending upon how you see them. And both points are valid," she drew the sentence out, as if she were in a kindergarten class repeating a lesson from her teacher.

"There'd be six of us sitting at a table, working on puzzle pieces. They were all mixed up. We could only do the puzzle if we worked together." She paused, then said "It was completely useless for us.

Afterwards, my boss suggested we have group meetings. *That* was the only difference."

For Bobby, it was his memory of the group "jump" that still drove him to distraction, long after it had taken place. "We spent three whole days together, off-site, dressed-down. You were required to go. One exercise was, how many different ways can you jump around the room?" So he and his colleagues jumped—on one leg, on both legs, with their hands in the air, with one hand covering an eye. They jumped and they jumped and they jumped some more. "Then the leaders would say things like, 'Look at how creative you are, how many different ways you can figure out to manage to jump around the room.' And we all did it," Bobby told me, his voice laced with contempt for everyone in the room, including himself. "We all did it."

The NYNEX seminar sent him into a spiral of self-disgust while generating even more powerful negative emotions toward his employer; yet the focus of "Winning Ways" was to feel upbeat, no matter what was going on within the corporation or the business world at large. "They'd bring up family big-time. Realize what you have: your family, your career—but *not* your job," Bobby pointed out. While everyone was thinking those good thoughts, soft music played in the background.

His voice faded away for a while as he recalled the scene to himself. "People would sit there and say, 'We can't believe we're doing this.' After all," he concluded, "at the end of day you've got a company that provides poor service, that is not well managed, and that is totally hostage to its union situation. They're spending money on things like this that are just fluff. That's the cynicism. That's the irony."

It's tough to quantify how much of the many billions of dollars spent each year on management consultants has paid for misguided internal PR efforts like these. But the landscape of corporate America has been littered in recent years with countless costly and ineffective counterparts to NYNEX's Winning Ways program: tiny testaments to the difficulty of brainwashing intelligent men and women into believing that they are better off than they once were within today's harsh new world of work.

Phillip was a veteran of the process. He had spent years in the marketing division of a chain of radio stations that went through a series of corporate mergers. Job conditions worsened each time his company got sold. One set of new corporate parents after another "kept cutting costs, cutting costs," he recalled. "They'd want a 10 percent decrease in the expense budget, but for sales to be increased by 10 percent or so. Then the next year, they'd say, cut it again by 10 percent and push up sales by another 10 percent."

In a pattern that has become all too predictable within the United States' large corporations, consultants were soon brought in to run employee motivational seminars. "I remember one set of meetings along the way," he told me, "when we had to all get together and stand up in front of the group and say what we were feeling. Our manager told us, 'We're going to talk about our feelings—there's a new openness here.' Some of us even started crying. We were really expressing our hopes."

That was only the beginning. "Then we had to get into a circle. Hold hands. Close our eyes. There were two different circles moving in two different directions. Then when the circle stopped moving, you had to fall backwards and trust that the person who was behind you would catch you. Then there was another exercise with boards and cinder blocks. The only way you could get across was if people would share their boards with you."

Since the program coincided loosely with a corporate era in which layoffs were rampant and other cutbacks continued, participants were dubious, to put it mildly, about the company's motives. With attendance mandatory and a clear corporate line to follow, this feel-good-fest was viewed by many people as yet another turn in their work lives over which they had no control.

The "spider webs" were a good example. "They tied up ropes between two trees so that it looked like a web," explained Phillip. "You literally had to lie on the ground and hold yourself stiff and be passed through the ropes. You had to hope that someone on the other side would catch you." He paused, as if searching for the right way to describe the experience. "This was the most uncomfortable thing for professional men and women. A lot of us," he confided, "felt uncomfortable, embarrassed, reluctant to play the games. But they kept at it. It was almost like it was designed to break you down. I think it was a way of humiliating us." He paused again. "If we would have been kept at our jobs, it would be one thing. But many people were fired anyway."

For Phillip, the equivalent of NYNEX's group "jumps" were the mandatory water sports. "There were dump tanks. We had to participate in that too. They gave everybody squirt guns and there were all these executives running around squirting each other. You felt you were under a microscope. One person refused to do it. I felt," he recalled, "if I don't squirt, will I be gone too?" Again, a pause. "In the end, plenty of people wound up getting fired—the squirters and the nonsquirters. What did it matter?"

The Public Relations Backlash

There was a pattern to the metaphors that people chose when describing their employers' internal public relations campaigns. "It's Orwellian," was a theme I heard repeatedly as men and women recounted the various ways that companies tried to convince them that bad things were really good. "It's like Vietnam," was another popular refrain (typically among people whose employers liked to deny that layoffs were really layoffs). One man went so far as to compare conditions at NYNEX to those in the Stalinist Soviet Union, since he felt that nothing the company told its employees could be trusted.

Clearly the public relations pitches were misfiring. White-collar workers particularly loathed the linguistic maneuvers that corporations relied upon to distance themselves from the human repercussions of their actions. Thus, layoffs were termed "releases of resources" by Bank of America, "career-change opportunities" by Clifford of Vermont, "schedule adjustments" by Stouffer Foods Corporation, and "elimination of employment security policy" by Pacific Bell. AT&T opted for a *Star Wars*-like phrase: "force management program." Bell Labs was notable during the nineties if only because its euphemism for downsizing hinted at something a bit closer to reality: "involuntary separation from payroll."[22]

Employee "reward" programs were often another enormous source of discontent. Since top executives usually aimed to control financial expenditures, at least when it came to people outside the executive suite, the popular trend was toward nonmonetary rewards. The theory behind them served the corporation's interests, if not the employee's: if you pay people a bonus to reward hard work, they will come to expect it and eventually stop working harder—so the safest course is never to get started. (Fortunately for top executives, their compensation packages weren't expected to produce the same result, although it's hard to know why not.) Investors and management consultants loved nonmonetary programs like these, since they had no impact on the company's bottom line.

But rather than bonding white-collar staffers closer to their employers, these initiatives nurtured widespread cynicism and resentment. "The company set up a 'Way to Go' program that recognized the very best ass-kissers," recalled "Keffo," a contributor to the Internet magazine *Temp Slave*. "It was all mucky-muck bullshit created to perpetuate the myth that the company cared about its workers. Of course, none of these workers ever got something real, like a raise in pay."[23]

Like the wolf in grandmother's clothing, motivational programs often boiled down to new and different corporate strategies to overwork staffers. Bank of America, one of the most notorious practitioners of layoffs and cutbacks during the past decade, came up with a noteworthy example in 1999, when it developed a program offering employees the chance to "adopt an A.T.M." machine.

This was not a profit-making venture for the employees; instead, bank volunteers were given the chance to clean an automatic teller machine and its surrounding area so long as they did so on their own time after work and without extra pay. The benefits from such adoptions were, presumably, lower janitorial costs for the bank and, perhaps, happier customers; it's hard to imagine much in the way of extra gratification for already busy staffers, who likely had more than enough cleaning tasks already waiting for them at home. More than 2,800 of the bank's 158,000 staffers signed up, perhaps because they hoped the extra work would shelter them whenever the next round of corporate cutbacks came along. Fortunately, California's state labor commissioner interceded, informing the bank that the program violated "basic precepts of wage and hour law."[24]

Without being quite so blatant, other programs have created new work for corporate staffers while pretending to add meaning to their lives. One popular, if often ineffective, internal spin technique links employee-motivation efforts with charitable activities. The corporate payoff includes plenty of positive buzz among lawmakers, potential investors, and the general populace. Staffers—whose regular workloads typically don't get reduced when "volunteer" assignments are layered on top—wind up with more job stress as they struggle to cope.

At HarperCollins, Annette (who worked in the publicity department) participated in the company's "Visions and Values" program. She and a group of colleagues from various job categories and departments were assigned to paint a facility owned by a nonprofit organization. It was not a matter of choice. "It was done very diplomatically, but you were given the sense, politely, that this was expected of you. So you did it."

The experience was anything but rewarding, she recalled. "It was a farce, really. We made a mess of it—after all, we weren't painters. We didn't know how to be careful and we didn't want to be doing this in the first place. I actually felt sorry for the people whose rooms we were painting." From Annette's vantage point, the only employee "bonding" that took place among the group's members was a kind of "reverse bonding, because we all felt so cynical about the whole process. After all, we had no choice about doing this. It only made our work lives harder, because we had to do this during the workweek and then find time during evenings or weekends to catch up on all the jobs we still needed to do."

She paused, then concluded, "All that 'Visions and Values' was about was making the company look good to the outside world. And that was a joke," she added, "because they really didn't give a s—— about anything but profit." Soon after her participation, in fact, HarperCollins made headlines because of a company-wide layoff.[25]

But despite the time and money that has been spent upon Visions and Values, Winning Ways, and countless variations on their ill-conceived management themes, corporate America's internal spin campaign has been far from successful during the 1990s. That's not too surprising, perhaps: it's easier for chief executives to sway readers with their aggressive certainties and stock market prowess than it is for employers to convince their white-collar staffers that all the changes they *know* have made work life worse are really just plain great after all. And within the ranks of workforce distrust and discontent—as well as popular resentment over excessive executive compensation levels—may come, finally, an effort to halt "sweatshop" corporate trends and to restore a more equitable balance to the twenty-first century workplace.

A Path Out of the White-Collar "Sweatshop"?

My book was nearly completed when I decided to make one more call to Gemma, the marketing executive from Scarsdale. Although we had spoken every couple of months by telephone, it had been more than three years since I had first interviewed her over lunch in a crowded Manhattan restaurant. I remembered marveling at how she, or anyone, could cope with a work and stress load quite like hers. There was no time to exercise, no time to see a physical therapist, no time during a workday even to replace a torn pair of stockings.

Had her work life changed during all these years, I asked her, during another rushed meal at another crowded restaurant. "Absolutely. The economy is so strong that we're all busier than ever." She paused for a moment, then added, "A few years ago, I told you about how I'd run out and get a sandwich for lunch and then spend twenty minutes in our conference room eating it with one of my friends from the office. Now I never take that kind of time away from work. I eat at my desk and make phone calls at the same time."

Her only time off now came during a few moments of her commute home. "You've got to be thankful for little things," she mused. "It takes the train a while to get out of Grand Central Station and all those tunnels. And that's time when I couldn't use my cell phone even if I wanted to."

The Toll Exacted by White-Collar "Sweatshops"

Workloads have gotten so heavy that free time really does seem an unimaginable luxury for men and women in all kinds of jobs and industries across the United States. Cell phones, laptops, and other workplace technologies loom as inescapable, since without them white-collar staffers cannot hope to meet the "24/7" demands of their employers. As layoffs, benefit cutbacks, and subtle forms of age discrimination have become ever more pervasive throughout the business world, long-term security for many people now seems to hang on the whims of the stock market, rather than on the strength of their careers.

The personal toll from changes like these is both vast and insidious. The speeded-up pace of work has exposed men and women to increasing risks associated with stress-related ailments at the same time that declining corporate benefit packages have left them with fewer protections. Although stock portfolios fattened for those fortunate enough to own them, many people became accustomed during the 1980s and 1990s to living with financial anxieties as they borrowed more, saved less, and watched pensions shrink or disappear.

Families paid an incalculable price for the business boom of the past two decades. As the culture of overwork overtook corporate America, frazzled parents on all rungs of the job ladder found themselves with less time to spend at home (as well as less "quality" time at home, free from distractions from the office). Gemma put it this way: "I feel as though there's an 'on' button at work and an 'on' button at home. When both on's are on at the same time, nothing is right for anyone. All systems burn out."

During an era in which economic prosperity could have supported a real enhancement in quality of life for people across the nation, many instead lost the ability to relax, concentrate on their families, and pursue leisure interests safe from intrusions from their workplaces. Despite the greatest bull market the world had ever seen, Americans were working harder by the end of the 1990s than their counterparts in Britain, France, Germany, and even Japan, the longtime symbol of workaholism.[1] What was it all for?

Many of the adults I interviewed over the past four years felt guilty or apprehensive about the long-term impact of their failure to supervise, motivate, or interact with their children in ways that their own parents had been able to manage, within a less demanding work world. Yet although a host of youth crises riveted public attention by the turn of the millennium—declining educational achievements, illicit drug use, underage crime, bizarre acts of violence—there was little recognition of the role that insatiable employers had played in eroding the bonds between parents and children, decreasing family stability, and damaging the nation's home life.

While the bull market charged ahead, self-help books, magazines, and Internet sites proliferated, all testaments to a general malaise felt by the overloaded, stressed-out, insecure denizens of the new American economy. By the close of the 1990s, many people may have had more money than ever, but they also had less time, physical stamina, and emotional energy to devote to activities unrelated to their all-consuming jobs. Interpersonal relationships of every kind deteriorated in ways that weakened communal structures while undermining the potential to live fulfilled, well-rounded lives. "Whatever Happened to Friendship?" was a question asked even by the *Wall Street Journal,* in an article arguing that "in this overstressed, hyperlinked age, some people seem wired to everything but each other."[2]

For the baby-boom generation and other Americans, the unparalleled prosperity of the past two decades could have helped to create better and more rewarding prospects for their golden years than the nation's economy had ever before offered. But instead, the Darwinian forces behind today's "sweatshop" corporations conspired to make the aging process *more* difficult and anxiety-producing than had been the case throughout much of the post–World War II period. Only those with stock portfolios thick enough to cushion them from the blows were spared.

Americans may be living longer than ever, but their earnings potential, job options, and marketability now peak and decline at earlier and earlier stages—in some industries and professions, for people as young as forty or so. Their parents may have had nine-to-five work lives and steady career paths, leading predictably to comfortable retirements. But for all the recent technological advances and record-breaking economic achievements, corporate staffers at the dawn of the twenty-first century were faced with the dismal prospect of working like dogs for a couple of decades while juggling the voracious demands of young children, aging parents, and corporate employers.

Then, as they age themselves, their prospects turn from bad to worse. Just when many white-collar men and women reach the maturity and experience levels that once might have seemed to justify a more comfortable and stable—even an *easier*—work-and-home-life balance, odds are strong that they will find themselves on the downhill track, squeezed into self-employment or increasingly precarious jobs for what could be another thirty or forty years of workplace grind. Given their declining pension prospects and the precarious financial health of the Social Security system, growing numbers of the nation's best and brightest may wind up unable to afford to retire.

The emotional impact of changes like these has gone far beyond exhaustion and anxiety for many corporate staffers. With the often-proclaimed "death" of mutual loyalty between employer and employee and the "commoditization" of once-valued jobs (through trends such as technological reengineering and increased use of contingent labor), educated and experienced men and women have come to feel marginalized and alienated from the careers that once added meaning and a sense of direction to their lives.

Such deteriorating workplace conditions have already begun to produce palpable changes in the American psyche. As corporations practically boasted of their lack of long-term commitment to employees during the past two decades—and prosperity's benefits were largely monopolized by top executives and professional investors—people of all ages and professions learned to replace traditional attitudes about hard work, just rewards, teamwork, and security with a new workplace ethos centered on cynicism, self-protection, and preoccupation with the quick "score." A new breed of careerists began to multiply, a group that felt as little attachment to their jobs or employers as the era's day-trading investors had for the stocks they bought and sold at a rapid-fire pace.

Negative changes in job conditions and attitudes have exacted a painful civic toll as well in recent years. When people have little choice but to obsess over workplace demands and career survival, they lack both the time and energy to devote to the wide range of volunteer activities that can enrich their communities while adding new dimensions to their own lives.

As a result, school systems across the nation now struggle to find parents willing and able to serve, the way their own parents did, as part-time classroom aides, fund-raisers, sports coaches, or PTA representatives. (Is that surprising? These same men and women often are too busy with office tasks even to help their children with homework.) Similarly, religious institutions and other nonprofit groups find themselves relying upon a shrinking, and usually aging, cadre of volunteers.

Despite the booming economy, there has been little in the way of a dollar-and-cents trade-off for all those missing bodies. During the 1980s and 1990s, corporate donations tended to go to large high-profile charities, rather than to the tiny grassroots organizations that seek to enhance a neighborhood's quality of life and opportunities in so many different, but unpublicized, ways. Moreover, some aggressive cost-cutters decided to reduce or eliminate their contributions entirely, thereby jeopardizing nonprofits and the communities they serve (as when the newly merged Citigroup stopped its practice of matching employees' individual donations, or then-CEO Al Dunlap axed plans for Scott Paper to make $3 million in annual gifts).[3]

On the education front, the 1990s were notable for a series of huge bequests by wealthy individuals; these mainly went, though, to the nation's leading universities. (Microsoft's Bill Gates proved an exception to this, with his foundation's support for public schools as well as higher education.) Still, most school systems, as well as day care institutions and urban after-school programs, remained as desperate for funds as they were for volunteers. The pattern repeated itself in the arts, social services, and elsewhere throughout the large and diverse nonprofit sector, to the detriment of the communities that have depended upon such institutions across the United States.

Large corporations, too, have begun to pay a price for their harsh new management practices: one that will only become more fully clear as the competititive and financial pressures upon them increase in the coming years, whether because of rising interest rates, stock market volatility, declining consumer demand, or continued shifts in global market conditions. That price, put simply, is less potential for future growth and stability, thanks to the serious and mounting difficulties these companies face when it comes to marshaling manpower and capital resources.

For most of the 1980s and 1990s, it seemed as though the leaders of big businesses had nothing to lose from the rupture of long-term ties and the end of workplace loyalty. They could hire and fire as they chose, cut costs to the bone, rely on mergers to camouflage stagnating results, and usually count on riding their stocks into the galaxy. But even the first few months of the twenty-first century gave hints of the problems that awaited America's once most-admired corporations.

More and more people who could do so "jumped ship" from the blue chips to the world of "dot-com's" and other upstart business ventures. From a potential employee's perspective, smaller entrepreneurial companies no longer seemed, as they once had, to be that much riskier or more demanding than mainstream employers; and they appeared to offer infinitely better prospects for financial reward, usually tied to generous stock-option packages.

Corporate flights near the top were the ones to capture media attention, as when Heidi Miller, the executive vice president and chief financial officer of Citigroup, left the banking giant to run Priceline.com. AT&T, no longer a symbol of workforce stability and long-term opportunity, lost more than a dozen top executives.[4] But similar decisions were made in growing numbers by skilled men and women on all rungs of the job ladder. Even the nation's top accounting, legal, and investment banking firms became fertile poaching grounds for start-ups in search of white-collar talent.

Within the traditional business world, those who stayed behind often were so shell-shocked by years of career insecurity, exhaustion, and demoralization that they lacked the energy and self-confidence to seek their fortunes elsewhere. One man who left the merger-wracked world of commercial banking to start his own Internet company called to tell me that he had run into several of his old colleagues at a New Year's party. "They're all hiding under their desks," is the way he put it. "Everyone's afraid of attracting attention. They're all counting the years until retirement and praying that they're going to be there to make it." With an employee profile like that (and rumors of more destabilizing mergers and layoffs to come), is it any wonder that many banks remained mired in mediocre results?

Yet banks were scarcely the only companies facing the prospect of toughening economic conditions in the new millennium with a very different—and far less reliable—workforce than that which had helped them weather the business crises of the late 1970s and early 1980s. Until recent years, large corporations could count on an ability to recruit, hire, and retain the best people that the United States' white-collar workforce could offer; they were besieged with qualified applicants.

But that is no longer the case. Whether the white-collar workers who now remain in the world of big business are burned out, stressed to their limits, or simply free from all workplace illusions and emotional attachments, they are not likely to make the kinds of sacrifices and extraordinary efforts that people once did when they cared about and identified with their employers. That should prove to be a huge handicap for big business, especially for those corporations that must now compete with smaller, more nimble business ventures whose staffers are motivated by stock options and the thrill of creating something new and different. When business leaders learn how much it can cost, in tough times, to buy a substitute for employee loyalty, they may learn to regret its absence.

But they have more to regret as well. By the turn of the century, the combined impact of all those layoffs in good times and bad, never-ending benefit cutbacks, insane levels of CEO compensation, and unrealistic bottom-line projections had tarnished corporate reputations across Main Street America. Big companies began to seem less worthy of respect as potential employers, as business neighbors, and, perhaps most significant, as investment opportunities.

One indication was the capital drain that quickly became even more pronounced among large corporations than the turn-of-the-century talent erosion. During ten single months between 1999 and 2000, Bank of America, Procter & Gamble, Coca-Cola, and seven other long-standing business leaders lost nearly $300 billion in market value as stock investors fled from them and other companies once viewed as the cornerstones of the U.S. economy. "What's an Old-Line CEO to Do?" asked one *BusinessWeek* headline, while noting, "Net-crazed investors sneer, no matter how sturdy the performance."[5] Declining share prices handicapped large-corporate executives in a variety of crucial ways: leaving them less capable of raising growth financing, less equipped to negotiate pricey strategic partnerships with other companies, and more vulnerable to outside takeover.

Executives outside the Internet loop complained that American investors had no interest in listening to their "stories." But the backlash from two decades' worth of "sweatshop" management practices—and the increasingly ineffective corporate spin campaigns that accompanied them—may have been partially responsible. That's because repeated rounds of layoffs and cutbacks eventually came to support an outside view, often quite accurate, of the large-corporate world as either out of control or out of ideas.

"I wonder sometimes," a marketing staffer at one of the weaker "Baby Bells" once told me, "if anyone here realizes that cutting costs down to zero doesn't add up to building a company with a future. Does anyone actually know the difference?" Investors may be learning. And when they choose to take unparalleled new gambles on Internet and other entrepreneurial ventures, they do so in part because they have been taught to distrust many of the United States' biggest companies and the people who run them.

Talent flight and declining investment appeal are problems that likely will compound at large workplaces across corporate America. After all, lower stock prices translate into less appealing compensation packages and thus weaker managements and skilled-manpower teams. Or they require companies to pay higher outright salaries in order to compete in a tight employment marketplace, pushing operating costs skyward. Both trends, already apparent by early 2000, fueled continued downward pressures on share prices.

During the 1990s, William Heffernan wrote a novel called *The Dinosaur Club*, about a downsized executive who carried out a revenge fantasy against his former employer. Many people identified with the scenario.[6] Yet by the beginning of the twenty-first century, it began to seem as though the United States' large old-line companies might turn out to be the real dinosaurs of the new economy.

Strategies to Reverse Deteriorating Job Conditions

The culture of overwork, extreme stress, and underreward is not yet inescapable. There are still large and successful companies that conduct business the "old-fashioned" way: building revenue and bottom-line growth by creating new products, services, or markets, rather than simply by buying results through mergers or acquisitions. They recognize that there is more to achieving profitability than cutting payroll and benefit costs and ratcheting up demands on overloaded staffers.

At companies like these, top executives value their so-called stakeholders (another word for employees) as highly as they do their investors and customers. Management efforts are directed at achieving key gains for all groups, because their leaders hold fast to the once-traditional notion that a corporation's long-term stability and future prospects depend upon a healthy triumvirate.

Are they altruistic institutions? Hardly. Most of these corporations remain convinced that benign workplace practices pay off in tangible and profitable ways, which run the gamut from reducing turnover and employee training costs to helping them keep unions out of the workplace (a goal that once motivated many companies to boost benefits and job conditions, especially during the early post-World War II decades). Their leaders care about productivity, the same way other business executives do. The difference is, they believe people will be more productive when they are permitted—

indeed encouraged—to lead well-rounded lives rather than simply pressed to work harder.

A group of well-tested strategies carried out by companies like these suggest that the United States' business community, stock markets, and larger economy could all thrive if more balanced and humane work policies and practices were incorporated into current management strategies. Before widespread improvements can occur, however, the nation's corporate leaders will need to rethink some of their long-held assumptions about work time.

One reason white-collar "sweatshop" practices spread like wild-fire throughout the 1980s and 1990s is that most business executives put in a lot of hours on their jobs and saw nothing wrong (in fact, everything right) with their employees doing the same. When new corporate challenges arise, such as increased market threats from foreign competitors or e-commerce ventures, only one option seems viable to them: work harder and longer. They're locked in a mind-set that tells them that the more hours their staffers spend on the jobs (preferably at the office, but at home if necessary), the better off the company will be. Not only do they accept this without question, they assume that the benefits of overwork are endless, that the more-hours/better-results equation is without limits.

In fact, the opposite may be true. There are numerous examples of U.S. companies that switched their overseas operations to shorter workweeks without suffering productivity or profitability losses. Packard-Bell even increased results by 30 percent in its French division when it readjusted jobs to accommodate the nation's new thirty-five-hour-workweek policy.[7]

Yet as Jeremy Rifkin noted in his *The End of Work*, despite similar experiences at companies that include Hewlett-Packard and Digital Equipment, "most American CEOs remain steadfastly opposed to the idea. A survey of 300 business leaders, conducted several years ago, soliciting their support for a shorter week did not receive a single positive response. One Fortune 500 CEO wrote back: 'My view of the world, our country, and our country's needs, is dramatically opposite of yours. I cannot image a shorter workweek. I can imagine a longer one . . . if America is to be competitive in the first half of the next century.'"[8]

During an era in which the U.S. economy was the indisputable world leader, work-less proposals struck many executives as somewhere between unrealistic and unpatriotic. With people like these at the helm of many corporations, corporate staffers have found themselves with no choice except to put in fifty, sixty, or more hours of work each week if they want to hold on to their jobs, let alone win promotions. But tight labor conditions, increased competition from entrepreneurial ventures, and the havoc played by a volatile stock market all may increase the pressure on chief executives to try a different approach toward time management. And if they decide to do so, there are a variety of models worth exploring, any of which would go a long way toward reducing excessive work and stress loads.

One approach would be for companies to mandate shorter workweeks. On Wall Street and throughout high-paced sectors such as technology, the decision simply to establish a forty-hour policy— and, more important, to enforce it—would give many employees back half of their lives to spend as *they*, and not their employers, choose. Some, the old-style workaholics, might not want the gift and might even look for employment elsewhere if they cannot find ways to subvert the new system. But if years' worth of employee surveys about overwork and job stress suggest anything, it is that many more people would welcome the change.

The software manufacturer SAS Institute took an aggressive approach to this strategy, with remarkable results. The company limited its full-time employees, including its chief executive, to a thirty-five-hour workweek, going so far as to shut down its switchboard at 5 P.M. and locking its main gate an hour later. And results did not suffer; in fact, sales grew at a double-digit rate for two decades. In addition, according to a Stanford Business School study, "not only did the company save tens of millions of dollars each year because its turnover rate was a fraction of the industry average, but it also gained by having more alert, less error-prone programmers."[9]

The decision to limit work hours can help improve conditions, of course, only if managers likewise agree to set reasonable productivity goals for individual workers and their departments. Many of the corporate world's most egregious offenders when it comes to employee overwork have work-time policies that sound perfectly manageable, at least on paper. When demands are too high, no one takes these policies seriously.

There's every reason to assume that a company willing to enforce a forty-hour week will *not* experience a decline in results comparable to the decrease in hours worked. But it's hard to know exactly what will happen, especially at first. So before killing the experiment by setting unrealistic goals, large businesses that explore this route will need to proceed cautiously: collecting information about the impact of shorter workweeks upon productivity, job turnover, and related costs before establishing appropriate new workloads and standards.

For those companies that balk at making workforce-wide time reductions, other strategies may help. Some large companies have tried a new concept called "work redesign." As the *Wall Street Journal* described it, "this bottom-up strategy demands that any gains in time or efficiency be shared with employees, usually by giving them more control over their work or more flexibility in hours." At Hewlett-Packard, BankAmerica, and the accounting firm Deloitte & Touche, all of which tested the technique, small groups of employees were allowed to reconstruct their own schedules, in part to give themselves more control over work flow and personal time.[10]

But even efforts like these are doomed to failure unless corporate leaders commit to nurturing real cultural changes in the ways that people within their organizations think about (and value) time. Conditions cannot be improved when companies offer job-redesign opportunities or flexible work arrangements but then subtly undermine the programs, as many do, by penalizing anyone who chooses to get off the overwork track (whether through bad performance evaluations, lower raises, fewer promotions, or lost benefits). Chief executives must believe—and then persuade their managers to act upon the notion—that quality personal time can raise an employee's productivity and improve the company's bottom line as surely as work time does.

Ah yes, personal time. It is a scarce and valuable commodity for the occupants of today's white-collar "sweatshops": people mourn its absence in the form of shorter vacation schedules, fewer holidays, lost personal days, and shrinking potential for sick days. Any company that truly seeks to improve conditions for its employees must find ways to give them more paid time off.

Here again, corporate managers need to overcome their preconceptions (this time, the ones that convince them that all manpower-related expenditures are bad and should be cut whenever and wherever possible). Vacation and personal days can accomplish wonders when it comes to reinvigorating stressed or exhausted men and women. When these benefits are cut back, as increasingly has been the case at big businesses across the country, angry and hurt staffers attach a symbolic value to lost days that can have a powerful impact, both eroding workplace relations and lowering productivity.

It does not cost much to add some enhancements in this area, whether in terms of a few more holidays and personal days, or expanded vacation schedules for longer-tenured employees. Some companies have won workplace brownie points even for instituting cost-free improvements, as when First Union created a paid-time-off bank (which lumped together people's sick days, vacations, and holidays and gave them more latitude about how and when to use them). Various studies suggest that corporate savings from changes like these may far outweigh their costs. According to one, conducted by the American Management Association, those companies that gave their employees "a life" by improving paid-time-off policies reported greater success in retaining staffers during tight labor conditions even than those that had offered them more cash.[11]

Benefit Enhancements That Can Pay Off

If harsh workplace conditions are to be alleviated, the balance between work time and personal time must be shifted, at least for all those white-collar staffers that desire it. But there are other types of changes—mainly on the benefit front—that could also produce real improvements in the lives of today's harried white-collar workers.

The erosion of health care plans and employee pensions has been widespread in all kinds of workplaces across the nation, but the time may finally have come for enlightened employers, or dissatisfied employees, to draw a line in the sand. For most executives, the very notion of spending more money to improve the quality of benefit packages seems a heresy. But here again, they are blinded by preconceptions (for instance, the idea that employee benefits are too costly and cushy). The big question in most business leaders' minds is not whether to cut back but by how much and how quickly.

That strategy is penny-wise and pound-foolish. Large companies are shrinking key benefits—and thus exacerbating their manpower problems—at the same time that four out of five corporate executives believe that the ability to attract and retain high-quality people is what will give companies the competitive edge in the coming decade.[12] It doesn't make sense. For big businesses that find themselves struggling to hold on to skilled employees, benefits offer an arena in which they could outperform entrepreneurial companies with relative ease (since they can purchase group insurance policies and administer retirement plans with far greater cost efficiencies).

As of now, unfortunately, there aren't too many corporate models for this strategy. Some large companies have plans that are less problematic than other companies' offerings, but few can boast of benefit packages that are not significantly worse than those they provided five, let alone ten, years ago. One exception again is SAS Institute, which, among other things, operates a free health care clinic for its employees. (Luxurious as that may seem, the company calculated in 1998 that its $1 million cost was actually about $500,000 cheaper than the price of providing traditional insurance for its 2,700 employees.)[13]

Companies need not go that far in order to make real improvements in their benefit packages. Rather than opting for bare-bones HMO plans, as many do, they could pay a bit more for other insurance options that would give employees the ability to consult doctors of their own choice so long as they are willing to shoulder a greater share of the fees. Whenever cash flow is strong enough to support it—as clearly was the case for many companies during the latter half of the 1990s—health care packages should be enhanced incrementally (by adding back dental or vision care, raising reimbursement levels, or reducing deductibles, to name a few possibilities). Meanwhile, corporations could make life easier for employees simply by deciding to switch insurance carriers less frequently than many now do.

In an era like this one, in which technological advancements create countless new opportunities while changing all the rules inside and outside the workplace, companies need to chart a course that can enhance their workers's lives as well as the bottom line. Ford and Delta came up with a benefit scheme that deserves emulation: providing inexpensive home computers and Internet access to employees throughout their organizations.[14] Again, there was a corporate as well as an employee payoff, since the companies stood to benefit from technologically savvier staffers, as well as reduced communication costs and hopefully lower turnover.

Even more important, companies can and should resist the temptation to monitor every keystroke that gets tapped or e-mail message that gets sent or received within the workplace. Their staffers deserve some respect and privacy—and in all likelihood, the vast majority will not abuse their employers' trust by spending workdays sending pornographic messages and electronically shopping until they drop. Employees also deserve (and will look for, within a tight labor market) companies that opt for workforce-friendly practices, such as the use of ergonomically correct furniture and the scheduling of frequent computer breaks, instead of relying upon new technologies simply to speed up results.

Then there's the pension issue. The brouhaha over IBM's switch to a "cash balance" pension plan suggests that if there is one single issue that has the potential to mobilize white-collar workers to fight back, it's the assault upon their retirement benefits. Indeed, by spring of the year 2000, disgruntled employees at Bell Atlantic, Duke Power, and SmithKline Beecham had followed their "Big Blue" brethren by setting up their own websites to educate fellow staffers about pensions and unite against cutbacks.[15]

Large companies could stand out from the pack—and increase their employment appeal—by taking a couple of fairly simple steps. The obvious one is to avoid pension switches or to introduce them so gradually that only new employees will be affected. (Actually, that might be in everyone's best interest, since cash-balance pensions really do seem to be better for younger people.) Those businesses with 401K retirement plans could make these more attractive by raising the level of corporate contributions.

The high-tech world's experience also suggests a powerful potential payoff from spreading a company's stock and options throughout the workforce, instead of only among top executives, as is often the case in large "low-tech" corporations. It might seem strange, at first glance, to suggest that businesses try to alleviate their own workplace problems by adopting a strategy that often accompanies abusive management practices at technology companies, at least when it comes to overworking and stressing employees. But there's nothing intrinsic to the notion of broad employee stock ownership that *requires* corporations to make staffers suffer for the financial reward.

One recent survey of the best corporations to work for in the United States found, in fact, that almost one third of them boasted a significant level of employee ownership: at least 10 percent through practices that ran the gamut from profit-sharing plans, ESOPs (employee stock ownership plans), to comprehensive option packages.[16] The companies that made the list included Southwest Airlines, Whole Foods, Hallmark, and A. G. Edwards. But even for those that did not, it's likely that their employment appeal was stronger within a tight labor market than that of many other corporations, especially for all the white-collar workers who fantasize about one day collecting their own version of the "Microsoft millionaire"'s payoff.

Employee ownership of options or stocks can translate into greater personal productivity, increased emotional attachment to the workplace, and reduced job turnover. But for executives hesitant to give the strategy a try, there is another advantage worth considering: companies with significant employee ownership stakes often outperform others in key stock market measures. According to one recent study, corporations that set up ESOPs averaged nearly 7 percent higher shareholder returns during the first four years after making the switch than all other publicly traded companies. Their annual returns on assets were also significantly higher.[17]

As with other employee-friendly policies, stock ownership offers a range of benefits for the corporate world that outweigh any initial costs; as a motivational tool, it may even outperform the harsh techniques to which many managers have grown accustomed. From the perspective of even the most bottom-line-obsessed executive, let alone working men and women of all ages and professions, it's a path out of the "sweatshop" that makes sense.

Restoring Trust and Workforce Ties

There is one final step that large corporations must take if they are to repair the damage caused by two decades' worth of harsh and inequitable management techniques. And that is to restore the confidence and respect they have lost among the nation's white-collar community.

Many approaches could help, so long as the companies adopting them were consistent about the messages they conveyed to the outside world and their employees, as well as the courses of action they followed. But that does not mean that success is guaranteed. Few top executives recognize, I believe, the extent of the animosity and distrust with which they—and their corporations—are now viewed.

Layoff policies are an obvious place to start for organizations that want to heal the breach: there may be no greater or more terrifying symbol of the lean-and-mean management practices of the 1980s and 1990s. Layoffs generate enormous anger, especially among white-collar staffers who believe they have become a blunt instrument of first rather than last resort among executives eager to blame anyone other than themselves for inadequate results. While people's increasing vulnerability to job loss undoubtedly encourages this perspective, the frequency with which layoffs now occur—and the matter-of-factness with which they are often greeted by the media and stock markets—reinforces the popular notion that these have become part of business-as-usual among large corporations.

Such cynicism can only be alleviated if top executives stop trying to spin layoffs as some kind of brilliant management decision and instead accept responsibility for whatever it was that, under their watch, produced conditions so disastrous as to necessitate mass firings. Forthrightness might help build credibility among white-collar employees and investors, especially if managers also displayed a commitment to resisting layoffs in all but the most unavoidable circumstances.

Jack Stack, the chief executive of Springfield Remanufacturing Corporation, has been noteworthy for his critique of current practices. "I have no patience with CEO's who make excuses for layoffs, who say they're cutting jobs only to make the company more competitive in the future, to protect the interests of shareholders, to avoid bigger layoffs down the road, or whatever. . . . Layoffs are a sign of management failure," he wrote in *Inc.* magazine. "You lay people off when you've screwed up, when you've guessed wrong about the market, when you haven't anticipated some critical development or created adequate contingency plans." He added, "When downsizing is the only choice, it's a sign of how badly management has failed, and the people who get hurt are invariably those who had nothing to do with creating the problems in the first place."

Straight talk like that would help, especially in a business era in which many people in the executive suite have chosen instead to hide behind public relations experts and linguistic maneuvers (like turning a layoff into a RIF, which makes "reduction in force" sound nothing if not jazzy and upbeat). What would also help would be a serious commitment to retraining rather than firing employees when their positions become unnecessary. This practice was largely shunned during the past two decades, since bottom-line-obsessed managers typically preferred to fire higher-paid and older workers and, as necessary, replace them with cheaper young staffers or temps. But it makes sense, especially in a tight labor market: it usually costs less to retrain people (who can build upon their experience within a corporation) than to recruit new hires and start training from scratch.

Another way to rebuild employee relations would be to set limits on the use of contingent labor, which at most large corporations continues to rise with no end in sight. By the end of the 1990s, many white-collar men and women felt as vulnerable to the threat of contingency as they felt to layoffs; the temporary employees and consultants who worked with them, often side by side, were an incessant reminder that most full-time permanent positions were ripe targets for job "redefinition" by employers eager to minimize their workforce commitments and expenditures.

In this age of corporate hype, some executives might argue that they would like to be less reliant on temps but have little choice, given the constraints of a low-unemployment marketplace. For most companies, though, that's far from the case. If nothing else, many could fill their positions by offering full-time posts to some of the temporary employees who pass through them. (Surveys indicate that the majority of temps are eager to make the change.) Or they simply might decide to stay at current levels of usage, which in itself would have a positive impact, just so long as executives also committed themselves to resist further job redefinitions.

Although clearly in the minority, some companies have decided to pull back from the trend, arguing that excessive use of contingent labor hurts them, as well as their staffers, more than it helps. Ford Motor is a good example: during the mid-1990s, it concluded that the company had too many contingent employees involved with core operations and set goals for a workforce-wide reduction. Its reasons included "concern for workforce harmony. . . . [W]hen the number of contingent workers grows too large, workforce morale suffers."

Excessive cost was also a factor. "There can be an illusion of savings," according to one company executive, "when in fact, if you add it all up—the temporary agency fees, the costs of turnover and so forth—what you end up finding out is that you've actually spent more money than you thought you were spending. . . . The contingent worker can ultimately be more expensive than the regular employee."[18]

Another way that U.S. corporations could begin to restore their credibility within the white-collar community would be to cap compensation for chief executives, which has reached levels in recent years that go almost unimaginably beyond the norm in any other country and any other period of history. From most people's perspectives, it doesn't really matter whether that compensation takes the form of outright stock grants, options, cash bonuses, or deferred pay: the overall package adds up to a picture of unparalleled greed and self-interest among a favored group who receive outsized awards when times are good and usually get treated pretty well even when they're not.

There are, of course, exceptions: companies and chief executives who have attracted headlines not because of astronomical pay levels but because they have attempted to restore a semblance of sanity, even decency, to the process. Back in 1998, Pepsico's chairman, Roger A. Enrico, who was already well heeled from years at the top, asked his board of directors to create a scholarship fund for the children of "front-line employees," rather than paying him his $900,000 annual salary.[19] That same year, the chief executive of Reebok, Paul B. Fireman, declined a bonus of 50 percent of his salary offered to him by his board, because he felt that the company's flagging performance did not warrant it.[20]

Other corporations have tried to enforce some degree of accountability so that their chief executives would pay a tangible financial price, beyond the decline in the paper value of their option holdings, when results slumped. Eastman Kodak, for example, decided not to pay CEO George Fisher a bonus back in 1997, during a year in which the company reported huge losses and decided to lay off nearly twenty thousand people. (His bonus had added up to nearly $2 million the previous year.) But most efforts along these lines still consist of baby steps: Fisher may have lost his bonus, but he still received a $2 million salary that year, as well as a corporate gift of $1.82 million in interest forgiven on loans and $27,180 in life insurance premiums.[21]

Various strategies could help on this front. Paychecks could be set at lower levels or forgone entirely by those chief executives willing to bet their financial futures on the potential value of their stock options. There are a few precedents: one-dollar (or lower) salaries were paid to James Barksdale of Netscape Communications, Lee Iacocca of Chrysler, and Dennis Hendrix of Panhandle Eastern.[22] Bonuses could also be paid in stock options rather than cash.

But since equity ownership is what has tended to create the over-the-top payoffs for chief executives, especially during the 1990s, I would suggest that companies explore ways to set some fair but reasonable limits on this reward as well. One approach might be to institute something along the lines of an excise tax, which would require top executives who earned large rewards from company stock to share a small portion of their profits with employees, perhaps through contributions to a bonus pool. A 5 percent toll on Al Dunlap's $100 million compensation package at Scott Paper thus would have provided $5 million to be distributed among all those employees (who had accomplished their own extraordinary feats, within the most unpleasant of corporate environments, in order to help his downsizing campaign succeed).

Another strategy that would enforce compensation accountability would be to require CEOs who exercise stock options to escrow a large portion of their profits—let's say 50 percent—for a significant period of time, perhaps three years. If the company's performance remained strong during this period and its stock price continued to trade at least within the range of the option-exercise price, he or she could then withdraw the escrowed funds and keep them. But if years of huge compensation were then followed by stock declines and mixed corporate results (as happened with Disney's Michael Eisner by the end of the 1990s), escrowed compensation funds could be seized by corporate boards and then either reinvested in the company as a growth-capital infusion or distributed as a shareholder dividend and company-wide bonus if that seemed more constructive.

These proposals may seem utopian and unrealistic; however, I believe that some type of change is inevitable, given the enormous resentment that executive compensation has generated across Main Street America during the past two decades. Companies can have these changes forced upon them through increasingly popular techniques such as proxy battles from shareholders.[23] Or they can seize the initiative and use reform efforts as a bridge to restore relations with distrustful employees and investors.

Personal Strategies for Change

Large corporations may decide, of course, to make only cosmetic adjustments or none at all in the "sweatshop" management practices that took hold during the 1980s and 1990s. Fortunately, however, white-collar men and women have a host of strategies worth exploring, which could help to improve their own working conditions and perhaps even compel real change across corporate America.

On the most basic level, people have an ability to resist harsh and excessive demands—and this is true now more than ever, thanks to the difficulties employers face in finding skilled replacements in a limited labor market. Yet many corporate staffers prove to be their own worst enemy when it comes to their inability to "just say no": They want to seem hardworking and cooperative, not to convey a sense of their own limitations. Driven by the goal of getting—and staying—on their company's fast track (or at least a secure career path), they are afraid of doing anything that might call attention to themselves in a negative way.

Yet throughout the course of my research, I heard stories from men and women about small victories that had had a real impact on their work lives. There were people who refused to carry beepers or cell phones; business travelers who made it a practice to stop work each night at 5 P.M.; commuters who never let anything get in the way of whatever train would get them home for the dinner hour. Some refused to buy personal computers or fax machines for their homes because they feared an intrusion from the office; others kept high-tech equipment in their children's bedrooms and denied its existence to their managers.

I am convinced that more people have the ability to assert limits like these than try to do so. But that doesn't mean that setting—and sticking to—workplace controls is simple. "There's tremendous social pressure to do the whole '24/7' thing," Alvin, a mid-level manager at Citigroup, told me, while noting proudly that he himself had been able to resist it. "I always cast myself as an outsider, someone who was going to carve out his own path. So I was able to keep myself to a pretty reasonable workday—probably 9 to 6 most of the time."

For those people whose employers simply will not tolerate a deviation from overwork norms, there's never been a better time to look for a new job, with the goal of finding one very different from their last. Bobbi, a financial staffer who had been laid off by Levi Strauss just weeks before I interviewed her, sounded an upbeat note. "My work life was so stressful. The amount of problems that I dealt with, every single day, was so enormous." She paused, then added, "Now, when I interview with prospective employers, I keep in mind the idea that I've got to be much more selfish and aggressive about getting what I want."

Unlike former colleagues who had lost jobs during Levi's earlier layoffs (when unemployment levels were higher and good jobs tougher to get), Bobbi felt confident that she had plenty of options. She planned to insist upon a checklist of demands before accepting any new post. These included the ability to work at home a couple of days each week on a high-powered computer system that she would expect her new employer to provide; she also wanted a commitment that would limit her business travel. "I've learned that salary just isn't the only thing that matters about a job," she concluded. "Even if you're earning a decent salary, what does it matter if you've got so much job stress that you can't enjoy anything?"

For people who want to change more than merely their jobs, there are also a number of promising alternatives. White-collar workers have traditionally resisted efforts at unionization. But there may be signs of change on this front, after two decades of layoffs and benefit cutbacks that have taught men and women on all rungs of the job ladder just how vulnerable they are as individuals, rather than members of a collective. When AT&T and Southern New England Telephone made changes in their pension plans, for example, their unionized blue-collar workers wound up with far better deals than managers and other non-unionized staffers did.[24]

For years now, the air traffic controller strike of the 1980s loomed as a symbol of the failure of the United States' white-collar union movement. But that image has been supplanted by the success of the more than fifteen thousand Boeing professionals who conducted a forty-day strike during the early months of the millennium because they were dissatisfied with wage-and-benefit offers that failed to match those made by the company to their unionized colleagues. Their victory included raises averaging 15 percent over three years, greater input into the management of the company, and the withdrawal of plans to make them pay more for their health insurance coverage—all concessions that are vital to the interests of white-collar workers.[25] This victory may inspire people at companies far beyond Boeing to give collective bargaining a chance.

Some people are already thinking in this direction. "I have gone so far as to opine," a senior manager at one the nation's largest banks told me during the Boeing strike, "that ten years from now the entire financial service sector will be unionized. Banks have backtracked on all the things they once did to keep unions out. And people are angry." In an economic environment in which even the American Medical Association has decided that it makes sense to organize doctors (at least those who are salaried employees of HMOs and hospital corporations), anything seems possible.[26]

One unforeseen consequence of harsh new management styles has been the invigoration of the white-collar union movement, most especially in the overworked high-tech sector. When IBM's disgruntled employees launched their Internet assault on the company's proposed pension cutbacks, the Communications Workers of America quickly hyperlinked its website to the group's and launched an electronic survey of working conditions at the company.[27] The AFL-CIO, meanwhile, has established Silicon Valley as an important target, with recent campaigns including one to improve conditions for temporary staffers, including secretaries, software testers, and bookkeepers.[28]

Other unions have gotten involved in white-collar issues in different ways. A coalition including 9to5, National Association for Working Women, as well as the AFL-CIO and some of the now-renowned permatemps from Microsoft launched a public relations and legislative drive in early 2000 to try to win limits to corporate America's use of contingent labor. United Airlines' unions (which together owned 60 percent of the company's stock) forced what may prove to be a landmark concession upon management: tying a portion of top-executive compensation to employee satisfaction levels, as measured by an independent survey firm.[29]

Despite the stresses of today's white-collar "sweatshops," some men and women—perhaps many—may continue to find the notion of joining a union incompatible with their self-perceived status in the employment marketplace. For them, there are other ways to unify: most effectively perhaps through the Internet. When I inter-viewed one of the founders of FACEIntel, the lobbying group com-posed of past and present employees of the high-tech company, he singled out the Internet as his greatest hope for change.

"What makes it possible for us to communicate, the only thing that brings you and I together, is the Internet," he told me during an early conversation that took place in 1997. "We don't have many resources. We don't have backing. But through the Internet, I have heard from many people at other corporations, as well as Intel." The group's extensive website attracted attention from men and women working in a wide range of industries and a surprising number of for-eign nations, as well as across the United States. It also brought FACEIntel in contact with journalists covering the high-tech world and work-related issues.

Like much else that relates to cyberspace, this trend is evolving. Websites clearly can be effective rallying devices, especially when organized around hot topics such as benefit cutbacks. When dis-gruntled employees at Bell Atlantic set up a chat room to discuss the company's cash-balance pension plan, they generated such an outpouring of complaints that they ultimately forced the company to negotiate a compromise with long-tenured employees, offering them the opportunity to keep a modified traditional pension instead. What was most amazing about this achievement was that the company had made the pension switch two years earlier—but back then, without the involvement of the Internet, few people understood its significance or believed they had a chance to fight back.[30]

Less successful, at least so far, has been the use of e-mail in resist-ing workplace downgrades. The medium offers all kinds of advan-tages for white-collar workers who want to organize in one way or another (including postage savings and ease of communication). But corporations are fighting hard to resist the trend. FACEIntel origi-nally used company-wide e-mailings to publicize its cause, but Intel sucessfully sued to prevent this, invoking common law concerning trespass. The case is currently under appeal. Other corporations, including Pratt & Whitney, have taken steps to block e-mail mes-sages from unions.

This battle is likely to continue for some time, with employees and unions struggling to find legally acceptable ways to make e-mails work for them. After all, as Michael Blain, of Washtech, an affiliate of the Communications Workers of America that is trying to organize software employees in the state of Washington, explained to a journalist, "It saves time. It saves money. We can reach 1,300 people by just hitting 'send.'"[31]

A New Kind of Investor Activism

Money is another weapon white-collar men and women can use to lobby for the alleviation of harsh management techniques. That's because even the most egregious of offenders—those companies whose management styles depend upon abusive levels of overwork, stress, layoffs, cutbacks, electronic surveillance, and any other "squeezing" technique they can come up with—all depend upon Main Street Americans, whether to buy their products or services or to invest in their stocks. If people chose to withhold their dollars from companies that mistreated them (or others like them), they could force real changes in the rewards and demands of the work-place.

This hasn't exactly been a popular strategy so far. Consumer boy-cotts, few and far between, have tended to center on the plight of the lowest-paid workers; current campaigns against companies such as Disney and Nike focus on their use of traditional sweatshop labor through overseas contractors. No one has yet attempted to rally consumers to protest the harsh conditions affecting white-collar workers. But this could change, especially given the Internet's abil-ity to publicize all kinds of workplace problems and initiatives.

Most individual investors likewise have overlooked white-collar issues, whether they make their investment decisions directly (through stock purchases) or indirectly (through the choice of mutu-al funds in which they place their personal savings or retirement funds). "We're all devouring ourselves," is the way that Marty, an art designer at one of the nation's largest publishing companies, assessed this trend. "We all own stock, and as stockholders, all we care about is profits. So we're the ones who are encouraging the con-ditions that make our work lives so awful."

So long as the stock market was rising with no end in sight, many people were uninterested in changing their perspective. Ben, the former savings-and-loan banker whom I interviewed during more than a year of his unemployment, dismissed my suggestion that people could use their investments to fight the very practices that had defeated him. "When I put on my hat as an investor, all I care about is, am I worth more today that I was yesterday," he told me. "I don't really care about Coca-Cola's employees. I care about its stock price."

But the business world has shifted since Ben made these statements to me back in 1997. Three years later—although he was employed—his paycheck was still significantly lower than it had been at his bank job; many of his investments had been sold, meanwhile, in order to maintain his family's standard of living. And the stock market now gave new meaning to the word "volatility." Even Ben's corporate icon, Coca-Cola, was in trouble, with worldwide losses, a depressed stock price, and the shocking layoff of one fifth of the company's global workforce.[32] It was now easier for Ben, and people like him, to recognize larger problems within the current business-world order, as well as a pressing need for change.

Given the breadth of opportunities within the investment universe, I believe that people could use their savings and retirement dollars to punish negative workplace practices, without suffering a financial setback. The model already exists in the socially responsible investment movement. The Domini Social Equity Mutual Fund, Pax World Fund, and Citizens Global Equity Fund Family all outperformed the S&P 500 index by multiyear measurements while screening for stocks that complied with environmental, antiviolence, health-oriented, or other goals.[33] There's no reason why other funds could not achieve similar results by likewise choosing only those companies that treat staffers like "stakeholders."

Some mutual funds have begun paying attention, if only broadly, to workplace issues. One study of 275 portfolio managers found that a company's ability to attract and retain talented employees ranked fifth among thirty-nine factors they relied upon when deciding which stocks to buy or sell.[34] Since new mutual funds keep starting up (often in response to perceived unsatisfied desires on the part of the investing public), more movement in this direction is likely to occur if people begin to express a desire to find funds that would avoid investing in companies that conducted layoffs, benefit cutbacks, electronic surveillance of employees, or other negative practices.

Mutual funds could accomplish a great deal in this regard. But an even greater source of financial-lobbying strength is the nation's enormous pension-fund bloc. As Jeremy Rifkin pointed out in *The End of Work*, the pension funds that manage the retirement savings of corporate and public employees account for "74 percent of net individual savings, over one-third of all corporate equities, and nearly 40 percent of all corporate bonds. Pension funds hold nearly one-third of the total financial assets of the U.S. economy."[35] During the 1980s and to a large extent the 1990s, many pension funds invested their dollars in companies whose bottom-line results were tied to harsh new management practices, whether related to merger-driven layoffs, technology-related downsizings, or even pension cutbacks.

But real change is taking place on this front. As the *Wall Street Journal* reported, the Council of Institutional Investors, a group of ninety-four pension funds that between them controlled $1 trillion in stock holdings, used a recent annual meeting to discuss "good workplace practices and how institutional investors can encourage their use."[36]

By spring 2000, the potential power behind those words was apparent: the California Public Employees Retirement System, known as Calpers, announced plans to vote its 9.2 million shares of IBM stock in support of a shareholder resolution that would require the company to give all of its 145,000 U.S. workers the right to hold on to their traditional pension plans if they didn't want to get switched to a cash-balance plan. (It was yet another indication of the power of that Internet site!)

Calpers president, William Crist, noted that he supported the resolution "because withdrawing promised benefits for any employee is not only morally reprehensible, it's plain bad business."[37] Where Calpers goes, other pension funds undoubtedly will follow. And as lobbying efforts succeed against pension cutbacks—right now the most visible focus of white-collar discontent—pension funds, socially responsible mutual funds, and other motivated investors may gain the confidence and motivation to target other workplace issues as well.

Is Improvement in Sight?

Four years after beginning this project, I conclude it with more optimism than I often imagined possible.

There were times early on when I felt as though the ever more difficult and demanding management practices that I was focusing upon were unstoppable in a world in which a company's stock could skyrocket simply upon the news that "Rambo" Al Dunlap had been hired to slash and burn his way through its workforce.

Again and again I heard stories that left me wondering whether my contemporaries had been overworked and stressed for so long that they had lost all sense of balance, let alone a vision of what a better work life could be. (What if they didn't even *know* that they were working under awful conditions, I asked myself, like the Wall Street executive who told me that he had no regrets about the holidays he had spent at the office—which included all holidays—although he did feel bad about having been forced to close an investment banking deal at the last minute, rather than attend his brother's wedding.) Maybe it was too late for change.

While writing my book, I kept hearing a popular radio advertisement, run by a job-search website warning people that they had only two choices in today's fast-changing workplaces: to become "distinct or extinct." Was I the only person, I wondered, whose heart pounded every time I heard the implicit threat behind the sales pitch?

For years it seemed easier to see signs of the relentless encroachment of work upon personal life than to point to significant improvements. People began giving me business cards that included not only their office phone numbers, office fax numbers, cell phone numbers, and e-mail address but also their home phone numbers, home fax numbers, and sometimes even personal e-mail addresses. At first, I felt guilty about even receiving these cards: wasn't I encouraging declining working conditions simply by accepting one? I finally compromised by accepting the cards, copying the office numbers onto a new Rolodex card, and then discarding the originals.

And yet, I conclude these pages with optimism.

With the weakening of the stock market, the accumulated effect of years' worth of deteriorating workplace conditions, and—if only symbolically—the downsizing of Al Dunlap, the "sweatshop" corporation no longer seems invincible. In the new millennium, white-collar Americans have begun voting with their feet and their pocketbooks. They don't like what they see in many large old-line corporations: whether it's a lack of new ideas, institutional cruelty, the vast gap between employee cutbacks and skyrocketing CEO compensation, or simply the unmistakable aroma of shrinking opportunities.

For a while, corporate men and women were blindsided by the negative workplace changes that were taking place around them. They were loyal; they so identified with their employers that they could not imagine work life without them; they deluded themselves about their value to their organizations; or they were scared to leave the large-corporate cocoon. Feelings like these made them easy prey for bottom-line-obsessed managers who believed, whether they chose to put it this way or not, that the only way to achieve results in the lean-and-mean 1980s and 1990s was to squeeze people dry and toss them out.

Those conditions are gone. And although many white-collar workers have changed because they had to—rather than wanted to—they are no longer unprepared to fight back. By the end of my research, many people told me proudly that they kept the phone numbers of a couple of headhunters on their Rolodexes or regularly visited employment websites. Some kept hidden files documenting their managers' errors so that they would have ammunition to fight back with if and when the time came for them to be downsized. Meanwhile, men and women I never would have imagined working for a small company or start-up contemplated making the switch; as they told me, their work lives could not get any riskier than they already were.

With the evolution of the Internet, the involvement of white-collar unions, and, perhaps most important, the support of major players in the investment community, white-collar workers were no longer isolated targets or helpless victims of a harsh new work world. Change seemed possible, even inevitable.

Perhaps, one day, I will try to interview someone after 5 P.M. and will be told that our conversation needs to wait until the next morning. I won't complain.

NOTES

Introduction: The Best of All Possible Worlds of Work?

1. Since most of the men and women I interviewed for *White-Collar Sweatshop* were, and still are, employed by the companies whose management and employment practices they described to me, I have taken steps to protect their confidentiality. These include, in all instances, changing their names; I have also disguised their job titles, departments, or personal characteristics in cases where these details might betray their identities. Likewise, I have omitted employers' names when specific anecdotes might place one of my sources in employment jeopardy. I have not changed people's quotes, however, nor have I altered their descriptions or anecdotes in any substantive manner.

2. One typical example: Carl Quintanilla, "Scenes from the *Insane* Job Market of '98: College Recruiting Becomes Lavish," *Wall Street Journal*, June 4, 1998, B1. According to an accompanying sidebar, "Now *THIS* is a job market," 63 percent of companies surveyed said that job candidates had the "upper hand" in negotiating for salary and benefits; 88 percent reported a shortage of qualified job candidates.

3. Louis Uchitelle, "Signing Bonus Now a Fixture Farther Down the Job Ladder," *New York Times*, June 10, 1998, A1.

4. Nina Munk, "The New Organization Man," *Fortune*, March 16, 1998 (on-line edition).

5. The Bureau of Labor Statistics (BLS) reports that in 1999 the average total size of the U.S. workforce was 133,488,000. Figuring out exactly how many of those workers fit the category "white-collar" isn't simple: the term itself is no longer officially in use, since the United States changed its job-category terminology with the Census of 1980. The BLS's last recorded use of the term was in 1982, when it reported 53,470,000 white-collar workers, out of a total 99,526,000-person

workforce. For the purposes of this book, it makes sense to combine two large job categories currently tracked by the bureau: managerial and professional specialty, of which there were 40,467,000, and technical, sales, and administrative support, at 38,921,000, as of 1999.

6. "It's the Best of Times—or Is It?," *BusinessWeek*, January 12, 1998, 35, reported that "[d]espite a robust economy, plenty of companies plan to downsize." Citing statistics from Challenger, Gray & Christmas, *BusinessWeek* noted that corporate downsizings had remained brisk throughout the then-seven years of the United States' economic expansion, with 1997's cuts occurring across major industry lines, including retail, industrial goods, financial, automotive, and aerospace/defense.

7. "New Era: New Economy Downsizing Defined," a press release issued by Challenger, Gray & Christmas, April 14, 2000.

Chapter 1: "The Pace Was Insane"

1. For more on the nature of this emotional attachment, see Charles C. Heckscher's study of mid-management employees at some corporations that experienced significant changes during the 1980s and 1990s, *White-Collar Blues: Management Loyalties in an Age of Corporate Restructuring* (New York: Basic Books, 1994). On page 34 he noted: "Middle managers in general—the overwhelming majority in my sample—*want to be loyal.* They want a community that goes beyond short-term performance and reward, that nurtures and supports, to which they can devote themselves. Though I myself, like many researchers before me, often felt the demands of the corporation on the individual to be excessive, I rarely heard this complaint from the managers themselves."

2. Juliet B. Schor, *The Overworked American: The Unexpected Decline of Leisure* (New York: Basic Books, 1992), 1. One remarkable aspect of the trend Schor reports on is that it runs counter to an earlier historical pattern in which hours of work declined gradually for Americans from the mid-nineteenth through the mid-twentieth century. "It was projected that economic progress would yield steady reductions in working time," she noted. "By today, it was estimated that we could have either a twenty-two-hour week, a six-month workyear, or a standard retirement age of thirty-eight" (p. 4).

3. These results are drawn from the Bureau of Labor Statistics' Current Population Survey (CPS) for 1999.

4. Based on CPS results for 1999, 57 percent of those working forty-nine to fifty-nine hours weekly were between twenty-five and forty-four years of age; of those working sixty or more hours, 56 percent fell into this age bracket.

5. Advertisements ran during 1999 in publications that included the *Wall Street Journal* and *The New Yorker*.

6. Rosabeth Moss Kanter, "Nice Work If You Can Get It: The Software Industry as a Model for Tomorrow's Jobs," *American Prospect*, no. 23 (Fall 1995): 52–59 (http://epn.org/prospect/23/23kant.html).

7. Daniel Q. Haney, "We're Working More and We're Not Happy About It," *Sun-Sentinel*, January 23, 1999, 13A.

8. Donna St. George, "The Incredible Shrinking Meal," *New York Times*, April 16, 1997, C1.

9. William L. Hamilton, "Power Lunch Is 2 in a Row, Just New York Minutes Each," *New York Times*, November 11, 1997, A1.

10. Witold Rybczynski, *Waiting for the Weekend* (New York: Penguin Books, 1992), 230.

11. Douglas A. Blackmon, "FedEx Delivers Sunday Punch for Expanding Workweek," *Wall Street Journal*, April 13, 1998, B4.

12. Schor, 32–33.

13. Thomas Goetz, "Hurry Up and Relax: The 24-Hour Vacation," *Wall Street Journal*, June 12, 1998, W1.

14. Survey results were quoted in Timothy D. Schellhardt, "Company Memo to Stressed-Out Employees: 'Deal with It,'" *Wall Street Journal*, October 2, 1996, B1.

15. American Management Association, "The Emotionally Charged Workplace," March 1995.

16. Cited in Alan Downs, *Corporate Executions: The Ugly Truth About Layoffs—How Corporate Greed Is Shattering Lives, Companies, and Communities* (New York: AMACOM, 1995), 201.

17. Cited in Schellhardt, B1.

18. George Bailey, "Manager's Journal: Fear Is Nothing to Be Afraid Of," *Wall Street Journal*, January 27, 1997, A22.

19. The Work Doctor (http://www.workdoctor.com), 1998.

20. L. M. Sixel, "Duking It Out in the Workplace: Office Fights More Frequent," *Houston Chronicle*, June 27, 1994, business section, 1.

21. Peter Coy, "Help! I'm a Prisoner in a Shrinking Cubicle," *BusinessWeek*, August 4, 1997, 40.

22. Neve Gordon, "The Cubicle-ization of the Workplace," *Chicago Tribune*, January 29, 1998, 19.

23. Cited in Charlene Marmer Solomon, "Stressed to the Limit," *Workforce*, September 1, 1999, 48.

24. Reported in Mike Snider, "Job Stress May Boost Cancer Risk," *USA Today*, August 30, 1993, 1A.

25. The study focused on nearly six hundred women who had graduated from Davis's law school during the years from 1969 to 1985. Cited in Jane E. Brody, "Health Watch: Women Under Stress," *New York Times*, June 11, 1997, C11.

26. Reported in AP, "Study Links Job Stress to Early-Birth Babies," *New York Times*, September 16, 1995, section 1, 47.

Chapter 2: "Working Three Times Harder and Earning Less"

1. These numbers are based upon pretax incomes and do not take account of capital gains from stock-related transactions. Cited in Gene Koretz, "Not Enough Is Trickling Down," *BusinessWeek,* January 31, 2000, 34.

2. Household debt levels increased by nearly 50 percent during the 1995–99 period, to a record level of $6.3 trillion. Cited in Gregory Zuckerman, "U.S. Boom: Living on Borrowed Dime?" *Wall Street Journal,* December 31, 1999, C1. By the end of the decade, the percentage of after-tax income saved by Americans dropped to its lowest on record, 1.5 percent. Cited in Yochi J. Dreazen, "Rate at Which Consumers Save Sinks to a Record," *Wall Street Journal,* February 1, 2000, A2.

3. Aaron Bernstein, Susan Jackson, and John Byrne, "Jack Cracks the Whip Again," *BusinessWeek,* December 15, 1997, 34.

4. See *1997 AMA Survey on Job Creation, Job Elimination and Downsizing* (New York: American Management Association, 1997). This membership survey conducted by the AMA found that 28 percent of respondents simultaneously eliminated and created jobs. In all, 41.1 percent of the AMA's surveyed firms reported job eliminations during 1997, while 19.0 percent reported actual "downsizings." Among these companies, the short-term benefits cited from cutbacks included increased operating profits (by 43.0 percent) and improved shareholder value (34 percent).

5. An analysis of business-cycle peaks (those years in which high corporate profitability could, at least in theory, best support wage and benefit improvements) helps document the declining reward structure for corporate employees. Back in 1979, "labor's share" of corporate income amounted to 82.6 percent; in 1989 it was 81.6 percent; by 1997 the figure had dropped to 78.4 percent. Lawrence Mishel, Jared Bernstein, and John Schmitt, *The State of Working America, 1998–1999* (Ithaca, N.Y.: ILR Press, 1999), 69.

6. Joseph B. White, " 'Next Big Thing': Re-engineering Gurus Take Steps to Remodel Their Stalling Vehicles," *Wall Street Journal,* November 26, 1996, A1. In its discussion of the personal problems caused by many reengineering campaigns is this report from one business analyst: "Companies are saying, 'Don't cut me any more.'"

7. The salary analysis that follows is drawn from statistical analysis by Mishel, Bernstein, and Schmitt, chapter 3, "Long-term Erosion and Growing Inequality," 118–218.

8. Expressed in 1997 dollars, that increase went from $11.64 to $13.21.

9. Robert Johnson and Paulette Thomas, "Christmas Bonus Goes Way of Organization Man," *Wall Street Journal,* December 22, 1999, A2.

10. Lester Thurow, "The Crusade That's Killing Prosperity," *American*

Prospect, no. 25 (March–April 1996): 54–59 (http://epn.org/prospect/25/25thur.html).

11. Back in 1975, 30 percent of all faculty at U.S. colleges and universities were part-time staffers; twenty years later, that figure had risen to 41 percent. Meanwhile, tenure rates declined, with 37 percent of postsecondary teachers having tenure in 1975, compared with 31 percent in 1995. These figures are cited by the American Association of University Professors, Washington, D.C., and drawn from surveys conducted by the National Center for Education Statistics.

12. Maria Mallory, Susan Brink, Katia Hetter, and David Fischer, "Professionals Feel the Heat," *U.S. News & World Report*, April 1, 1996, 44–48.

13. Although the effort has met with varying degrees of success, there was at least one two-year period during the decade, 1993–94, when the average income for all physicians declined by 3.6 percent, despite the United States' 2.6 percent inflation rate. "Socioeconomic Characteristics of Medical Practice," American Medical Association, New York, 1997.

14. Milo Geyelin, "Crossing the Bar: If You Think Insurers Are Tight, Try Being One of Their Lawyers," *Wall Street Journal*, February 9, 1999, A1.

15. White-collar workers as a whole earned 5 percent more during the first quarter of 1999 than they had a year earlier. For college-educated men, the year's increase was 5.2 percent; for their female counterparts, it was 2.7 percent. Jared Bernstein, "Real Median Wages Finally Recover 1989 Level," *Quarterly Wage and Employment Series*, vol. 1, table 1B (1999).

16. Patrick Barta, "Rises in Many Salaries Barely Keep Pace with Inflation," *Wall Street Journal*, February 1, 2000, A2.

17. Mishel, Bernstein, and Schmitt, 211.

18. Nina Munk, "The New Organization Man," *Fortune*, March 16, 1998 (on-line edition).

19. Mishel, Bernstein, and Schmitt, 161.

20. Ibid.

21. Cited in Gene Koretz, "Economic Trends: Gen-X Gets Short-changed," *BusinessWeek*, May 11, 1998, 24.

22. 1997 statistics cited from the Bureau of Labor Statistics' second biennial survey on contingent work in the United States. As one indication of how disproportional this statistic is, consider that only 13 percent of noncontingent jobs across the nation were held by those under twenty-five. Steven Hipple, "Contingent Work: Results from the Second Survey," *Monthly Labor Review*, November 1998.

23. Excerpted from http://www.disgruntled.com/temps.html, September 16, 1997.

24. The survey conducted by the International Society of Certified Employee Benefits Specialists was cited in Donald J. McNerney, "Contingent Workers," *HR Focus*, vol. 73, no. 10 (October 1996): 1.

25. That contrasted with only 12 percent of respondents in 1990. Helen Axel, "Contingent Employment," *HR Executive Review* (New York: Conference Board, 1995), vol. 3, no. 2.
26. Ibid.
27. Hipple, table 8, p. 29.
28. Their rate of multiple-job holding is 8.9 percent, compared to 6.7 percent for noncontingent workers. Ibid., p. 26.
29. Ibid., table 3, p. 25.
30. Jeremy Rifkin, *The End of Work: The Decline of the Global Labor Force and the Dawn of the Post-Market Era* (New York: G. P. Putnam's Sons, 1995), 193.
31. The Department of Labor (DOL) has been tracking this trend, on a biennial basis, since 1984. As defined by the Department of Labor, displaced workers are "persons aged 20 years and older who lost or left jobs because their plant or company closed or moved, there was insufficient work for them to do, or their position or shift was abolished." Cited in http://stats.bls.gov/newsrels.htm in a release dated August 19, 1998.
32. The DOL's survey looks at displacement and reemployment rates at two-year intervals, measuring among other things how many of those who were laid off managed to find full-time noncontingent positions during the same period. Since 1984, the full-time reemployment rate has averaged about 55 percent, although it dropped as low as 46.5 percent for those who were laid off during the 1981–83 recessionary period and 48.1 percent for the group displaced during the years 1989 through 1991.
33. A breakdown of this trend is revealing, since the typical salary impact of a layoff differs on a year-to-year basis but is invariably—and sometimes quite significantly—negative. According to the Bureau of Labor Statistics, the percent change in median weekly earnings for long-tenured displaced workers who became reemployed in full-time jobs ranges as follows: for those displaced during the period 1981–83, a decline of 12.5 percent; 1983–85, -2.9 percent; 1985–87, -15.2 percent; 1987–89, -7.4 percent; 1989–91, -7.7 percent; 1991–93, -16.0 percent; 1993–95, -12.3 percent; 1995–97, -2.0 percent.
34. Excerpted from http://www.dinosaurclub.com.
35. The study examined the death rates of people forty-five and older during the years 1972–89. Cited in Gene Koretz, "Economic Trends: Income Swings Can Be Deadly," *BusinessWeek*, March 2, 1998, 32.
36. "Big Knives of 1997," *BusinessWeek*, December 15, 1997; Patrick McGeehan, "Merrill Cuts 3,400 Jobs, Reports Loss," *Wall Street Journal*, October 14, 1998, C1; Carl Quintanilla, "Broad Round of Job Cuts Hits U.S. Firms," *Wall Street Journal*, October 16, 1998, A2; Deborah Lohse, "Met Life Sets 10% Cut in Nonsales Force as It Weighs Switch in Corporate Status," *Wall Street Journal*, September 9, 1998, A6; Sam

Howe Verhovek, "Boeing Plan for Job Cutbacks Is Bitter Pill for Seattle Area," *New York Times,* December 3, 1998, A1.

37. Job cuts reported in "Challenger Employment Report," conducted by Challenger, Gray & Christmas, Chicago, Illinois, which has been surveying the trend since 1989.

Chapter 3: "This Is the Way of the World"

1. The contrast between earlier years is stark: during 1973–79, the annual increase in the value of nonwage benefits (which include employer-sponsored health care plans, pension plans, and payroll taxes) averaged 4.9 percent. From 1979 to 1986, that increase dropped to 0.8 percent; since then the annual increase has averaged just 0.2 percent. Lawrence Mishel, Jared Bernstein, and John Schmitt, *The State of Working America, 1998–1999* (Ithaca, N.Y.: ILR Press, 1999), table 3. 14, p. 144.

2. In 1980, 97 percent of all full-time employees at "medium and large private establishments" participated in employer-sponsored medical plans. Coverage levels first showed signs of erosion by the middle years of the decade; by 1988, only 90 percent of full-timers participated. By 1993 this figure had dropped to 82 percent, and in 1995 to 77 percent. Historical figures are drawn from *Report on the American Workforce* (Washington, D.C.: Department of Labor, 1995), table 46, p. 198. Current figures are drawn from the DOL's 1997 survey of "Employee Benefits in Medium and Large Private Establishments."

3. In 1991, 67 percent of the full-time employees of medium and large private companies were covered by traditional fee-for-service plans, while the remainder participated in some type of managed-care arrangement. By 1997 the situation had more than reversed itself: only 27 percent of full-time employees were in a fee-for-service plan, while 73 percent had managed-care coverage. Source: table 5, p. 9, of the DOL's 1997 employee-benefits survey, cited in note 2 above.

4. In 1980, only 46 percent of employees opting for family coverage were required to pay a portion of costs; by 1991 that figure had risen to 69 percent, and by 1997 it was up to 80 percent. A similar trend held true for single workers: in 1980, only 26 percent were required to pay part of their policy costs; by 1991, 51 percent were required to do so, and by 1997 it was up to 69 percent. *Report on the American Workforce,* table 46; "Employee Benefits in Medium and Large Private Establishments," table 5.

5. Back in 1984, more than three quarters of U.S. companies provided dental coverage to their employees; by 1995, only 57 percent did—and most required employees to pay for part of its cost. No author, *Working USA,* January–February 1999, 4.

6. Steven Hipple, "Contingent Work: Results from the Second Survey," *Monthly Labor Review,* November 1998, table 10, p. 30.

7. Richard A. Oppel, Jr., "Giving Benefits to Partners of Gay Workers," *New York Times*, December 1, 1999, C1; Oppel, "When Corporate Worlds Collide: Exxon's Decision on Benefits," *New York Times*, December 8, 1999, C12.

8. Arlie Russell Hochschild, *The Time Bind: When Work Becomes Home and Home Becomes Work* (New York: Metropolitan Books, 1997), 26–27, 239.

9. The study, conducted by Michael K. Judiesch and Karen S. Lyness of the City University of New York's Baruch College, found that multiple leave-takers were penalized even more heavily. Reported in Gene Koretz, "Economic Trends: Hazardous to Your Health," *Business-Week*, January 17, 2000, 26.

10. Meanwhile, pension costs amounted to a shrinking share of overall nonwage benefit costs: in 1979 they added up to 18.2 percent of total benefit costs; by 1996 that level had dropped to 11.8 percent. Mishel, Bernstein, and Schmitt, table 3.14, p. 144.

11. As with compensation and insurance cutbacks, this trend gained momentum during the mid-eighties. Whereas in 1980 84 percent of all those working full-time for medium-to-large employers were covered by defined-benefit plans, by 1986 that number had dropped to 76 percent. Eight years later, it was down to 63 percent, and by 1995, 52 percent. Cited in *Report on the American Workforce*, table 46, p. 198; "Employee Benefits in Medium and Large Private Establishments," 1997 survey.

12. Ellen E. Schultz, "Pension Terminations: '80's Replay," *Wall Street Journal*, June 15, 1999, C1.

13. There is some overlap between this percentage and the statistics cited in note 11 above, relating to defined-benefit plans. That's because the DOL report and BLS statistics include corporations whose pension plans contained both defined-benefit and defined-contribution elements.

14. Here again, there is some overlap, this time between tax-deferred savings plans and defined-contribution plans (since 401Ks, for example, may include a commitment on the part of companies to make some matching contribution). Still, the trend indicates clear increases, especially during the nineties. Back in 1991, only 44 percent of men and women working full-time for medium-to-large private employers participated in one of these plans; by 1995 that percentage was 54 percent.

15. Ellen E. Schultz, "Many Workers Are Missing Out on 401(k) Plans," *Wall Street Journal*, December 16, 1999, C1.

16. "The Flaw in Private Savings," *BusinessWeek*, April 27, 1998.

17. Diana B. Henriques and David Cay Johnston, "Managers Staying Dry as Corporations Sink," *New York Times*, October 14, 1996, A1.

18. Excerpted from http://clubs.yahoo.com/clubs/ibmpension. As of February 2000, the club reported 2,132 members, more than 26,000 messages posted, and over 2.7 million page views in total.

19. Ellen E. Schultz and Jon G. Auerbach, "IBM Pension-Plan Changes Spark Ire-Filled Web Site," *Wall Street Journal*, June 14, 1999, C1.

20. No author, "IBM Ready to Adopt 'Cash-Balance' Plan for Pension Program," *Wall Street Journal*, May 4, 1998, A8; Bethany McLean, "The Latest Twist," *Fortune*, October 28, 1996, 234.

21. Excerpted from http://clubs.yahoo.com/clubs/ibmpension.

22. Richard A. Oppel, Jr., "IBM Does an About-Face on Pensions," *New York Times*, September 18, 1999, C1.

23. Danielle Sessa, "IBM Employees Honored for Protest Against Cash-Balance Pension Plans," *Wall Street Journal*, December 31, 1999, B2.

24. Hipple, table 12, p. 32.

Chapter 4: "They Used to Use a Ball and Chain"

1. Excerpted from correspondence from "tickler," May 6, 1999, on http://alex.bla-bla.com/bla/go.cfm?goto=3644.

2. Survey conducted by Stanford Institute for the Quantitative Study of Society. Cited in John Markoff, "A Newer, Lonelier Crowd Emerges in Internet Study," *New York Times*, February 16, 2000, A1.

3. Amy Harmon, "Plugged-in Nation Goes on Vacations in a New Territory," *New York Times*, July 13, 1997, section 1, 1.

4. The respective sources for these statistics, all cited by Data Analysis Group at its website, http:www.cif1.com, are: "1999 Industry Outlook—Forecast: Consumer," *Appliance Manufacturer/CEMA*, January 1, 1999, 92; "1998 Buyers Guide," *Presentations*, December 1, 1997, A10; *EDN*, April 1, 1999, 80.

5. Ownership statistics come from Dataquest, a division of Gartner-Group. According to Census Bureau projections, there were 102,118,600 households in the United States during 1999.

6. Statistics from *EDN*, see citation in note 4 above.

7. 1997 estimate provided by IDC Corporation, cited in Harmon, 14.

8. Katie Hafner, "For the Well Connected, All the World's an Office," *New York Times*, March 30, 2000, G1.

9. Cited in Sue Shellenbarger, "Business Travelers Reshape Work Plans in Rush to Get Home," *Wall Street Journal*, March 18, 1998, B1.

10. Tom Mainelli, "Working While You're Away," *Smart Computing*, February 1998, 79; Patricia J. Bell, "Travel Journal: Taking the High-Tech Road," *Gourmet*, March 1998, 72.

11. Excerpted from correspondence from "technoid," April 20, 1999, on http://alex.bla-bla.com/bla/go.cfm?goto=3644.

12. Statistics from the "Casio PhoneMate Report: Managing Messages in a Wired World," research conducted by Yankelovich Partners, March 10–22, 1998.

13. Harmon, 14.

14. June Fletcher, "*Really* Casual Friday: The Floating Office," *Wall Street Journal*, June 5, 1998, W1.

15. Bell.

16. Correspondence from "WallyK," April 19, 1999, on http:// alex.blabla.com/bla/go.cfm?goto=3644.

17. "Technology and the 24 Hour Day," *Harvard Business Review*, November–December 1996, 85.

18. "Casio PhoneMate Report."

19. *Inter@ctive Week/Forrester Research*, August 10, 1998, 39, cited by Data Analysis Group, http://www.cif1.com.

20. Arlie Russell Hochschild, *The Time Bind: When Work Becomes Home and Home Becomes Work* (New York: Metropolitan Books, 1997), 129.

21. Christopher Grimes, "As 'Bandwidth' Goes By, Tech Workers in Silicon Valley Coin Timely Phrase," *Wall Street Journal*, June 8, 1999, B4A.

22. "Messaging Practices in the Knowledge Economy," Pitney Bowes survey released on June 21, 1999; Tammy Reiss, "You've Got Mail, and Mail, and Mail . . . ," *BusinessWeek*, July 20, 1998, 6.

23. Craig Brod, *TechnoStress: The Human Cost of the Computer Revolution* (Reading, Mass.: Addison-Wesley Publishing, 1984), 68–69, 41.

24. Barbara Garson, *The Electronic Sweatshop: How Computers Are Transforming the Office of the Future into the Factory of the Past* (New York: Penguin Books, 1988), 10.

25. Ibid., 60.

26. Jeremy Rifkin, *The End of Work: The Decline of the Global Labor Force and the Dawn of the Post-Market Era* (New York: G. P. Putnam's Sons, 1995), 144.

27. Ibid., 194.

28. Gene Koretz, "Solving a Labor-Market Puzzle," *BusinessWeek*, April 26, 1999, 26.

29. Nick Wingfield, "More Companies Monitor Employees' E-Mail," *Wall Street Journal*, December 2, 1999, B8.

30. "A Different Type of Computer Monitor," *New York Times*, August 27, 1998; Michael J. McCarthy, "Thinking Out Loud: You Assumed 'Erase' Wiped Out That Rant Against the Boss? Nope," *Wall Street Journal*, March 7, 2000, A1.

31. McCarthy, A1.

32. Bill Machrone, "The Depersonalization Continues," *PC Week*, September 2, 1996, 63.

33. Cited in Daniel S. Levine, *Disgruntled: The Darker Side of the World of Work* (New York: Berkley Boulevard Books, 1998), 118–19.

34. Statistics based upon an American Management Association survey of 1,054 member companies, cited in "Upfront: The Big Picture," *BusinessWeek*, May 31, 1999, 8.

35. Ellen Joan Pollock, "Inhuman Resources: Sir: Your Application for a Job Is Rejected; Sincerely, Hal 9000," *Wall Street Journal*, July 30, 1998, A1.

36. Press release from Challenger, Gray & Christmas, Northbrook, Illinois, June 29, 1999.

37. Rifkin, 187.

38. Grimes, B4A.

39. Founded in 1995 by financial journalist Daniel Levine, www.disgruntled.com combined a raucous and irreverent style with relentless, often well-researched criticisms of the workplace. (Its revenue-producing ventures included the sale of advertising, antiwork T-shirts, and a range of books, among them a published collection of articles and letters excerpted from the website.) In his "memo from the boss" to new visitors, Levine wrote, "We work because we need food, shelter, clothing and anything that numbs the pain of work itself. If it weren't for the fact that the only thing that sucks worse than work is being unemployed, who'd do it." The Internet magazine ceased publication in early 2000.

40. Excerpted from http://www.disgruntled.com/anonymous1297.html.

41. Excerpted from http://www.disgruntled.com/mailroom.html, name withheld, posted February 24, 1996.

42. http://www.disgruntled.com/anonymous1297.html.

43. Excerpted from http://www.grrl.com/stories.html.

44. Excerpted from http://www.dinosaurclub.com/page22.html.

45. Mike France and Joann Muller, "A Site for Soreheads," *BusinessWeek*, April 12, 1999, 86–90.

Chapter Five: "My Full Intention Was to Be There Forever"

1. "Growth is the word that best characterizes the economy of the United States for the two decades after World War II," reported Mansel G. Blackford and K. Austin Kerr, "The Company in the Postwar World," in Harold G. Vatter and John F. Walker, eds., *History of the U.S. Economy Since World War II* (Armonk, N.Y.: M. E. Sharpe, 1996), 129. Between 1945 and 1960, the nation's real GNP rose by 52 percent; during the next decade, it went up by another 46 percent.

2. Alfred Chandler, Jr., *The Visible Hand: The Managerial Revolution in American Business* (Cambridge, Mass.: Belknap Press of Harvard University Press, 1977), 476. The act initially generated significant opposition from a business community that aimed to minimize government interference; by the 1950s, though, "businessmen in general and professional managers in particular had begun to see the benefits of a government commitment to maintaining aggregate demand. They supported the efforts of both Democratic and Republican administra-

tions during the recessions of 1949, 1957, and 1960 to provide stability through fiscal policies . . ." (Chandler, 496–97).

3. William H. Whyte, Jr., *The Organization Man* (New York: Simon & Schuster, 1956), 71–72.

4. Earl S. Willis, "General Electric's Plan for Financing Retraining," *Management Record*, vol. 24, no. 4 (April 1962). Published in New York by the Conference Board, which was then known as the National Industrial Conference Board.

5. Harold Stieglitz, "Conference Board Reports: Recognition for Long Service," *Studies in Personnel Policy*, no. 106 (New York: National Industrial Conference Board, 1950), 2.

6. Quoted in Joseph Nocera, "Living with Layoffs," *Fortune*, April 1, 1996, 69–71.

7. Charles C. Heckscher, *White-Collar Blues: Management Loyalties in an Age of Corporate Restructuring* (New York: Basic Books, 1994), 24.

8. Amanda Bennett, *The Death of the Organization Man* (New York: William Morrow, 1990), 36.

9. During this recession, long-term unemployment skyrocketed for professional and technical workers, with 9.3 percent of the group reporting unemployment of twenty-seven weeks or longer in 1970, compared with a 3.8 percent average since 1957. Cited in "Table 74: Long-Term Unemployment, by Major Industry and Occupational Group, 1957–74," *Handbook of Labor Statistics: 1975 Reference Edition* (Washington, D.C.: U.S. Department of Labor, Bureau of Labor Statistics), bulletin 1865, 174. Analyzing the trend for the Conference Board, Karen Kelly speculated about whether white-collar workers were now as susceptible as their blue-collar colleagues had long been to the potential for layoffs. Karen Kelly, "A White-Collar Recession," *Conference Board Record*, vol. 8, no. 9 (September 1971).

10. "The fringe benefit was by no means entirely new, but its widespread adoption during the war gives it a special, war-related character. It too turned out be an irreversible and expanded change," commented Harold G. Vatter, "The War's Consequences," in Vatter and Walker, eds., 5.

11. Francis X. Sutton, Seymour E. Harris, Carl Kaysen, and James Tobin, *The American Business Creed* (Cambridge, Mass.: Harvard University Press, 1956), 63, 137.

12. Jeremy Rifkin, *The End of Work: The Decline of the Global Labor Force and the Dawn of the Post-Market Era* (New York: G. P. Putnam's Sons, 1995), 169–70.

13. No author, *Profile of Employee Benefits, 1974* (New York: Conference Board, 1974), report no. 645.

14. Cited in "Briefs on Personnel Practices," *Management Record* (New York: National Industrial Conference Board), vol. 24, no. 1 (January 1962): 31.

15. "About the only thing that everyone agrees on is that 1973 was a break year. After 1973, income growth slowed significantly." No author, "American Living Standard," excerpted from *The Economist*, November 10, 1990, in Vatter and Walker, eds., 19–22.

16. Dorothy R. Kittner, *Monthly Labor Review* (Washington, D.C.: U.S. Department of Labor, Bureau of Labor Statistics), vol. 93, no. 2 (February 1970).

17. Whyte, 320.

18. F. Beatrice Brower, untitled article, *Management Record* (New York: Conference Board), vol. 12, no. 10 (October 1950): 390.

19. According to the IRS, 13,899 pension, profit-sharing, and stock bonus plans existed at large corporations by 1950. Statistics cited in Brower, ibid., 390.

20. F. Beatrice Brower, "Trends in Employee Benefit Plans," *Management Record* (New York: Conference Board), vol. 12, no. 1 (January 1950): 14.

21. Murray W. Latimer, *Monthly Labor Review* (Washington, D.C.: U.S. Department of Labor, Bureau of Labor Statistics), vol. 93, no. 5 (May 1970): 47.

22. Roger F. Murray, *Economic Aspects of Pension: A Summary Report* (New York: National Bureau of Economic Research, 1968). Statistics appear in table 5: "Past and Projected Growth of Private Pension Plans, 1940–80," and include private-pension programs run by corporations, labor unions, and nonprofit organizations.

23. Sloan Wilson, *The Man in the Gray Flannel Suit* (New York: Simon & Schuster, 1955), 10, 277.

24. Witold Rybczynski, *Waiting for the Weekend* (New York: Penguin Books, 1992), 144.

25. Geoffrey H. Moore, "Measuring Leisure Time," *Conference Board Record*, vol. 8, no. 7 (July 1971).

26. William S. Dutton, *Adventure in Big Business: A Stirring Account of America's Industrial Giants . . . How They Grew . . . How They Affect Your Life* (Philadelphia: John C. Winston Company, 1958), 110.

27. Juliet B. Schor, *The Overworked American: The Unexpected Decline of Leisure* (New York: Basic Books, 1992), 79.

28. Whyte, 142–43.

29. Heckscher, 4.

30. Schor, 4.

31. Moore, "Measuring Leisure Time."

32. Alan Downs, *Corporate Executions: The Ugly Truth About Layoffs— How Corporate Greed Is Shattering Lives, Companies, and Communities* (New York: AMACOM, 1995), 22–23.

33. Albert J. Dunlap with Bob Andelman, *Mean Business: How I Save Bad Companies and Make Good Companies Great* (New York: Times Business, 1996), 196–97.

34. No author, "Our Company and How It Operates: A Text of General Information for Employees of the Long Lines Department, American Telephone and Telegraph Co., March 1941."

35. Excerpted from a talk given by W. L. Lees, vice president, Bell Telephone Company of Pennsylvania, in *Management Record* (New York: Conference Board), vol. 12, no. 12 (December 1950): 452.

36. Chris Tilly, "The Good, the Bad and the Ugly: Good and Bad Jobs in the United States at the Millennium," Russell Sage Foundation, June 1996, http://epn.org/sage/rstil-jo.html.

Chapter 6: "Ma Is Dead"

1. Peter Coy, "When Is the Jobless Rate Too Low?," *BusinessWeek*, November 1, 1999, 170; Gretchen Morgenson, "Dow Finishes the Day over 10,000 Mark for the First Time," *New York Times*, March 30, 1999, C12.

2. Bruchey, "Some Deeper Currents in the Recent Past," in Harold G. Vatter and John F. Walker, eds., *History of the U.S. Economy Since World War II* (Armonk, N.Y.: M. E. Sharpe, 1996), 36.

3. Coy; Louis Uchitelle, "Productivity Gains Help Keep Economy on a Roll," *New York Times*, March 22, 1999, A16; Jacob M. Schlesinger, Tristan Mabry, and Sarah Lueck, "Charting the Pain Behind the Gain," *Wall Street Journal*, October 1, 1999, B1.

4. James Surowiecki, "Company Man," *The New Yorker*, January 19, 1998, 72.

5. Mansel G. Blackford and K. Austin Kerr, "The Company in the Postwar World," in Vatter and Walker, eds., 136.

6. Connie Bruck, *The Predators' Ball: The Inside Story of Drexel Burnham and the Rise of the Junk Bond Raiders* (New York: Penguin Books, 1988), 268.

7. Lawrence Kudlow, "The Road to Dow 10000," *Wall Street Journal*, March 16, 1999, A26.

8. Michael Useem, *Investor Capitalism: How Money Managers Are Changing the Face of Corporate America* (New York: Basic Books, 1996), 2.

9. Alan Downs, *Corporate Executions: The Ugly Truth About Layoffs— How Corporate Greed Is Shattering Lives, Companies, and Communities* (New York: AMACOM, 1995), 136–37, reports, "During the 1980s and early 1990s, nearly 2,000 corporations dipped into pension funds for at least $1 million each, bringing the total take from the funds set aside for the retirement of older workers to just over $21 billion."

10. The source of all statistics relating to the mutual fund industry is the Investment Company Institute, Washington, D.C.

11. Bruck, 94.

12. Useem, 25. "These developments help explain," he added, "why mergers and acquisitions at publicly traded companies more than doubled between 1980 and 1988, and leveraged buyouts rose by a factor of 10."

13. All statistics are drawn from the Bureau of Labor Statistics' Current Population Survey.

14. Cited in "Executive Summary to *The State of Working America, 1994–95*" (Washington, D.C.: Economic Policy Institute, 1995), http://epn.org/epi/epi-swa01.html.

15. Barry Bluestone and Stephen Rose, "Overworked and Underemployed: Unraveling an Economic Enigma," *American Prospect,* no. 31 (March–April 1997): 58–69 (http://epn.org/prospect/31/31blue.htm).

16. According to David R. Howell, "The Skills Myth," *American Prospect,* no. 18 (Summer 1994), "By the 1980's, concession bargaining had become widespread." He cites the following statistics for workers with private-sector union contracts, whose wages were frozen or cut: The percentage "ranged from 0 to 5 from 1964 through 1980, rose to 8 percent in 1981, jumped to 44 percent in 1982 and 37 percent in 1983. While dropping to 23 percent in 1984 and 26 percent in 1985, by historical standards these rates have remained at remarkably high levels."

17. Bruck, 91.

18. In order to preserve his anonymity, I agreed to omit all written details that might disclose his identity to former colleagues or others, and also to skip over those sections pertaining mainly to family matters. In all other regards, however, the excerpts I have selected are quoted verbatim.

19. This compared to an 11 percent level in the 1970s. Cited in Downs, 17.

Chapter 7: "Raising the Bar"

1. *IEEE-USA Perspectives,* March 1999.

2. Challenger, Gray & Christmas survey dated January 7, 1999.

3. Andrew S. Grove, *Only the Paranoid Survive: How to Exploit the Crisis Points That Challenge Every Company and Career* (New York: Currency, Doubleday, 1996), 6.

4. Dr. Norman Matloff, "Debunking the Myth of a Desperate Software Labor Shortage," testimony to the U.S. House Judiciary Committee, Subcommittee on Immigration, presented on April 21, 1998, and updated on April 4, 1999 (http://heather.cs.ucdavis.edu/itaa.html).

5. Ibid.

6. Aaron Bernstein and Steve Hamm, "Is There Really a Techie Shortage?" *BusinessWeek,* June 29, 1998, 93.

7. The differential was only 59 percent for those with twenty years' experience. From the 1998 study by economists Clair Brown, Ben Campbell, and Greg Pinsonneault, Department of Economics, University of Cali-

fornia at Berkeley, "The Perceived Shortage of High-Tech Workers," cited by Matloff in "Debunking. . . ."

8. Staffing survey released on April 23, 1999, National Association of Temporary and Staffing Services, Alexandria, Virginia; historical statistics are drawn from the Bureau of Labor Statistics.

9. The study, conducted by the South Bay AFL-CIO Labor Council, was reported in Leslie Helm, "Microsoft Testing Limits on Temp Worker Use," *Los Angeles Times,* December 7, 1997, D1.

10. Rosabeth Moss Kanter, "Nice Work If You Can Get It: The Software Industry as a Model for Tomorrow's Jobs," *American Prospect,* no. 23 (Fall 1995): 52–59 (http://epn.org/prospect/23/23kant.html).

11. Steven Greenhouse, "Equal Work, Less Equal Perks," *New York Times,* March 30, 1998, D1.

12. Comments from "Beejay," http://alex.bla-bla.com/bla/docs/msg.cfm?nextmsg=17, posted on April 21, 1999.

13. Helm, D14.

14. Eric Herman, "Elizabeth Spokoiny: A Piece of the Pie," *Smart Money,* June, 1998, 96. The so-called Vizcaino case was catalyzed, in part, by an Internal Revenue Service audit that took place around 1990, which concluded that "Microsoft's independent contractors were common-law employees," according to Herman. Two years later, a class action suit was filed against the company by the Seattle law firm of Bendich, Stobaugh & Strong on the part of a group of long-term temporary employees who argued that they were entitled to the same benefits earned by full-time noncontingent employees—including access to the company's stock-purchase plan, which permitted workers to buy discounted stock.

15. Conversation with Microsoft public relations representative in April 1999.

16. Greenhouse, D1.

17. Ibid., D6.

18. Helm, D14.

19. Quoted in Helm, D1.

20. Ralph T. King, Jr., "Microsoft Loses Ruling over Temporary Workers," *Wall Street Journal,* May 14, 1999, A3; Chuck Wolfred, "Revenge of the Temps: Independent Contractors' Victory in Microsoft Case May Have Wide Impact," *Washington Post,* January 16, 2000, H01.

21. King, A3.

22. No author, "Microsoft Says Temps Must Take a Hiatus After Working a Year," *Wall Street Journal,* February, 22, 2000, A32.

23. Helm, D1.

24. Excerpted from entry by "joeoverwork," http://alex.blabla.com/bla/go.cfm?goto=3644, dated April 23, 1999. This chat room was established with help from, and links to, the work-related Internet magazine www.disgruntled.com.

25. Clint Willis, "Using Change to Corner the Market," *Your Turn* (Forbes Special Interest Publications Group), Spring 1998, 22.

26. At that point, which was during autumn 1997, the website's address was http://www.igc.apc.org/faceintel/whoweare.htm. Among the information provided in this three-page site was a description of FACEIntel, which had organized in early 1996 in Folsom, California, under the original name of AXEI ("Associated X-Employees of Intel").

27. Excerpted from FACEIntel's website, whose address during the winter of 1999 was http://www.face@castle.com. Its current address is http://www.faceintel.com.

28. Grove, 4, 7–23. Steve Lohr, "Intel's Chief Steps Down After 11 Years," *New York Times*, March 27, 1998, D1.

29. As of the time of this writing, these e-mails had been temporarily halted by the Sacramento County Superior Court. Jonathan Rabinovitz, "Anti-Intel E-mail Halted," *San Jose Mercury*, December 4, 1998, A1. But the case proceeded through the appeals process, with amicus brief motions filed on Ken Hamidi and FACEIntel's behalf by the American Civil Liberties Union and the ACLU of Northern California and by the Electronic Frontier Foundation (assisted by the Berkman Center for Internet and Society of Harvard University Law School). Cited in http://www.intelhamidi.com

30. Tim Jackson, *Inside Intel: Andy Grove and the Rise of the World's Most Powerful Chip Company* (New York: Plume, 1997), 240.

31. "Many industry officials have admitted they have shifted their hiring focus to new college graduates. Intel has such an interest in this group that its recruiting literature is riddled with the acronyms NCG and RCG, 'new college graduate' and 'recent college graduate,' respectively," noted Dr. Norman Matloff in "Debunking the Myth," 4.

32. Jackson, 112.

33. Grove, 117.

34. Oscar L. Vidal, "Intel," *Value Line*, April 23, 1999.

35. Grove, 6.

36. Excerpted from http://www.igc.apc.org/faceintel/weeklypostings.htm.

37. Vidal.

38. Dean Takahashi, "Intel Beats Lowered Earnings Forecasts," *Wall Street Journal*, April 15, 1998, A3.

39. Matloff, 14.

40. Vidal.

Chapter 8: "Like a Boulder Rolling Downhill"

1. Rick Brooks, "Major Banks Raise Y2K-Upgrade Costs, Signaling Some Unanticipated Expenses," *Wall Street Journal*, August 20, 1999, A2.

2. David Greising with Peter Galuszka, Kathleen Morris, Andrew Osterland, and Geoffrey Smith, "1,000,000,000 Banks: Are Megabanks—

Once Unimaginable, Now Inevitable—Better . . . ?," *BusinessWeek*, April 27, 1998, 33.

3. Cited from the Banking Industry Databank that appeared on www.snl.com, August 24, 1999.

4. Greising, 35.

5. No author, "Wells Fargo to Cut Its Work Force by 5% in Wake of Merger," *Wall Street Journal*, March 29, 1999, A6.

6. The source for this statistic is Challenger, Gray & Christmas, in a release dated June 14, 1999.

7. Alan Downs, *Corporate Executions: The Ugly Truth About Layoffs— How Corporate Greed Is Shattering Lives, Companies, and Communities* (New York: AMACOM, 1995), 31.

8. Matt Murray, "Citigroup Expecting to Chop 8,000 Jobs," *Wall Street Journal*, September 13, 1998, A3.

9. Paul Beckett, "Citigroup Makes Move to Change Pension Benefits," *Wall Street Journal*, April 2, 1999, A4. To lessen the blow, the company planned to allow some of its longer-tenured employees to continue with their existing pensions.

10. Richard Sennett, *The Corrosion of Character: The Personal Consequences of Work in the New Capitalism* (New York: W. W. Norton, 1998), 82, 84.

11. N. R. Kleinfield, "The Company as Family, No More," *New York Times*, March 4, 1996, A1.

12. Ibid., A12.

13. Rick Brooks, "Those Were the Days Before We Had to Lay You Off," *Wall Street Journal*, May 5, 1998, A1.

14. Rosemary Metzler Lavan, "Fleet and NATW in $3.2 Billion Deal Will Cut 1,800 Jobs Here," *Daily News* (New York), December 20, 1995, 48.

15. Greising, 35.

16. Rick Brooks, "How Bad News of First Union Caught Many Analysts Napping," *Wall Street Journal*, May 28, 1999, C1.

17. Gretchen Morgenson, "A Cautionary Note on Mergers: Bigger Does Not Necessarily Mean Better," *New York Times*, December 8, 1998, C1.

18. Matt Murray, "Missed Opening: Key Corp. Fails to Prove It Can Unlock Promise of a Merger of Equals," *Wall Street Journal*, August 25, 1998, A1.

19. Melissa Wahl, "Wall Street Pummels Bank One; Credit Card Unit Woes Shock Analysts, Investors," *Chicago Tribune*, August 26, 1999, 1; David S. Cloud and Glenn R. Simpson, "Money-Laundering Case Is Difficult to Unravel," *Wall Street Journal*, September 10, 1999, A2; Michael R. Gordon and Neela Banerjee, "Full Speed Ahead in Fog of Russian Economy, Bank of New York Hit a Shoal," *New York Times*, September 23, 1999, A8; Karen Talley, "Chase Stock Down 5.2% on Rumor of Weak Profits," *American Banker*, September 10, 1999, 1.

20. Rick Brooks, "Bank Stocks Are Facing Added Pressure from Worry over Loans, Portfolio Losses," *Wall Street Journal*, September 14, 1999, C1.

21. Mike McNamee, Pamela L. Moore, Dean Foust, and Geoffrey Smith, "Invasion of the Superbanks?," *BusinessWeek*, November 1, 1999, 176.

22. Jeffrey E. Garten, "Mega-Mergers, Mega-Influence," *New York Times*, October 26, 1999, A27.

23. Ron Chernow, "The Birth of a Bureaucratic Mastodon?," *Wall Street Journal*, April 9, 1998, A22.

24. Matt Murray, Thomas Kamm, and Christopher Rhoads, "BNP Joins Bank Quest for Bigness, but It Is No Industry Cure-All," *Wall Street Journal*, March 11, 1999, A1.

25. Jeffrey E. Garten, "Economic Viewpoint: Megamergers Are a Clear and Present Danger," *BusinessWeek*, January 25, 1999, 28.

26. Dean Foust, "Commentary: If This Safety Net Snaps, Who Pays?," *BusinessWeek*, April 27, 1998, 38.

27. Source: Challenger, Gray & Christmas, "Merger Job Cuts Shoot Past 250,000," news release dated May 11, 1999.

28. Doreen Carvajal, "The More the Books, the Fewer the Editors," *New York Times*, June 29, 1998, E1.

29. Larry Black, "The Bottom Line: Divorce, Wall Street-Style," *New York*, September 8, 1977, 40. This article cites research conducted by Mark L. Sirower, a professor at New York University's Stern School of Business and the author of *The Synergy Trap*. Morgenson, C12.

30. Morgenson, C12.

31. Allen R. Myerson, "For Oil Workers, Merger Is Just Another Word for More Layoffs," *New York Times*, November 30, 1998, A1.

32. Gordon Fairclough, "P&G to Slash 15,000 Jobs, Shut 10 Plants," *Wall Street Journal*, June 10, 1999, A3.

33. Jim Carlton, "At Packard Bell, Survival Mode Means Big Cuts," *Wall Street Journal*, June 3, 1999, B1.

34. Sennett, 51.

35. Amanda Bennett, *The Death of the Organization Man* (New York: William Morrow, 1990), 217.

36. Downs, 78–79.

37. Ibid., 15.

38. Ibid., 13.

39. Claudia H. Deutsch, "Kodak to Lay Off 10,000 Employees in a 10% Cutback," *New York Times*, November 12, 1997, A1; Ross Kerber, "Kodak Boosts Layoff Plan, Restructuring Charge," *Wall Street Journal*, December 19, 1997, A3.

40. Alec Klein, "Shutter Snaps on Fisher's Leadership at Kodak," *Wall Street Journal*, June 10, 1999, B1.

41. William Wolman and Anne Colamosca, *The Judas Economy: The Triumph of Capital and the Betrayal of Work* (Reading, Mass.: Addison-Wesley Publishing, 1997), 67.

Chapter 9: "Career-Change Opportunities"

1. Albert J. Dunlap with Bob Andelman, *Mean Business: How I Save Bad Companies and Make Good Companies Great* (New York: Times Business, 1996), 31.
2. John A. Byrne, "Chainsaw," *BusinessWeek*, October 18, 1999, 128–49; James R. Hagerty and Martha Brannigan, "Inside Sunbeam, Raindrops Mar Dunlap's Parade," *Wall Street Journal*, May 22, 1998, B1; Martha Brannigan and Joann S. Lublin, "Dunlap Faces a Fight over His Severance Pay," *Wall Street Journal*, June 16, 1998, B1.
3. Jeff Papows, *Enterprise.com: Market Leadership in the Information Age* (Reading, Mass.: Perseus Books, 1998), xi.
4. Dunlap, ix.
5. Excerpted from http:www.amazon.com/exec/obidos/ts/book-custome, November 19, 1999.
6. Andrew S. Grove, *Only the Paranoid Survive: How to Exploit the Crisis Points That Challenge Every Company and Career* (New York: Currency, Doubleday, 1996), 3.
7. Grove, 108.
8. John Cassidy, "Wall Street Follies," *The New Yorker*, September 13, 1999, 32. Cassidy cited statistics from a study jointly published by the Insitute for Policy Studies and the advocacy group United for a Fair Economy.
9. Dunlap, 177.
10. Jennifer Reingold, "Executive Pay," *BusinessWeek*, April 27, 1997, 59; Jennifer Reingold, "Executive Pay," *BusinessWeek*, April 20, 1998, 65; Jennifer Reingold, "Executive Pay," *BusinessWeek*, April 19, 1999, 72; William M. Carley, "GE Chairman Defends Pay, Stresses Quality," *Wall Street Journal*, April 24, 1997, A4.
11. Lawrence Mishel, Jared Bernstein, and John Schmitt, *The State of Working America, 1998–1999* (Ithaca, N.Y.: ILR Press, 1999), 211.
12. Jennifer Reingold with Amy Borrus, "Even Executives Are Wincing at Executive Pay," *BusinessWeek*, May 12, 1997, 40.
13. Reingold, April 19, 1999, 72; Paul Beckett, "Citigroup Makes Move to Change Pension Benefits," *Wall Street Journal*, April 2, 1999, A4; Matt Murray, "Citigroup Expecting to Chop 8,000 Jobs," *Wall Street Journal*, September 13, 1998, A3.
14. Bernie Sanders, "IBM Workers Fight Back," *The Nation*, January 24, 2000, 6; Joseph Pereira, "IBM CEO in 1999 Exercised Options Nearly Triple '98's," *Wall Street Journal*, March 14, 2000, B8.
15. Reingold, April 20, 1998, 108; John J. Keller, "AT&T Will Eliminate 40,000 Jobs and Take a Charge of $4 Billion," *Wall Street Journal*, January 3, 1996, A3; John J. Keller, "AT&T Handsomely Rewarded Top Brass," *Wall Street Journal*, March 27, 1998, A3; Reingold, 1999, 114; John J. Keller, "AT&T Revamping to Trim 18.000 Jobs," *Wall Street Journal*, January 17, 1998, A3.

16. Raju Narisetti, "Xerox's Chief Has Rise of 51% in Salary, Bonus," *Wall Street Journal*, April 10, 1998, B7.
17. Cassidy.
18. Jim Carlton, "Apple Paid Ex-CEO $9.2 Million After Ouster," *Wall Street Journal*, December 8, 1997, B10.
19. Timothy D. Schellhardt, "Anatomy of an Unusual Stock-Option Windfall," *Wall Street Journal*, June 2, 1999, B1; Adam Bryant, "Stock Options That Raise Investors' Ire," *New York Times*, March 27, 1998, D1, D5.
20. Cassidy.
21. William C. Ferguson, "Ethical Foundations," *Executive Excellence*, vol. 14, no. 6 (June 1997): 15–16.
22. Cited from William Lutz's *The New Doublespeak*, in Steven Levy, "Work Is Hell: Why Dilbert Is No Joke," *Newsweek*, August 12, 1996, 57.
23. Jeff Kelly, ed., *The Best of Temp Slave!* (Madison, Wis.: Garrett County Press, 1997), 21.
24. Jeffrey L. Seglin, "The Right Thing: Playing It the Company Way, After Hours," *New York Times*, February 20, 2000, section 3, 4.
25. Doreen Carvajal, "$270 Million HarperCollins Charge Is Set," *New York Times*, August 5, 1997, D1.

Conclusion: A Path out of the White-Collar "Sweatshop"?

1. Suzanne Daley, "A French Paradox at Work," *New York Times*, November 11, 1999, D1.
2. Nancy Ann Jeffrey, "Whatever Happened to Friendship?," *Wall Street Journal*, March 3, 2000, W1.
3. Albert J. Dunlap with Bob Andelman, *Mean Business: How I Save Bad Companies and Make Good Companies Great* (New York: Times Business, 1996), 199.
4. Steve Rosenbush, "The Talent Drain at AT&T," *BusinessWeek*, March 13, 2000, 94.
5. John A. Byrne with Debra Sparks, "What's an Old-Line CEO to Do?," *BusinessWeek*, March 27, 2000, 38.
6. William Heffernan, *The Dinosaur Club* (New York: Pocket Books, 1999). An affiliated website, www.dinosaurclub.com, attracted a steady stream of confidences from readers, mainly veterans of the large-corporate world.
7. Daley.
8. Jeremy Rifkin, *The End of Work: The Decline of the Global Labor Force and the Dawn of the Post-Market Era* (New York: G. P. Putnam's Sons, 1995), 227.
9. Leslie Kaufman, "Some Companies Derail the 'Burnout' Track," *New York Times*, May 3, 1999, A1.
10. Sue Shellenbarger, "Are Saner Workloads the Unexpected Key to More Productivity?," *Wall Street Journal*, March 10, 1999, B1. Shellenbarger's

weekly column, "Work & Family," does a good job of tracking quality-of-life improvements in corporate America.

11. Cited in Sue Shellenbarger, "Employees Who Value Time as Much as Money Now Get Their Reward," *Wall Street Journal*, September 22, 1999, B1.

12. According to a survey by Andersen Consulting, Economist Intelligence Unit, 75 percent of executives worldwide believe that human performance matters more than productivity and technology in terms of its strategic importance; even more, 80 percent, believe that by 2010 the most important strategic accomplishment will be attracting and retaining people. Survey cited in John Byrne, "The Search for the Young and Gifted: Why Talent Counts," *BusinessWeek*, October 4, 1999, 114.

13. Timothy D. Schellhardt, "An Idyllic Workplace Under a Tycoon's Thumb," *Wall Street Journal*, November 23, 1998, B1.

14. Kathleen Kerwin, Peter Burrows, and Dean Foust, "Workers of the World, Log On," *BusinessWeek*, February 21, 2000, 52.

15. Virginia Munger Kahn, "The Electronic Rank and File," *New York Times*, March 8, 2000, G1.

16. No author, cited in "Employee Ownership Companies Top 'Best 100 Places to Work' List," *Employee Ownership Report* (a publication of the National Center for Employee Ownership), vol. 18, no. 2 (March–April 1998).

17. The study, which was conducted by management consultants Hewitt Associates and Northwestern University's Kellogg Graduate School of Business, focused on 380 large U.S. companies that made the switch between 1971 and 1991. Cited in Gene Koretz, "Economic Trends: ESOP Benefits Are No Fables," *BusinessWeek*, September 6, 1999, 26.

18. Cited in Donald J. McNerney, "Contingent Workers," *HR Focus*, vol. 73, no. 10 (October 1996): 1.

19. Nikhil Deogun and Joann S. Lublin, "Who's News: PepsiCo's Enrico Forgoes 1998 Salary, Asks Firm's Board to Fund Scholarships," *Wall Street Journal*, March 24, 1998, B10.

20. No author, "Reebok's Chairman and Chief Executive Declines 1998 Bonus," *Wall Street Journal*, March 29, 1999, B2.

21. No author, "Kodak Cuts Chairman's Pay to $2 Million," *New York Times*, March 20, 1998, D2.

22. Deogun and Lublin.

23. According to the Investor Responsibility Research Center, Washington, D.C., there were 103 proxy battles over executive compensation in 1999, up from 72 in 1998.

24. Ellen E. Schultz, "'Cash' Pensions Trigger Protest of New Allies," *Wall Street Journal*, January 21, 1999, C1.

25. Steven Greenhouse, "Unions Predict Gains from Boeing Strike," *New York Times*, March 21, 2000, A14.

26. Steven Greenhouse, "A.M.A.'s Delegates Vote to Unionize," *New York Times*, June 24, 1999, A1.

27. http://clubs.yahoo.com/clubs/ibmpension.

28. Steven Greenhouse, "The Most Innovative Figure in Silicon Valley? Maybe This Labor Organizer," *New York Times*, November 14, 1999.

29. No author, "Work Week," *Wall Street Journal*, January 25, 2000, A1; David Leonhardt, Aaron Bernstein, and Wendy Zellner, "UAL: Labor Is My Co-Pilot," *BusinessWeek*, March 1, 1999, 38.

30. Kahn, G1.

31. Noam S. Cohen, "Corporations Battling to Bar Use of E-Mail for Unions," *New York Times*, August 23, 1999, C1.

32. Constance L. Hays, "Coca-Cola to Cut Fifth of Its Staff After Woes at Home and Abroad," *New York Times*, January 27, 2000, A1.

33. http://www.business-ethics.com.

34. The study, which was conducted by Ernst & Young's Center for Business Innovation, found that success in attracting and retaining workers ranked just behind strategy execution, management credibility, quality of strategy, and innovation. Cited in Sue Shellenbarger, "Investors Seem Attracted to Firms with Happy Employees," *Wall Street Journal*, March 19, 1997, B1.

35. Rifkin, 227.

36. Shellenbarger, "Investors Seem Attracted. . . ."

37. Reuters, "I.B.M. Workers Get Backer in Pension Fight," *New York Times*, March 28, 2000, C27. The resolution, which was also backed by the New York State Common Retirement Fund, was defeated in April 2000, but it won enough support—28.4 percent of votes, or nearly 300 million shares—to guarantee its place on the 2001 ballot if its backers resubmit it. Ellen E. Schultz and Jon G. Auerbach, "IBM Holders Defeat Pension Resolution," *Wall Street Journal*, April 26, 2000, A2.

SELECT BIBLIOGRAPHY

Bennett, Amanda. 1990. *The Death of the Organization Man*. New York: William Morrow.

Brod, Craig. 1984. *TechnoStress: The Human Cost of the Computer Revolution*. Reading, Mass.: Addison-Wesley Publishing.

Bruck, Connie. 1988. *The Predators' Ball: The Inside Story of Drexel Burnham and the Rise of the Junk Bond Raiders*. New York: Penguin Books.

Chandler, Alfred D., Jr. 1977. *The Visible Hand: The Managerial Revolution in American Business*. Cambridge, Mass.: Belknap Press of Harvard University Press.

Downs, Alan. 1995. *Corporate Executions: The Ugly Truth About Layoffs—How Corporate Greed Is Shattering Lives, Companies, and Communities*. New York: AMACOM.

Dunlap, Albert J., with Bob Andelman. 1996. *Mean Business: How I Save Bad Companies and Make Good Companies Great*. New York: Times Business.

Dutton, William S. 1958. *Adventure in Big Business: A Stirring Account of America's Industrial Giants . . . How They Grew . . . How They Affect Your Life*. Philadelphia, Pa.: John C. Winston Company.

Garson, Barbara. 1989. *The Electronic Sweatshop: How Computers Are Transforming the Office of the Future into the Factory of the Past*. New York: Penguin Books.

Grove, Andrew S. 1996. *Only the Paranoid Survive: How to Exploit the Crisis Points That Challenge Every Company and Career*. New York: Currency, Doubleday.

Heckscher, Charles C. 1994. *White-Collar Blues: Management Loyalties in an Age of Corporate Restructuring*. New York: Basic Books.

Heffernan, William. 1999. *The Dinosaur Club*. New York: Pocket Books.

Hochschild, Arlie Russell. 1997. *The Time Bind: When Work Becomes Home and Home Becomes Work*. New York: Metropolitan Books.

Jackson, Tim. 1997. *Inside Intel: Andy Grove and the Rise of the World's Most Powerful Chip Company.* New York: Plume.

Kantor, Rosabeth Moss. 1977. *Men and Women of the Corporation.* New York: Basic Books.

Kelly, Jeff, ed. 1997. *The Best of Temp Slave!* Madison, Wis.: Garrett County Press.

Krass, Peter, ed. 1997. *The Book of Business Wisdom: Classic Writings by the Legends of Commerce and Industry.* New York: John Wiley & Sons.

Levine, Daniel S. 1998. *Disgruntled: The Darker Side of the World of Work.* New York: Berkley Boulevard Books.

Mills, C. Wright. 1956. *White Collar: The American Middle Classes.* New York: Oxford University Press.

Mishel, Lawrence, Jared Bernstein, and John Schmitt. 1997. *The State of Working America, 1996–1997.* Armonk, N.Y.: M. E. Sharpe.

————.1999. *The State of Working America, 1998–1999.* Ithaca, N.Y.: ILR Press.

O'Boyle, Thomas F. 1998. *At Any Cost: Jack Welch, General Electric, and the Pursuit of Profit.* New York: Alfred A. Knopf.

Papows, Jeff. 1998. *Enterprise.com: Market Leadership in the Information Age.* Reading, Mass.: Perseus Books.

Rifkin, Jeremy. 1995. *The End of Work: The Decline of the Global Labor Force and the Dawn of the Post-Market Era.* New York: G. P. Putnam's Sons.

Rudolph, Barbara. 1998. *Disconnected: How Six People from AT&T Discovered the New Meaning of Work in a Downsized Corporate America.* New York: Free Press.

Rybczynski, Witold. 1992. *Waiting for the Weekend.* New York: Penguin Books.

Schor, Juliet B. 1992. *The Overworked American: The Unexpected Decline of Leisure.* New York: Basic Books.

Sennett, Richard. 1998. *The Corrosion of Character: The Personal Consequences of Work in the New Capitalism.* New York: W. W. Norton.

Sprouse, Martin, ed. 1992. *Sabotage in the American Workplace: Anecdotes of Dissatisfaction, Mischief and Revenge.* San Francisco, Calif.: Pressure Drop Press.

Sutton, Francis X., Seymour E. Harris, Carl Kaysen, and James Tobin. 1956. *The American Business Creed.* Cambridge, Mass.: Harvard University Press.

Useem, Michael. 1996. *Investor Capitalism: How Money Managers Are Changing the Face of Corporate America.* New York: Basic Books.

Vatter, Harold G., and John F. Walker, eds. 1996. *History of the U.S. Economy Since World War II.* Armonk, N.Y.: M. E. Sharpe.

Whyte, William H., Jr. 1956. *The Organization Man.* New York: Simon & Schuster.

Wilson, Sloan. 1955. *The Man in the Gray Flannel Suit.* New York: Simon & Schuster.

Wolman, William, and Anne Colamosca. 1997. *The Judas Economy: The Triumph of Capital and the Betrayal of Work.* Reading, Mass.: Addison-Wesley Publishing.

INDEX

MECHANICS' INSTITUTE